Events That Changed the World Through the Sixteenth Century

The Greenwood Press "Events That Changed the World" Series

Events That Changed the World in the Twentieth Century
Frank W. Thackeray and John E. Findling, editors

Events That Changed the World in the Nineteenth Century
Frank W. Thackeray and John E. Findling, editors

Events That Changed the World in the Eighteenth Century
Frank W. Thackeray and John E. Findling, editors

Events That Changed the World in the Seventeenth Century
Frank W. Thackeray and John E. Findling, editors

Events That Changed the World Through the Sixteenth Century

edited by
Frank W. Thackeray
&
John E. Findling

THE GREENWOOD PRESS
"EVENTS THAT CHANGED THE WORLD" SERIES

GREENWOOD PRESS
Westport, Connecticut • London

Library of Congress Cataloging-in-Publication Data

Events that changed the world through the sixteenth century / edited by Frank W. Thackeray and John E. Findling.
     p. cm.—(The Greenwood Press "Events that changed the world" series, ISSN 1078–7860)
    Includes bibliographical references and index.
    ISBN 0–313–29079–2 (alk. paper)
    1. History, Modern—16th century. I. Thackeray, Frank W. II. Findling, John E. III. Series.
    D228.E95 2001
    909'.5—dc21   00–052132

British Library Cataloguing in Publication Data is available.

Library of Congress Catalog Card Number: 00–052132
ISBN: 0–313–29079–2
ISSN: 1078–7860

First published in 2001

Greenwood Press, 88 Post Road West, Westport, CT 06881
An imprint of Greenwood Publishing Group, Inc.
www.greenwood.com

Printed in the United States of America

The paper used in this book complies with the Permanent Paper Standard issued by the National Information Standards Organization (Z39.48–1984).

10 9 8 7 6 5 4 3 2 1

Contents

Illustrations

Preface

This volume, which describes and evaluates the global impact of ten of
the most important events in the world during the fifteenth and sixteenth
centuries, is the fifth in a multi-volume series intended to acquaint readers with the seminal events of world history. Earlier volumes, published
between 1996 and 1999, highlighted events in the twentieth, nineteenth,
eighteenth, and seventeenth centuries. There is also an ongoing series of
volumes addressing the American experience, and a forthcoming series
will deal with events that changed Great Britain.

Our collective classroom experience provided the inspiration for this
project. Having encountered literally thousands of entry-level college
students whose knowledge of the history of the world is sadly deficient,
we determined to prepare a series of books that would concentrate on
the most important events affecting those students (and others as well)
in the hope that they would better understand the world and how it
came to be. Furthermore, we hope these books will stimulate the reader
to delve further into the events covered in each volume and to take a
greater interest in history in general.

The current volume is designed to serve two purposes. First, the editors have provided an introduction that presents factual material about

each event in a clear, concise, chronological order. Second, each intro-duction is followed by a longer interpretive essay by a specialist explor-ing the ramifications of the event under consideration. Each essay concludes with a selected bibliography of the most important works about the event. The ten chapters are followed by three appendices that provide additional information useful to the reader. Appendix A is a glossary of names, events, organizations, and terms mentioned but not fully explained in the introductions and essays. Appendix B is a timeline of key fifteenth- and sixteenth-century events, and Appendix C lists the most important ruling houses and dynasties during the fifteenth and sixteenth centuries.

The events covered in this volume were selected on the basis of our combined teaching and research activities. Of course, another pair of editors might have arrived at a somewhat different list than we did, but we believe that we have assembled a group of events that truly changed the world in the fifteenth and sixteenth centuries.

As with all published works, numerous people behind the scenes de-serve much of the credit for the final product. Barbara Rader, our editor at Greenwood Publishing Group, has encouraged us from the very be-ginning. The staff of the Photographic Division of the Library of Con-gress provided genial assistance to us as we selected the photographs that appear in this book. Our student research assistants, Sandra Taylor and Laura Blandford, read and made perceptive comments on many of the essays in this volume. We are especially grateful to Brigette Colligan, who was always ready to type or retype whatever we asked her to. Various staff members of the Indiana University Southeast computer center cheerfully unscrambled disks and turned mysterious word-processing programs into something we could work with. We benefited from funds that IUS provided to hire student research assistants and pay for other costs associated with the project. Special thanks to Roger and Amy Baylor and Kate O'Connell for making their establishment available to us, enabling us to confer about this project and discuss its many facets with our colleagues and former students in a congenial atmosphere at a time when our campus administration was not inclined to provide that sort of supportive environment. Among those who helped us in one way or another to make this a better book are John Newman, Sam Sloss, Sheila Anderson, Kim Pelle, Yu Shen, and Glenn Crothers. And, most important, we thank our authors, whose essays were well-conceived and thoughtful and whose patience when the project seemed to lag was much appreciated.

Finally, we wish to express our appreciation to our spouses, Carol Findling and Kathy Thackeray, and to our children, Jamey and Jenny Findling and Alex and Max Thackeray, whose patience with us and interest in our work made it all worthwhile.

Frank W. Thackeray
John E. Findling

The *Reconquista,* c. 711–1492

INTRODUCTION

A map of the Iberian peninsula (present-day Spain and Portugal) after the Muslim conquest in 711 shows the remaining Christian areas stretched in a narrow band across the northern edge of the peninsula. Composed of the principalities of Asturias-Leon, Navarre, Aragon, and Catalonia, this territory is nowhere more than 200 miles wide and then only in the remote northwest. By contrast, the Muslim-held territory, called al-Andalus, occupies some 80 percent of the peninsula, including virtually all of its major cities except Barcelona.

Compare that map with one of Iberia in 1492, the year the *reconquista* (or, literally, the reconquest) ended. An independent Portugal occupies the southwest part of the peninsula, and Christian Spain is divided into three kingdoms—Aragon in the northeast, incorporating Catalonia, Castile, the largest by far, extending from the northwest across the center of the peninsula into the southeast, and Navarre, still a small northern state nestled in between Aragon and Castile. As for the Muslims, their territory has been reduced to the tiny emirate of Granada, huddled along the southern coast of Iberia and incorporating the city of the same name. The *reconquista* is the story of the struggle that lasted some 780 years to bring Spain back into the circle of Christian nations. It is important to note that the *reconquista* was not a long, protracted war but a conflict that flared into open warfare occasionally. Over time, the resurgent

The Patio of the Lions in the Alhambra, Granada, Spain. Although the Spanish *reconquista* drove the Moors from Spain, a great deal of exquisite Moorish architecture was left behind. (Reproduced from the Collections of the Library of Congress)

Christians gradually gained the upper hand, but it was not until 1492 that the last of the Muslims were finally expelled from Spain.

Muslims first came to Spain from north Africa in significant numbers early in the eighth century, when enemies of King Rodrigo (r. 710–711) sought their help in deposing the king. A north-African chieftain named Jebel al Tarik (from which the name Gibraltar is derived) brought his soldiers over to Spain, defeated Rodrigo in a battle near Cadiz, and then stayed on in Iberia. More Muslims came, and they overran virtually the entire peninsula in a short period of time. A small number of Christian Spaniards hid in the northern mountains as Tarik's forces brought Spain into the Islamic world. Because they came from Mauritania (now Morocco), they came to be called Moors and presided over what was then the liveliest civilization in Europe.

The Christian *reconquista* began with a victory at the cave of Covadonga in 722, just 11 years after the completion of the Muslim conquest. Under the leadership of a Visigoth soldier named Pelayo, Christian forces ambushed a Muslim army and won a decisive victory. The importance of the battle may have been more psychological than practical; Muslim leaders had not seriously tried to conquer the rugged mountainous areas of northern Spain, whose people were thought to be primitive and whose resources were not worth the effort. Moreover, quarrels within the Muslim leadership further blunted their efforts to root out the last of the Christian resistance. At any rate, Pelayo's victory and Muslim distractions allowed Christian Spain to take the offensive after the year 740 under King Alfonso I and his successors.

The *reconquista* moved slowly in the period between 740 and 850 as Christians solidified their control over northern Iberia. Between 850 and 950, however, Christian control expanded into central Catalonia, in the vicinity of Barcelona, and farther west and south, into the remote areas of what is now northern Portugal. In the eleventh century, the reunification of the kingdoms of Leon and Castile under Fernando I in 1037 marked an important step forward in the political fortunes of Christian Spain. During Fernando's reign, military victories brought areas of the central plateau of Spain and central Portugal under Christian rule and placed other regional emirates, called *taifa* kingdoms, under a tribute system in which their Muslim chieftains were forced to make monetary payments to ensure their continuing security.

Fernando died in 1058, and it took seven years of intense family infighting among his five children before the second son emerged as Alfonso VI of Castile and Leon. Among the highlights of Alfonso's 44 year reign was the capture of Toledo, an important market city in Spain's central plateau. Alfonso VI also strengthened the social fabric of Castile and Leon by promoting the immigration of merchants and craftsmen who formed the basis of a middle class and fortified the religious community by bringing in monks. This served to bring prosperity to the region and fostered artistic endeavors, church construction, and population growth.

In the late eleventh century, the progress of the *reconquista* stalled as a dynamic new Muslim dynasty, the Almoravids, established their power in north Africa and then came to Iberia in 1084 at the invitation of the beleaguered *taifa* kingdoms. A major battle was fought at Sagrajas (near present-day Badajoz), and the Muslims, using black African troops and a camel cavalry, prevailed. Alfonso's forces retreated, but the Almoravids failed to pursue, instead returning to Africa. The Almoravids paid another visit to Iberia in 1090 and occupied much of what was left of al-Andalus, a move that stabilized the frontier, since neither side felt strong enough to attack the other.

During this time, the most famous and romantic figure of the *reconquista* was at the peak of his career. Rodrigo Diaz, or El Cid (roughly, "the boss"), born into an aristocratic family in the 1040s, served the royal family as a soldier and quasi-diplomat until Alfonso VI of Castile exiled him in 1081, apparently for some extracurricular military activity against certain Moors with whom Alfonso was trying to negotiate. Diaz went to Zaragoza, where he worked as a mercenary soldier, fighting Christian or Muslim enemies as requested. In 1082, he captured the count of Barcelona and two years later, he defeated the king of Aragon and took most of the royal court prisoner. Exploits like these made Diaz famous (and wealthy) and brought him back into the favor of Alfonso in 1086.

The reconciliation was short-lived, however, and by 1089, El Cid was once again a free-lance (literally) soldier. His wealth and fame enabled him to put together his own army for hire, and he fought both Christians and Muslims in eastern Spain, as the occasion demanded. In 1092, the Muslim-controlled city of Valencia was in turmoil between pro- and anti-Almoravid partisans. El Cid's forces laid down a long and highly-effective siege and then subsequently defeated two Almoravid attacks to retake the city. Even Muslims praised the military exploits of their adversary. For the next five years, El Cid maintained control in heavily Muslim Valencia through his ability to understand and appreciate Muslim custom and tradition in ways that allowed them to submit to his rule. After El Cid's death in 1099, his successors could not sustain Christian rule, and Alfonso VI was forced to evacuate and burn Valencia in 1102.

After Alfonso's death in 1109, dynastic problems disrupted the *reconquista* and led to civil war in Leon in 1110. This struggle lasted until 1117 and ushered in a period of economic decline and continuing political instability that prevailed for the remainder of the twelfth century. Alfonso VII, who emerged as the king of Castile and Leon in 1126, did manage to extend Christian rule farther to the south in the 1140s after the collapse of the Almoravid dynasty, but he was not able to hold on to his conquests.

Alfonso VIII succeeded his father in 1158, when he was just three years old, but by the late 1170s he had come of age and established his rule over Castile. Another of Alfonso VII's sons became Fernando II, king of Leon, signifying a split between the two kingdoms that lasted until 1230, by which time Castile had replaced Leon as the politically and economically dominant kingdom. After 1230, the kingdom, by far the largest in Spain, was known simply as Castile.

By the 1170s, a new Moorish dynasty, known as the Almohads, consolidated under its rule what the Almoravids had controlled. More culturally sophisticated than their predecessors, the Almohads set up their capital in Seville and brought to Iberia a brief period of high culture, expressed in art and architecture as well as both secular and religious literature. They also brought political stability to southern Iberia and raised a formidable army that inflicted a major defeat on Alfonso VIII at Alarcos in 1195. However, Alfonso took his revenge in 1212 by destroying the Muslim army at the important battle of Naves de Tolosa, where as many as 50,000 soldiers may have fought on each side. This led to another period of significant Christian expansion; over the next 50 years, the area under Castilian control increased by about 50 percent, mainly in the southwest corner of the peninsula, and included the important cities of Cordoba (1236) and Seville (1248). Most historians consider Naves de Tolosa to have been the most decisive battle of the entire *reconquista*.

The capture of Seville was another decisive victory for Christian Spain, one that involved what might be considered an act of Muslim treachery. In 1246, the ruler of the *taifa* kingdom of Granada had offered to pay tribute and assist Fernando III (sometimes referred to as San Fernando III), the king of Castile, in capturing Seville in return for Granada security. Fernando accepted the offer, and in the summer of 1247, naval forces loyal to Fernando took control of the Rio Guadalquivir, Seville's link to the sea. The following spring, they destroyed the pontoon bridge across the river that was the city's last link to its Muslim allies in north Africa. Seville was under siege from the combined forces of Fernando and Granada. Summers in Seville were (and still are) very hot, and disease, food shortages, and a lack of potable water finally broke the morale of Muslim leaders in the city. In the terms of surrender, signed in November 1248, all Muslims were forced to leave the city, taking with them only what they could carry. As for Granada, it was left in a semi-autonomous state for the next 250 years.

Although Granada was nominally independent during this time, it was poor and needed almost constant assistance from Muslims in north Africa. Tax rates were high in order to allow the emirs to pay the annual tribute to Castile, and the population was increased to an unhealthy level by the influx of immigrants from parts of Spain that had been returned to Christian rule. But Granada was well-fortified, with frontier outposts every few miles and watchtowers throughout the territory. Granadan armies were well-trained and their light cavalry units, recruited in Morocco, were especially effective. In addition, Granada enjoyed good relations with the Merinids, the Muslim power in Morocco that had succeeded the Almohads. During the early fourteenth century, there were occasional battles or sieges involving Castilian and Merinid armies, but they resulted in little territorial change. The most important event was the successful siege of Algeciras in 1342–1344, where contingents of English and French soldiers fought alongside the Castilians. Shortly after the fall of Algeciras, the plague epidemic known to history as the Black Death swept over Spain (and, indeed, the rest of Europe), killing Alfonso XI, the king of Castile, and forcing the abandonment of military campaigning. Following the plague, internal squabbling in Christian Iberia and Spanish involvement in the Hundred Years' War meant that Granada was left in peace.

This peace was first broken in 1410 when Castilian forces captured the strategically important town of Antequera. In 1415, the Portuguese took Ceuta, the port city that controls the straits of Gibraltar. Meanwhile, the Merinid dynasty had collapsed, leaving the Moors in Granada bereft of allies and making their defeat inevitable once the political conflicts in Iberia were resolved. This happened in 1474 when Ferdinand of Aragon married Isabella of Castile and united the two most important Spanish kingdoms.

The conflict that led to the capitulation of Granada in 1492 began with a frontier incident in the winter of 1481–1482. Conflict escalated over the next several years, although it was clear that the Castilian army was much superior in all respects to that of Granada. Moorish political problems also helped. The emir of Granada was Abu-l-Hasan, and his son, Boabdil, rebelled against him in 1483 and became a loyal partisan of Ferdinand. In 1485, Abu-l-Hasan was overthrown by his brother, al-Zagal, who, in turn, was driven to an outpost in eastern Granada by Boabdil in 1487, where Christian forces defeated him in 1489. Amidst all of this, important Granadan strongholds inexorably fell to Ferdinand's troops: Ronda (1485), Loja (1486), Malaga (1487), and Almeria (1490). Although Boabdil might have been expected to surrender Granada peacefully to Ferdinand, he did not, and an eight-month siege was necessary to bring about the surrender of the city. On January 2, 1492, Ferdinand and Isabella, dressed in Moorish costume, formally accepted control of Granada from Boabdil. One of those present was Christopher Columbus, then pursuing royal sponsorship for a voyage west across the Atlantic Ocean.

INTERPRETIVE ESSAY
Pamela Beattie

On January 2, 1492, Ferdinand and Isabella, the rulers of the Spanish kingdoms of Castile and Aragon, entered the city of Granada in triumph. The monarchs were clothed in Moorish costume and accepted the keys to the city as a symbol of surrender. After almost 800 years, the Spanish *Reconquista* was over. The conquest of Granada spelled the end for an independent Muslim state in the Iberian Peninsula. And in many respects, the successful Granadan campaign was the crowning achievement of the reign of the so-called Catholic Kings who received this sobriquet in recognition of their conquest. But the conquest of Granada was not the only event worthy of note in this momentous year. With the successful conclusion of the ten year campaign against Granada, the Spanish rulers found themselves more inclined to look outside the peninsula for glory, and later that same January, Christopher Columbus convinced the queen to assist in funding the famous voyage that resulted in the "discovery" of the New World. And finally, in the spring of 1492, the monarchs of Spain issued an edict forcing the expulsion of all Spanish Jews. All three events were linked—the conquest of Granada, the discovery of the New World, and the expulsion of the Jews—and the conquest can be understood as the culmination of one chapter of Spanish history and the beginning of another.

Reconquista is the term used to describe the struggle by Iberian Christians to recover territories in the peninsula which were conquered by Muslim forces in the early eighth century during the heady days of Islamic expansion and the creation of the Arab empire. The Muslim conquest of the Christian kingdom of the Visigoths in 711 occurred almost as an accident, the result of fortuitous circumstances, treacherous Visigothic vassals, and enterprising Muslim leaders. Eventually, an independent Caliphate was established in Spain and the Muslims became firmly entrenched there. Part of the conquered Christian population eventually converted to Islam; part retained their Christian beliefs and lived as protected communities, or *dhimmi*, under Muslim rule and became known as Mozarabics; and part retreated to the northern reaches of the peninsula and survived as best they could. By the late eighth century, these northern Christian principalities began gradually expanding their territories southwards again and the movement known as the *reconquista* was underway. Over time, rhetoric and ideology stressing the "recovery" of Christian lands from Muslim enemies of the true faith was developed to support the expansion. The *reconquista* became a crusade against the infidel, a series of military expeditions designed to seize land and acquire wealth, and eventually a popular migration.

It is difficult to generalize about the character of the *reconquista*. One reason is the longevity of the movement. Over the course of nearly 800 years, the *reconquista* took on many different forms; it was not a steady, gradual expansion of Christian kingdoms southwards, but took place in fits and starts, with great advances (usually corresponding to periods of Muslim disunity) followed by lengthy periods of minimal progress. For example, the frontier between the Muslim kingdom of Granada and the rest of Spain remained virtually unchanged between approximately 1250 and 1492. Between 1350 and the start of the Granada campaign in 1482, Christians and Muslims engaged in sporadic official warfare for a total of only 25 years. Over such a broad sweep of time, motivations for participating in the *reconquista*, military tactics, and associated institutions varied. What is remarkable is that the political and religious objectives of the movement could survive for so long.

Generalization about the *reconquista* is also difficult because of the diversity of the Iberian peninsula. Everything from political institutions to language varied from kingdom to kingdom in medieval Iberia. The major principalities north of Muslim territories eventually coalesced into three independent states which were frequently at war with each other: Portugal, Castile, and Aragon. The shifting alliances between and against co-religionists further complicated the course of the *reconquista*. Muslim rulers of Granada often allied with Iberian Christians to resist the aggressions of the North African princes. Similarly, the Christian rulers of Castile or Aragon were willing to ally with Muslim Granada to protect and advance their dynastic and territorial interests against each other.

Finally, the geographical terrain, economic opportunities, and settlement patterns in the various regions of Spain were such that the rulers and inhabitants of these regions resorted to different measures to advance the *reconquista* and aid in the consolidation of vast territorial gains. In the course of the *reconquista*, the major Christian states almost doubled their territories. However, territory acquired by Aragon in the Balearic islands and the regions of Valencia and Murcia was oriented towards the Mediterranean and North African coasts, was relatively thickly populated, and thus provided different economic and political challenges than did the rugged and largely under-populated territories conquered by Castile in central Spain. Portugal, naturally, tended to be more oriented to the Atlantic and the western coast of Africa as its portion of the *reconquista* progressed.

Even when one takes into consideration the longevity of the *reconquista*, the shifting alliances of the Spanish kingdoms, and the variation in *reconquista* experience from region to region, the fact remains that much of Spanish history was shaped by the *reconquista* and that the people, culture, and institutions of the Iberian peninsula were strongly influenced by the frontier, both ideological and physical, between the Muslim and Christian worlds. The frontier of the *reconquista* was fluid and shifting, although at certain times and in specific places it had the character of a border, complete with customs officials and a medieval variation of a passport system. It was itself a region rather than a specific dividing line. Just as many communities of Christians lived under Muslim rule following the Islamic conquest, so many Muslim communities now found themselves under Christian rule in the wake of the *reconquista*, further confusing the concept of frontier. Depending on the region under examination, these Muslims (or *Mudejars*) lived in specific (often walled) sections of medieval Spanish towns, formed an independent hamlet or village, or were somewhat more integrated in agricultural areas. Thus the success of the *reconquista* and the influence of the frontier led to another incredibly important aspect of medieval Spanish life: *con-*

vivencia or co-existence, the way in which the Christian, Muslim, and Jewish populations of Spain lived together and interacted throughout the Middle Ages.

The idea of *convivencia* has had a varied history. The concept was originally embraced to emphasize the significance of all three religious groups, Christians, Muslims, and Jews, in shaping a Spanish cultural identity. Some historians have stressed the positive side of *convivencia*, pointing to instances of cooperation between members of different religions, tolerance, and acculturation. For example, many Muslim craftsmen such as tilemakers, masons, and stoneworkers were involved in the construction of public buildings (even churches) and thus many medieval buildings in Spain display a distinctive Arabic architectural style. For example, some parish churches in Aragon are modeled after Islamic minarets. Members of the substantial Jewish communities in urban centers throughout Spain were renowned as physicians and businessmen. Christians, Muslims, and Jews worked side by side to create flourishing economies in cities such as Barcelona, Valencia, and Toledo. Communities of Muslims (known as *aljamas*) and of Jews were permitted to practice their respective religions. Muslim neighborhoods could be identified by the presence of a mosque and ritual calls to prayer five times a day. Assurances that Muslim communities could retain their religious freedom often comprised extensive clauses in the surrender treaties signed in the wake of the *reconquista*. This was particularly the case in regions such as Valencia, where Christian overlords were outnumbered by their Muslim subjects. *Convivencia* also entailed juridical, economic, and political freedoms. Muslim communities were allowed their own officials who ruled in accordance with *sharija*, or Muslim sacred law. Muslims could have their own cemeteries and on occasion were even allowed to retain their own fortresses. Christian rulers were willing to make such accommodations because of their great dependence (primarily economic) on the subjugated population. The Muslims living in the territories of Aragon were not known as the "royal treasure" for nothing.

Muslims and Jews under Christian rule possessed a legal status defined with some uniformity in the great law codes of the medieval Spanish kingdoms; laws protected minority communities and clearly established their privileges. For example, the twelfth-century *Usages of Barcelona* stressed that the ruler was the protector of all his subjects regardless of class or religion. But it is possible to paint an overly rosy view of *convivencia*. Although individuals representing different cultures and religions could tolerate one another, do business, and perhaps even be friends, the modern concept of toleration meant nothing in the Middle Ages. The general laws of the great codes could differ greatly from the municipal codes, and the way Muslims were supposed to live under Christian rule and the way they DID live were often two different things. Despite acculturation in many areas, the *convivencia* of medieval Spain also created a culture of separation. Fathers were allowed to disinherit sons who converted to Islam. Muslims lived in walled barrios. They wore distinctive clothing (by law) for easy identification to guard against unacceptable social interaction. Laws promised large rewards for returning Muslim slaves who had fled their masters. In reality, communities of both Muslims and Jews found their actions carefully circumscribed, and as the centuries progressed, their situation became increasingly difficult. Frequent *mudejar* rebellions made these communities even more vulnerable. Because *convivencia* was the flip-side of the *reconquista*, a Christian could simultaneously allow a Muslim worker a break for prayer to Allah at the appropriate time of day, and view war against Islam as a divine mission, and all Muslims as agents of the Antichrist. Other Europeans who traveled to Spain to participate in the *reconquista* as a crusade found it difficult to understand such a dichotomy, and frequently criticized the Spanish for their complex interactions with various Muslim communities.

Following the conquest of Toledo in 1085, the *reconquista* increasingly assumed the character of religious warfare. The development of the crusading movement in Europe had an obvious impact on the nature of the struggle for territory between Christians and Muslims in Spain. Religious leaders regarded the *reconquista* as the western theater of the war against Islam. Unlike the majority of Crusades in the Holy Land, the *reconquista* was successful, and many crusade theorists and propagandists hoped that the war against the "infidel" in the East would benefit from the experiences of crusaders in Iberia. Some authors, such as the famous thirteenth-century missionary Ramon Llull, suggested that the most likely path to the conquest of the Holy Land lay through Spain to North Africa and then toward the East. As the *reconquista* became a more integral part of general crusade theory in Europe, it increasingly enjoyed the economic and spiritual benefits of crusade status. From the time of Urban II and the First Crusade to the campaign against Granada 400 years later, Spanish rulers were periodically allowed to collect various percentages (known as tenths or other fractions) of ecclesiastical revenues to use as subsidies for the *reconquista*. Papal bulls extended crusaders' indulgences to participants in the *reconquista*, and civilians could receive indulgences for material support. Once the *reconquista* had crusade status it attracted knights from across Europe. As the *reconquista* became more closely associated with the Christian ideology of holy war, resistance on the part of Muslims similarly emphasized the religious character of the struggle. Some Muslim propagandists viewed participation in Granada's struggle to withstand Ferdinand's and Isabella's attacks as the most noble and important religious duty of Allah's faithful.

If medieval Christians were to view the *reconquista* as an essential element of the expansion of Christendom, they needed to address the problem of Muslims living under Christian rule. The nature of the relationship between Muslims and Christians in Iberia was all the more interesting because the Muslim "enemy" was anything but barbarous, and Iberian Christians could not help but be aware of this. Angus MacKay has argued that although Christianity expanded at the expense of Islam, it was the richer and more cultivated civilization of Islam which influenced Spain and western Europe rather than the reverse. An important element of the *reconquista* was the continual process of accommodation and acculturation among Christians, Muslims, and Jews. There is much debate about the extent of the cultural debt which Christian Spain owed to the Islamic world, primarily because scholars can also discern important cultural developments during this period that clearly belonged to the sphere of European Christian civilization. Nevertheless, the influence of Islamic civilization can be seen in the both the material culture (architecture, art, dress, weaponry) and the intellectual culture of the Iberian world (philosophy, theology, literature). Of outstanding importance is the work of the medieval translators of the twelfth and thirteenth centuries. These scholars, associated particularly with the city of Toledo, translated many scientific and philosophical works from Arabic into Latin. Some of these works were masterpieces of the ancient Greco-Roman civilization that the Islamic world had inherited through its conquests. Thus, the Muslims of Spain acted as cultural transmitters to Europe. Other works translated from Arabic were masterpieces of Islamic scholars such as the celebrated Averroes of Cordoba, whose interpretations of Aristotle had a profound impact on medieval thought. When Peter the Venerable, abbot of Cluny, visited Spain in 1142, he even commissioned a translation of the *Qur'an*, the holy text of the Muslims.

The work of the medieval translators in Spain made apparent a shared philosophical and theological tradition between Christians and Muslims. This inspired Christians, especially Dominican and Franciscan friars, to embark on missionary programs designed to bring Muslims under Christian rule into the Catholic Church. The experience of missionaries in Spain, with their emphasis on understanding the language and character of their audience, added significantly to Christian missionary programs which were eventually taken to places such as India, China, and the New World. The experiences of crusaders in *reconquista* Spain and the Holy Land also stimulated important developments in Church law and theology. It raised questions such as: What is a just war? What is a Holy War? Is forced conversion valid? Can crusades be declared to conquer territory for evangelization? Is slavery permissible? Both Christian and Muslim theologians argued that forced conversion was against God's law; both groups embraced ideologies of Holy War. Following Columbus's discovery of the New World, ecclesiastical and political leaders drew upon these ideas to justify and interpret the conquest of the Americas. In his bull *Inter Caetera*, Pope Alexander VI traced the history of the *reconquista* through the conquest of Granada. Now that the *reconquista* was over, the rulers of Castile and Aragon could turn towards the important task of extending the bounds of Christendom in new lands.

The legal and theological questions raised by the *reconquista* as Holy War point to the second aspect of the movement, namely its character as a war of expansion. Although the Spanish kingdoms all expanded their territory dramatically during the *reconquista*, the effect of the physical frontier was especially profound for Castile, which was the only Iberian kingdom to have a land-based frontier with a Muslim state after the mid-thirteenth century. The conquest of Granada further increased Castilian territory. Because the *reconquista* lasted for so many centuries, Spanish society retained its military character for generation after generation. The famous epic poems of Spain, such as the *Song of Roland* and the *Cantar de Mio Cid* (or El Cid), dramatically illustrate the predominance in Spanish life of the idea of warfare against the Muslims, and in the case of El Cid, the complexity of the military relationship between Muslims and Christians.

Because of the ideals of the *reconquista*, the frontier with Islam was constantly changing. Consequently, institutions designed to deal with frontier life were also impermanent. Truces were signed, rather than permanent treaties. Both sides developed laws, regulations, and methods for dealing with the realities of the frontier. For long periods after 1250, the conditions along the Iberian frontier were comparable to a Cold War. Fairly amicable coexistence, which included tolerance and respect, could and did develop between periods of militancy and zeal. Documents even report the existence of a frontier shrine dedicated to a saint venerated by both Christians and Muslims and therefore made accessible to both groups. But frontier life also included regular skirmishes, frequent raids, and surprise attacks. During the long period of relative inactivity in *reconquista* efforts, frontier ballads kept the ideals of the movement alive and violent encounters along the frontier continued. Such activity provided opportunities for booty, land, and fame. According to Derek Lomax, it is less true that peaceful coexistence along the frontier was occasionally disrupted by war provoked by religious and political officials than that kings made occasional and ineffectual attempts to limit the endless warfare from which their subjects often benefitted.

An interesting problem associated with the *reconquista* was the large number of captives held by both Muslims and Christians. Special officials known as *alfaqueques* were entrusted with the job of ransoming such prisoners and negotiating payments for release. Occasionally their task became even more complicated when captives converted to the religion of their captors. A popular frontier ballad called the *Ballad of Bovalias el Pagano* describes the religious confusions posed by a man who had converted and reconverted at least eight times. Some captives refused to come home once they had converted or experienced new opportunities across the frontier. In those cases, *alfaqueques* sometimes could arrange visitation rights. Religious orders called Trinitarians and Mercedarians were also created specifically for ransoming captives and related charitable activities. Judges, known as *alcaldes*, resolved frontier disputes and conflicts. Special investigators, called *rastreros*, who were responsible for bringing cross-border criminals to justice, assisted the judges. Other officials dealt with complex economic transactions across the frontier. Trade in some types of goods, particularly those that would aid military efforts, was forbidden, and Muslims and Christians employed customs officials and collected export and import taxes across the Castilian-Granadan frontier. Even after 1492, these institutions continued to exist because of a new coastal frontier dominated by pirates and relationships with the Ottoman Turks.

Because the *reconquista* was a war of expansion, it also became a popular motive for migration. Christian rule over conquered territories was often consolidated through colonization or *repoblacion*. In places like Valencia, under the rule of Aragon, *repoblacion* was easier because capitulation documents allowed many Muslims to retain their lands under Christian lordship making massive Christian migration to these areas unnecessary. In Castile, however, *repoblacion* was a daunting task. It followed different patterns corresponding to the stages of the *reconquista*.

After conquering Toledo in 1085, the Castilians undertook their first systematic attempts to create an authentic frontier society organized for war. This required firm royal control over settlement, organization of lands, resolution of conflicts, and preparations for defense. Settlement of both warriors as well as peasants (farmers) was essential. Each colonist had clearly defined military and economic obligations according to the urban law codes, which also regulated the sharing of spoils. The result was a pattern of settlement spread over vast territorial regions, characterized by numerous frontier towns that served as centers of administration, markets, and fortresses. Settlers were encouraged to colonize these lands by various royal incentives including tax exemptions, military privileges (payments, free grain for subsistence), and asylum for those accused of various crimes. Official documents of land division were called *repartimientos*; the same term was used to describe divisions of land and authority in the New World after 1492. But in spite of the many privileges offered, some areas had to be populated over and over again.

South of Toledo, an acute shortage of population and manpower led to great instability. In these regions, the Castilian monarchy bestowed vast grants of land upon two major groups in order to stimulate economic development and stability. The first of these groups consisted of great noble families and royal vassals whose power thus became so great that they profoundly influenced the development of political institutions in Castile. These nobles contributed to the civil war and dynastic struggles which plagued Castile between 1350 and the reigns of Ferdinand and Isabella. The second group receiving vast land grants were the Spanish military orders. The orders of Calatrava, Santiago, Alcantara, and others were founded in the twelfth century and modelled on the great crusading orders of the Templars and Hospitallers to combine piety and monastic discipline with knightly ideals. Military orders became vital to the garrisoning of strongholds and the resettlement of border areas. Eventually the Iberian monarchs were able to restrain the power of these orders by appointing their leaders or taking over the leadership themselves (which King Ferdinand did in the sixteenth century).

Repoblacion provided social and economic opportunities for all levels of society. Some scholars have argued that feudalism never really developed in medieval Iberia as it did in other parts of Europe because the *reconquista* involved almost the entire society in military endeavors. The primary responsibility of defending the land belonged to the settlers who were given houses and lands by the king in return. These settlers were more than simple farmers and enjoyed increased opportunities for social mobility. Because military service was indispensable, many free men could aspire to noble status by performing a legitimizing military role in society. This created many different levels of knights characterized by their military specialty, which in turn increased social stratification. Concepts of honor and valor in the context of military success helped determine social mobility. Distinctive institutions such as the *hermandades*, associations of lesser nobles, townspeople, and bishops who grouped together for mutual protection, also developed along the frontier. Out of this society came the conquistadors of the Americas, making their culture another product of the medieval *reconquista*.

The challenges of *repoblacion* contributed to the economic development of medieval Spain. Both the Aragonese and the Portuguese developed maritime economies in the Mediterranean and Atlantic respectively and experienced different economic pressures than did Castile. In Castilian territory, the nature of the terrain as well as the large grants of land made ranching a major part of the economy because rural labor was scarce, crop-farming was hazardous and the mobility of ranching was attractive. In fact, cattle-ranching was unique to Iberia in the Middle Ages. The economic role of ranching provides another link between Old World and New after 1492. Along with the methods of colonization, frontier institutions, and social mobility, ranching was exported to the New World, as many of the colonists who followed in the wake of the conquistadors came from the cattle-ranching areas of Old Spain. They brought with them cattle and the organization, methods, and customs of ranching (including bull fighting, cowboys, and the economic divisions of land called *encomiendas*).

After a lengthy period of civil war, Ferdinand and Isabella renewed the *reconquista* by embarking upon their campaign against Granada in 1482. The war actually began in response to a Muslim raid that captured the Spanish fortress of Zahara in 1481, and rapidly escalated into an organized campaign. Granada was still a formidable enemy due to contacts with North Africa, significant wealth and population, and mountainous terrain. But after 1482, Granada entered into civil war when Boabdil rebelled against his father, King Abu-l-Hasan. As in early stages of *reconquista*, Spanish rulers took advantage of internal dissension to divide and conquer. But Spain's greatest advantage in 1482 was the fact that for the first time in many, many years, the Christian rulers in Spain were united through Ferdinand and Isabella's dynastic marriage.

In most respects, the war against Granada followed traditional *reconquista* policies and techniques. The campaign was extremely popular and served as a unifying force for Spain. It acquired crusade status and was financed largely by percentages of ecclesiastical revenues. Participants received indulgences and the popes published bulls supporting the campaign. What was novel about this campaign was the degree of royal control over battles and financing, the use of professional soldiers, the number of soldiers engaged in combat, and the extensive use of artillery. In these military details, the campaign against Granada took on the character of an early modern war. The war also took place in the context of a rejuvenated royal prestige and authority during a period when many early modern political institutions were being shaped. This meant that for Spain the conquest of Granada helped to create an important link between royal policy and divine mission which in turn helped to shape the ideology of conquest in the New World.

This relates to another important element of the campaign. Throughout the fifteenth century, the European imagination was increasingly captured by eschatalogy (ideas pertaining to the end times). In the late fifteenth century, prophecies pointing to Ferdinand as the key figure in the last events of world history circulated throughout Europe but were especially popular in Spain. The prophecies predicted that Ferdinand would expel the Muslims, conquer Granada, cross the sea and defeat all Islam, convert the Jews, recover Jerusalem, and create a new Christian world empire. As Ferdinand and Isabella experienced success, the prophecies multiplied and gained greater currency. Such prophecies emphasize the importance of the religious aspect of royal policy and help to explain many of the similar ideas expressed in the writings of Christopher Columbus. Ferdinand and Isabella repeatedly declared that they were not undertaking the campaign against Granada (and later the conquest of the Americas) simply for wealth and personal glory, but for the expansion of Christendom and the glory of God. It was a holy cause. Thus the *reconquista* generated many of the ideals which underlay the conquest of the New World.

The signal importance of the conquest of Granada is explained by its results. First of all, it concluded the *reconquista*. For the first time in 780 years, Christian rulers controlled the entire Iberian peninsula. Initially, the Muslims of Granada were guaranteed property rights and religious freedoms if they chose to stay in Granada; they could also choose to receive assistance for emigration to North Africa. The first Archbishop of Granada, Ferdinand of Talavera, was given the task of converting the Muslims of Granada, and he attempted to do this with sensitivity and patience, making distinctions between Moorish customs and Islamic beliefs. But the attitude towards religious pluralism had changed in Spain and the rest of Europe and, frustrated with the slow progress of conversion, the monarchs sent Archbishop Cisneros of Toledo to Granada to speed things up. His controversial mass baptisms provoked a series of rebellions. In 1500, worried about cooperation between North Africa and the Granadan Muslims, the monarchs gave the Muslims of Granada a choice between baptism or emigration on much less favorable terms than in 1492. Given that the Spanish Inquisition had been established in 1478 and that the Jews had been expelled in 1492, this decision was not surprising. Throughout the sixteenth century, increased attempts at creating a country with a uniform religion and culture were made, including decrees forbidding the speaking and writing of Arabic in Granada. Finally, in 1609, the Moriscos (baptized Muslims) were also expelled from the entire peninsula. The conquest of Granada in 1492 not only marked the end of the *reconquista* but also the end of *convivencia*. Such an emphasis on religious unity was characteristic of all of Europe in the Reformation era and points towards the early modern wars of religion and attempts to convert the indigenous peoples of the Americas. It was also an important characteristic of the early modern nation state, of which Spain was an example.

If the *reconquista* per se was over, its ideals persisted well after 1492. This can be seen in three different areas. The first is a planned expedition for advance into North Africa. This was not an entirely new concept; Aragon and Portugal had been pursuing such plans for many years. But after 1492 these plans tied into the development of European ideas of diplomacy and defense against the Ottoman Turks. The campaign against Granada was seen by many European rulers, including the pope, as a necessary prerequisite for a campaign against the Turks. Secondly, *reconquista* ideals survived in Spain's internal policy. Military orders and the collection of ecclesiastical tithes continued to play a pivotal role in the Spanish economy and society. The money was used to finance wars in the Mediterranean, wars against the Dutch Protestants, and activities in the New World. The military orders provided the clearest institutional link between reconquest and conquest, crusade, and empire. Many of the conquistadors who traveled to the New World proudly sported the *habito*, or membership in one of the military orders.

The third area in which *reconquista* ideals persisted was the New World. Contemporary Spaniards realized that the creation of the overseas Spanish empire formed a continuation of the *reconquista* with all its problems of settlement and organization. Authors such as Lopez of Gomara grandly announced that the conquest of the Indies began when that of the Moors was over, for the Spanish had always fought against the infidels. Following the conquest of Granada, Spain found itself with many unemployed soldiers who were unwilling or unable to return to civilian life. Overseas expansion for Spain was logical because it would lead to peace at home and royal profit abroad. Spanish conquest in the New World is virtually inconceivable without the success of Granada in 1492. It has been argued that no other European country could have taken advantage of discovery of the New World at that date. As Derek Lomax concluded, Spain's experience with the *reconquista* enabled it to conquer, administer, Christianize, and Europeanize the New World. For good or ill, the *reconquista* changed the world in the fifteenth and sixteenth centuries because it marked the point at which the Old World met the New.

SELECTED BIBLIOGRAPHY

Bishko, C. J. "The Spanish and Portuguese Reconquest, 1095–1492." In *A History of the Crusades*, edited by Kenneth Setton, pp. 396–456. Madison: University of Wisconsin Press, 1975. This lengthy article is one of two works dedicated to the history of the *reconquista* that have been published in English.

Boswell, John. *The Royal Treasure: Muslim Communities Under the Crown of Aragon in the Fourteenth Century*. New Haven: Yale University Press, 1977. A basic study of *convivencia* in medieval Aragon.

Burns, R. I. *The Crusader Kingdom of Valencia: Reconstruction on a Thirteenth-Century Frontier*. 2 vols. Cambridge, MA: Harvard University Press, 1967. A seminal work in understanding *convivencia* and *reconquista* institutions under the Crown of Aragon.

———. *Islam under the Crusaders: Colonial Survival in the Thirteenth-Century Kingdom of Valencia*. Princeton, NJ: Princeton University Press, 1973. Another key study by a leading historian of the *reconquista* in Spain.

———. *Medieval Colonialism: Postcrusade Exploitation of Islamic Valencia*. Princeton, NJ: Princeton University Press, 1975. Complements Burns's earlier two studies.

Cook, Weston F., Jr. "The Cannon Conquest of Nasrid Spain and the End of the Reconquista." *Journal of Military History* 57, no. 1 (January 1993): 43–70. Studies the early modern military tactics of the Granadan campaign.

Dillard, Heath. *Daughters of the Reconquest: Women in Castilian Town Society, 1100–1300*. Cambridge, Eng.: Cambridge University Press, 1984. An interesting study of social roles for women in the context of the *reconquista*.

Edwards, John. "A Conquistador Society? The Spain Columbus Left." *History Today* 42 (1992): 10–16. A well-written brief introduction to the continuity of the *reconquista* mentality in the New World.

Elliott, J. H. *Imperial Spain 1469–1716.* Harmondsworth, Eng.: Penguin Books, 1963. Standard account of imperial Spanish history that discusses the relationship between the *reconquista* and the New World in Chapter 2.

Fernandez-Armesto, Felipe. *Before Columbus: Exploration and Colonisation from the Mediterranean to the Atlantic, 1229–1492.* Houndsmills, England: Macmillan Education, 1987. An interesting study that establishes the context for later exploration of the New World.

Goni Gaztambide, J. "The Holy See and the Reconquest of the Kingdom of Granada, 1479–1492." In *Spain in the Fifteenth Century (1369–1516): Essays and Extracts by Historians of Spain,* edited by Roger Highfield. New York: Harper and Row, 1972. Traces the involvement of the papacy in the Granadan campaign and studies the crusade bulls and ecclesiastical financing of the conquest.

Gonzalez Jimenez, Manuel. "Frontier and Settlement in the Kingdom of Castile (1085–1350)." In *Medieval Frontier Societies,* ed. Robert Bartlett and Angus MacKay, pp. 49–74. Oxford: Clarendon Press, 1989. Studies different phases of *repoblacion* and the role of resettlement in the *reconquista.*

Hillgarth, J. N. *The Spanish Kingdoms 1250–1516.* 2 vols. Oxford: Clarendon Press, 1976–78. This is one of the standard authoritative histories of Spain in English and deals with the conquest of Granada in volume two.

Housley, Norman. *The Later Crusades, 1274–1580. From Lyons to Alcazar.* Oxford: Oxford University Press, 1992. Chapters 9 and 10 deal with the *reconquista* from 1274 to 1580 (beyond Granada).

Johnson, H. B., ed. *From Reconquest to Empire: The Iberian Background to Latin American History.* New York: Knopf, 1970. A collection of essays tracing continuities between medieval and imperial Spanish history.

Kagay, Donald J. "Columbus as Standardbearer and Mirror of the Spanish Reconquest," *American Neptune* 53 (1993): 254–59. Traces continuities in ideology between the *reconquista* and Columbus.

———. "The Essential Enemy: The Image of the Muslim as Adversary and Vassal in the Law and Literature of the Medieval Crown of Aragon." In *Western Views of Islam in Medieval and Early Modern Europe: Perception of Other,* ed. David R. Blanks and Michael Frassetto. New York: St. Martin's Press, 1999. Studies the realities of *convivencia* in the medieval Crown of Aragon.

Lomax, Derek W. *The Reconquest of Spain.* London: Longman, 1978. This is the only book-length treatment of the *reconquista* available in English.

Lopez de Coca Castaner, Jose Enrique. "Institutions on the Castilian-Granadan Frontier, 1369–1482." In *Medieval Frontier Societies,* ed. Robert Bartlett and Angus MacKay, pp. 127–50. Oxford: Clarendon Press, 1989. Examination of frontier influence on Castilian institutions.

MacKay, Angus. "Religion, Culture and Ideology on the Late Medieval Castilian-Granadan Frontier." In *Medieval Frontier Societies,* ed. Robert Bartlett and Angus MacKay, pp. 217–43. Oxford, Eng.: Clarendon Press, 1989. Examines the impact of religion and ideology on Spanish frontier culture.

———. *Spain in the Middle Ages: From Frontier to Empire, 1000–1500.* London: Macmillan Press, 1977. A wonderful introduction to the main events of medieval Spain with an emphasis on Spain's frontier experiences.

Meyerson, Mark. *The Muslims of Valencia in the Age of Fernando and Isabel: Between Coexistence and Crusade*. Berkeley: University of California Press, 1991. An important study of *convivencia* in late medieval–early modern Spain.

Muldoon, J. *Popes, Lawyers and Infidels: The Church and the Non-Christian World 1250–1550*. Philadelphia: University of Pennsylvania Press, 1979. An important study of the theological and canonical implications of crusade, *reconquista*, and conquest.

O'Callaghan, J. F. *A History of Medieval Spain*. Ithaca, NY: Cornell University Press, 1975. One of the few single volume histories of medieval Spain available in English, this work studies the *reconquista* but stops before Granada.

Phelan, J. L. *The Millennial Kingdom of the Franciscans in the New World*. 2nd ed. Berkeley: University of California Press, 1970. A fascinating book which traces the continuity of religious and eschatologial ideas in the New World.

Wright, L. P. "The Military Orders in Sixteenth and Seventeenth-Century Spanish Society: The Institutional Embodiment of a Historical Tradition," *Past and Present* 43 (1969): 34–70. Examines the endurance of an important *reconquista* institution following the conquest of Granada.

A woodcut of a sixteenth-century Florentine merchant. The woodcut shows typical Renaissance dress, furniture, and "tools of the trade." (Reproduced from the Collections of the Library of Congress)

2

The Renaissance, c. 1300–1630

INTRODUCTION

David Dale, writing in the *Sydney Morning Herald* (November 27, 1999), makes a case for the use of the Italian word, *renascimento*, instead of Renaissance to describe the wave of cultural changes that appeared first in Italy in the fourteenth century and was sponsored by wealthy Italians in Florence, Milan, and Venice and by the Catholic Church hierarchy in Rome. The French, whose word for the movement has been Anglicized and is universally used in the English-speaking world, had very little to do with it, especially in its early stage. Regardless of what word we use, the Renaissance did begin in Italy, and then spread to other parts of Europe in the fifteenth century. It came about as a result of significant economic growth that began as early as the eleventh century in the northern Italian cities mentioned above. These cities prospered from foreign trade with the Middle East, northern Europe, and eventually, the Orient. Technological improvements in shipbuilding greatly facilitated the growth in trade, and Italian cities took advantage of their convenient geographical location on or near the Mediterranean Sea.

Although it is an inland city, Florence is regarded as the site of the first flowering of Renaissance culture. That city prospered from its privileged position as bankers to the papacy and became, as a result, the banking center for all of Europe. In addition, Florence developed a prosperous wool industry, employing thousands of workers in spinning and weaving wool into fine cloth that was sold all over the world. Florence and other northern Italian cities were ruled by small groups of wealthy men—a form of government called an oligarchy. They ruled rather despotically, though usually not brutally, and maintained lavish courts and sumptuous lifestyles. Their society was far more secular than that of the Middle Ages, and it accommodated well the rising interest in humanism that began to flourish in the early fourteenth century.

While it is hard to date precisely the beginning (or the end) of the Renaissance, most historians choose Francesco Petrarch (1304–1374) as the first major figure, although others look further back and see signs of the Renaissance in the work of the painter Giotto or the writer Dante Alighieri, both of whom preceded Petrarch by a generation or so. As historian Peter Burke points out in *The European Renaissance*, "whatever date is chosen for the beginning of the Renaissance, it is always possible to make a case for going back still further."

Humanism, literally the study of humanity, emerged from a renewed interest in ancient Greek and Roman society and, particularly, Greek and Roman intellectual life. As Petrarch expressed it, humanism represented a return to what was thought to be the high point of human civilization and an escape from the sterile "Dark Ages," as he called the preceding centuries. While Petrarch and other humanists did not reject Christianity, they placed new emphasis on the examination of human achievements and potential.

Humanism was therefore closely linked to a rising sense of secularism, which connotes concern with the present-day material world instead of the spiritual world of faith and eternal life. While Renaissance scholars no doubt prayed to go to heaven, they and their less intellectual friends also developed a new interest in the acquisition of personal wealth and worldly goods. Sensual gratification was important in Renaissance life, and writers found ample justification for living the "good life" in the works of the Greeks and Romans they admired. Church leaders never protested much, indeed, many of the popes and other ranking Catholics of the time indulged themselves in the sensual pleasures of fourteenth and fifteenth century Italy.

We can best view the Renaissance and the changes it brought through its art and architecture. New generations of painters and sculptors broke away from the stylized forms of religious medieval art and created artworks that were more anatomically realistic and often more secular in content. Indeed, much of what we know about such things as Renaissance dress and furniture is drawn from evidence found in contemporary paintings. It is also significant that much of the painting and sculpture was commissioned or sponsored by individual civic leaders or business-men as a way of flaunting their wealth and heightening their prestige. In architecture, new buildings designed in strict classical styles based on Greek and Roman models signified the intellectual and aesthetic influence of antiquity on the Renaissance.

Apart from art and architecture, the Renaissance also brought about genuine social changes rooted in the new concern for secularism. Education became a higher priority for families of wealth and status; young gentlemen (and to a lesser extent, young ladies) of the court were expected to have some knowledge of the classics, to have a religious education, and to have at least a passing acquaintance with music and art. On another level, the Renaissance also witnessed the publication in 1513 of Niccolo Machiavelli's *The Prince*, a highly secular political tract that explores an individual's relationship with the state and advocates aggressive and cunning manipulation of human nature to achieve the natural end of politics, the implementation of effective rule by a powerful ruler.

With the invention of printing by use of movable type in the mid-fifteenth century (see Chapter 6), the spread of knowledge became much easier. By the end of the century, printing presses were at work all over Europe and works of classical literature were far more accessible than ever before. Printing also provided the public with religious publications, government propaganda, contemporary fiction, and, increasingly, scientific treatises.

The printing press helped spread Renaissance culture from Italy to the rest of Europe, but cultural diffusion also came from students who traveled to Italy and brought what they learned back home. In general, historians see the Renaissance in northern Europe as being more religiously centered than it was in Italy. Scholars looked for ways to meld the best of classical and Christian teachings in order to guide people to a richer but more ethical life on earth, and, unlike Machiavelli, they had confidence that human nature was essentially good. Education, if properly applied, could work to make good men even better in the eyes of God.

The northern European Renaissance was typified by the English thinker Thomas More (1478–1535) and the Dutch cleric Desiderius Erasmus (1466?–1536). More, whose opposition to Henry VIII's church reforms in England led to his martyrdom, wrote a treatise, *Utopia*, (literally, "nowhere"), about a place in which people are well-educated, live in a classless society, and are never motivated by greed. It was an ideal society but one that spurned the influence of the church, a factor that earned More some criticism from his religious superiors. Erasmus was a monk who developed a keen appreciation for the Latin and Greek languages and their literature. Like More, Erasmus believed in the value of education, though one based more on a combination of the Bible and classical works than More advocated. Erasmus believed that the key to a good life was found in the "philosophy of Christ," which he equated to a kind of spiritual attitude. Of all the northern European humanists, Erasmus was probably the most distinguished, in large part because he was able to take advantage of printing to have his work widely distributed. His humanist writings made him famous all over Europe in his lifetime, and he had dedicated followers everywhere, whom he encouraged through frequent correspondence. However, he was less than impressed with many Italian humanists, who, he thought, were imitating Greek and Roman models to the extent that they were "paganizing" their culture and losing sight of the importance of the church.

Northern European art and architecture also reflected the more religious character of the Renaissance there. Although painters worked in a realistic style and, indeed, were just as skillful as the Italians, their paintings more frequently had religious themes, sometimes combined with folklore or fantasy. Public buildings in northern Europe lacked the disciplined attention to Greek and Roman forms seen in Italy and appeared more like religious shrines, even when they had a secular purpose.

Between 1490 and 1530, there was such a concentration of artistic and literary output of high quality that scholars refer to the period as the High Renaissance. Leonardo da Vinci, Raphael, and Michelangelo were all in mid-career during these years, and Rome had emerged as the center of Renaissance culture, although Florence and Venice remained important cities of cultural distinction. Pietro Bembo, papal secretary to Pope Leo X after 1513, wrote Latin poetry and edited the works of Dante and Petrarch. Leonardo, Raphael, and Michelangelo were all recognized as master painters. There was a new interest in classical culture, seen in the zeal for discovering and collecting ancient sculpture and in the production of new works, such as Michelangelo's *David* (1501). In architecture, renewed enthusiasm for the work of the Roman architect Vitruvius inspired the building of carefully designed palaces for wealthy families.

The High Renaissance is generally considered to have ended with Charles V's invasion of Rome in 1527, an event that caused considerable destruction. By this time, some of the great figures had died or left Rome;

the invasion further dispersed the cultural community to the extent that even contemporary writers noted that it was the end of a special epoch.

When did the Renaissance end? Clearly, the movement underwent important changes around 1530, but most modern scholars reject the notion that the Renaissance came to a screeching halt at that time. History does not usually work that way, and in the case of the Renaissance, it can be argued that significant elements continued on for a hundred years after 1530. Classical sources of inspiration became more varied; for example, artists and literary humanists from places other than Rome (especially the Netherlands) helped spread Renaissance ideas to the peripheries of Europe and even beyond, to India, China, Mexico, and Peru, where a *mestizo* humanist named Garcilaso melded pagan Inca culture with Christian tradition.

The late Renaissance also saw a spreading of humanist interests in sources other than Greek and Roman antiquity. Some scholars have seen in this a fragmentation of the humanist movement, while others interpret it as a natural evolution of humanism. This "fragmentation" or "evolution" can be found in the rise of interest in Arabic language and culture, in ancient Egypt, in the Celtic druids, and in the philosophies of Eastern cultures. Perhaps even more importantly, later humanists began to take a renewed interest in the long-scorned Middle Ages, a trait particularly evident in marginal places like Denmark, Poland, and Hungary.

Another feature of the later Renaissance is what historian Peter Burke calls the "domestication" of the movement. By this, he means the growth of interest in the Italian culture of the High Renaissance, evidenced in increased travel to Italy and in flattering writing about Italy (which, in turn, caused a flurry of anti-Italian writing). Others tried to imitate Italian architecture, interior design, and decorative arts. Formal sculpture gardens on the Italian model proliferated in northern Europe, as did private museums of art or antiques. Education focused on the classics, and handwriting styles and type fonts imitated those of the Romans. Even leisure activities such as dancing, horseback riding, and fencing were carried out with reference to Italian practices.

It is just as hard to date the end of the Renaissance as the beginning, but it is probably safe to say that there was a gradual fading of enthusiasm for humanism and the classics that coincided with increased interest in what came to be called the "scientific revolution." The ideas of Nicholas Copernicus, Johannes Kepler, René Descartes, and Galileo Galilei represented a conscious break with classical thinking in their rejection of the notion that the classics represented the pinnacle of civilization. This was especially obvious in the area of astronomy and ideas about the place of the earth in the universe.

Yet humanism survived in the writings of a number of authors and playwrights in the seventeenth and eighteenth centuries, especially in England and northern Europe. Some writers continued to revere Erasmus, while others perpetuated what might be called the cult of antiquity. Similar evidence can be found in the history of art and sculpture. And even in our own day, the popularity of Renaissance revivals attests to the lasting significance of this event that changed the world.

INTERPRETIVE ESSAY
Blake Beattie

The Renaissance produced some of the most distinctive ideas and images in the western tradition, yet scholars remain deeply divided over what exactly it was—some have even denied that it existed at all, except in the minds of the eighteenth- and nineteenth-century historians who coined the term "Renaissance." While such a view goes too far, scholars have often overestimated the scope and influence of the Renaissance. It was chiefly a literary and artistic phenomenon whose influence on politics is undeniable, though less thoroughgoing than is often maintained—its role in inspiring the voyages of the "Age of Discovery" has been greatly exaggerated, and it contributed very little to the "Scientific Revolution" of the early modern period. Nor does it account for any significant changes in the broader societal and economic contours of European life. It was not a distinct historical period, but a transitional phase between the medieval and early modern periods in European history. Ultimately, the Renaissance might best be seen as a distinctive cultural attitude that prevailed in fifteenth- and sixteenth-century Europe—an attitude that, paradoxically, looked with great excitement to the future even as it drew its inspiration from the distant past.

The word "renaissance" means "rebirth." It was first used by eighteenth-century scholars to describe the revival of interest in classical studies and values, especially among Italian intellectuals, in the fourteenth and fifteenth centuries. Interest in classical antiquity was not unique to later medieval Italy: the Middle Ages witnessed several earlier "renaissances," and most medieval educational programs were based on the seven liberal arts, a curriculum established in late antiquity. But the Italian classicism of the later Middle Ages went much farther than its predecessors in exploring the history and letters of classical antiquity. Later medieval classicists had access to a much larger corpus of classical texts, relatively few of which circulated in Europe before the thirteenth century. By 1200, an influx of texts from the Muslim world, where the classics had been preserved and studied for centuries, was providing European scholars with ancient works that were previously unknown in the West. European classicists began to search actively for lost or forgotten manuscripts after 1350, thus further increasing the number of available texts. And when Constantinople fell to the Turks in 1453, many Greek intellectuals fled to the West, bringing a number of ancient Greek works with them. Thus, later medieval scholars could delve much more deeply than their predecessors into the study of western antiquity.

Eventually, the classical studies of the later Middle Ages generated the educational and literary program known as humanism, which lies at the heart of Renaissance thought and culture. The first scholar to use the term "humanism" was the Florentine historian and statesman Leonardo Bruni (1370–1444), who took it from the lexicon of the ancient Romans. To the Roman orator and statesman Cicero (106–43 B.C.E.), *humanitas* signified a body of literary and historical studies that were essential to the education of any truly civilized person. In recreating this body of studies, the humanists established the ideas and values on which nearly the whole of Renaissance culture came to rest.

The "Father of Humanism" was the great Italian poet Francesco Petrarca (1304–1374), better known as Petrarch. Though Petrarch always considered himself a Florentine, his family had been exiled from Florence on political grounds in 1301, and he was actually born in Arezzo. He spent much of his life at Avignon, where the popes resided from 1309 to 1375. He became a cleric and entered the service of Cardinal Giovanni Colonna (c. 1294–1348), whose liberal patronage allowed Petrarch to devote himself to literary pursuits. He scoured the monastic libraries of southern France in search of classical texts, and discovered several lost works by his literary hero, Cicero. Dismissing contemporary Latin styles and forms as debased, Petrarch emulated the classical Latin of Virgil and Cicero, and dabbled in new literary forms based on classical genres. His *De viris illustrious* is a series of biographies of famous Romans, inspired by the works of Plutarch; his *Familiares* are an epistolary memoir containing Petrarch's reflections on his life and times; his (unfinished) *Africa* is a Latin epic celebrating the Roman general and statesman Scipio Africanus. These works broke sharply with medieval literary conventions to revive forms and themes that had not been used in the West since classical antiquity. After the ravages of the Black Death (1347–1351), Petrarch began to look more to the salvation of his soul than the resurrection of Roman antiquity, and his work assumed a much more overtly Christian character. In the first half of his career, however, he defined what became the humanist program: the active search for sources; linguistic precision in the study of ancient texts; the adoption of classical styles, themes, and forms; and the cultivation of classical models and ideals in one's own lifestyle.

Petrarch's work was advanced by another famous Florentine, Giovanni Boccaccio (1313–1375). In his youth, Boccaccio studied commerce and law at Naples, a major center of classical scholarship in early fourteenth-century Italy. He soon developed a fascination with the world of antiquity and embarked on a literary career. His first ventures were decidedly "lightweight"—at the urging of Petrarch, who recognized Boccaccio's talent, he undertook more serious classical studies. His *De genealogia deorum (On the Genealogy of the Gods)*, for example, is a detailed study of Greek and Roman mythology, intended as a reference for authors who wished to write on mythological themes. In 1362, Boccaccio introduced humanism to the academy by inaugurating the Dante Lecture Series at the University of Verona. Boccaccio is best known for his *Decameron* (1350), a collection of one hundred short stories, ostensibly told by ten young Florentines seeking refuge from the Black Death in a remote rural villa. Masterfully written, inventive, irreverent, and often ribald, the *Decameron* quickly became one of the most popular works of the fourteenth century. It exercised a great influence on later medieval popular literature; Chaucer, Christine de Pisan, Marguerite de Navarre, and Cervantes all acknowledged their debt to it. While there is little in the *Decameron* that can properly be described as humanist content, the work's enormous popularity drew attention to Boccaccio's classical scholarship, and helped indirectly to bring humanist ideas to a much broader audience.

Petrarch, Boccaccio, and other early humanists treated humanism primarily as a literary enterprise; during the fifteenth century, humanism acquired a broader application. Perhaps the greatest of the fifteenth-century humanist scholars was the Roman Lorenzo Valla (1407–1457), a linguist and textual critic who applied humanist methods and techniques to a number of different fields. He wrote an influential manual of classical Latin style and developed the techniques of critical editing, by which the language of ancient texts was recreated in contemporary editions. He proved on linguistic grounds that the Donation of Constantine was not an authentic fourth-century document, but an eighth-century forgery. With his keen appreciation for the historical circumstances in which ancient writings were composed, Valla pioneered a humanist reading of scripture that became extremely influential in northern Europe. He also wrote philosophical treatises on a variety of important subjects. Thus, Valla's work demonstrated the potential applicability of humanist methods and techniques to a wide range of disciplines and fields.

As humanism developed, it came to acquire a large following among Italian intellectuals. Major humanist circles grew up in Florence, Rome, Venice, and a number of lesser Italian cities. By 1450, humanism had not only become the dominant intellectual form in Italy, but was beginning to spread into other parts of Europe. Several factors account for the rapid dissemination of humanist ideas after 1400. Certainly, the support of princely patrons was extremely important. Humanism has been described quite appropriately as "a program for the ruling classes." Ancient writers from Plato and Aristotle to Cicero and Caesar wrote extensively on political practice and theory—their works provided fifteenth-century rulers with a wellspring of ideas. Humanist studies promoted certain skills that were ideally suited to the task of governing. The study of rhetoric and oratory, for example, could be indispensable to the art of effective persuasion. Indeed, most humanists were themselves very persuasive writers, and rulers were quick to recognize the potential benefits of patronizing such skillful propagandists. Princes who curried the favor of humanist scholars, like Duke Federico III of Urbino (1444–1482), were bathed in glowing panegyrics; princes who earned the enmity of the humanists learned to fear their artfully venomous invective: the reputation of Pope Paul II (1464–1471), for example, who arrested and tortured the humanist Bartolomeo Platina (1421–1481), was vilified by humanists to the point of irreparable damage. The celebrated humanist Aeneas Silvius Piccolomini (1405–1464), who reigned as Pope Pius II from 1458 until his death, penned a description of his archenemy, Sigismondo Pandolfo Malatesta, lord of Rimini (1417–1468), which ranks among history's most brilliant character assassinations. Thus, while rulers were eager to acquire reputations as patrons of scholarship and the arts, their patronage afforded many more tangible benefits, and contributed significantly to the growing influence of humanism and humanist thought in the fifteenth century.

Elements of humanist thought also managed to appeal to people outside of politically and intellectually elite circles. The language of humanist scholarship was often difficult and technically demanding, but its ideas were accessible to most literate laypeople. While humanists typically regarded classical Latin as the only proper language for serious scholarship, many were skillful "popular" writers who applied their literary skill to vernacular works, infused with a humanist sensibility, which reached large audiences. Petrarch wrote some of the most beautiful poetry in the Italian tradition; Boccaccio's *Decameron* was written in the vernacular; a number of Renaissance masterpieces, from Lodovico Ariosto's (1474–1533) *Orlando Furioso* and Pietro Bembo's (1470–1547) *Gli Asolani* to Baldassare Castiglione's (1478–1529) *Libro del corteggiano* and Niccolo Machiavelli's (1469–1527) *Il Principe*, were written not in Latin, but in the language of ordinary Italians.

Humanist ideas appealed especially to urban society. The distinctive environment of the cities engendered new attitudes and values, apart from and often at odds with those of medieval Europe's ecclesiastical and feudal traditions. In the socially kinetic and predominantly commercial context of urban society, material success and social status were, at least in theory, less an accident of birth than a consequence of private initiative. It says a lot about the origins of the Florentine Medici, one of fifteenth- and sixteenth-century Europe's richest and most powerful families, that their coat-of-arms incorporated the three balls that symbolized the pawnbroker's trade. Energetic public activity and self-invention thus emerged as urban social virtues—the man who achieved success in a turbulent but exciting world became an urban ideal. As an educational program that offered instruction in the arts of public activity and accomplishment, humanism provided a programmatic justification for the activities and upwardly mobile aspirations of the urban middle and upper classes.

The humanist outlook also responded meaningfully to the troubled circumstances of the later Middle Ages, when many of the institutions and practices that had guided European society for centuries began to falter or break down. An over-sized population began to outstrip its agricultural resources after about 1270 and found itself afflicted by famines and epidemics in the fourteenth and fifteenth centuries. Major changes in commerce engendered economic instability and, in some areas, economic contraction. Continuing political changes spawned brutal conflicts, such as the Hundred Years' War (1338–1453), that made use of fearsome new technologies like gunpowder. Humanists not only acknowledged these changes, but also actively sought to negotiate them. From the time of Petrarch, humanist scholars believed that they stood at the dawn of a "New Age" in Europe—far from dreading the prospect of change, they expressed enormous confidence in the human ability to overcome all challenges and build a glorious future. Leon Battista Alberti (1404–1474) summed up the lofty humanist view of the human condition when he declared, "Men can do all things if they will." Not surprisingly, such a view offered hope to many in a troubled and uncertain age.

Still, nothing accounts for the rapid spread of humanism and humanist ideas more than printing. The invention of the printing press around 1450 sparked a revolution in the dissemination of information and ideas beside which the Internet pales in significance. As publication ceased to depend on the painfully slow and expensive process of copying books by hand, the volume of texts in circulation increased astronomically. By 1400, some 2,000 copies of Boccaccio's *Decameron* circulated in all of Europe, making it by far one of the "best-sellers" of the fourteenth century. A century later, just 50 years after the invention of printing, some 7.5 million books circulated in Italy alone. As the first intellectual movement to be transmitted by mass publication, humanism could reach unprecedented numbers of people at unprecedented speed.

As humanism spread during the fifteenth century, its ideas came to influence spheres of human activity beyond literature and scholarship. The result was a "humanist culture" with which the Renaissance is most accurately identified, characterized by an interest in classical antiquity and by a focus on human activity. It differed from earlier medieval cultural perspectives and anticipated many modern ones in two principal ways. First, it was highly individualistic. Compared to their twelfth- and thirteenth-century forebears, later medieval Europeans were strikingly self-conscious and self-expressive; they were fascinated by the notion of the private self, and often asserted the interests of the individual above those of the community. The humanist emphasis on the activity of the individual, inventing himself as he made his way through the world, created a Renaissance ideal: the "Universal Man," who attained fame and expressed his individual genius by mastering a wide variety of different fields. Dante Alighieri (1265–1321), a politician, poet, and political theorist; Leon Battista Alberti, a historian, mathematician, musician, moralist, architect, and artist; and above all Leonardo da Vinci (1452–1519), an artist, scientist, musician, architect, and engineer embodied the triumphant self-actualization that the Renaissance celebrated as the height of human achievement. Renaissance culture exhibits an almost obsessive interest in individual personalities and achievements, including one's *own*. In the fifteenth century, scholars, artists, politicians, and even ordinary citizens produced more autobiographical writings than appeared in the entire period between 500 and 1400. It is an exaggeration to claim, as some scholars have, that the Renaissance witnessed "the discovery of the self" in western society—nevertheless, the Renaissance did impart an unprecedented importance to "the self" that endures in the modern period.

The humanist culture of fifteenth-century Italy was also largely secular in its focus. Renaissance secularism has often been misrepresented as indifference or even hostility to religion. One of the twentieth-century's greatest scholars of medieval philosophy, Etienne Gilson, actually proclaimed that "the Renaissance is not the Middle Ages plus Man, but the Middle Ages minus God." Anyone who has ever gazed upon Leonardo's *Last Supper*, Michelangelo's *Pieta*, or Raphael's *Transfiguration* will recognize the absurdity of the claim. Most Italian humanists were devout (if sometimes unconventional) Catholics; many were churchmen. They may have believed, like the Greek philosopher Protagoras (c.485–415 B.C.E.), that "man is the measure of all things," but they did not surrender their belief in the divine. If anything, they believed that the glories of human achievement redounded to the even greater glory of God. In his definitive manifesto on the human condition, *Oratio de dignitate hominis (Oration on the Dignity of Man)*, the Renaissance philosopher Giovanni Pico della Mirandola (1463–1494) argued that the freedom to act and to choose set man at the pinnacle of universal creation. Yet he stressed that human freedom, like the hope of salvation through Christ's resurrection, is a gift from God. For Pico, humans are special because they are created in the image of God, without whom humanity itself, let alone human achievement, is inconceivable.

Still, it is true that most Italian humanists preferred secular subjects to religious ones, and some contemporaries criticized the humanist proclivity for "pagan" themes like ancient history and mythology as inimical to Christian belief. The humanists defended themselves by arguing that many of the ancients were virtuous and wise, and therefore worthy of emulation, in spite of their pagan beliefs. They believed that the human condition, and the worldly affairs that attended it, were valid subjects, even when they did not impinge directly on spiritual or moral matters.

Unlike the Scholastic theologians of the twelfth and thirteenth centuries, who believed that God is knowable through the study and rational analysis of his creation, Italian humanists often assumed that the divine lay beyond the realm of human understanding. Given the hardships that afflicted later medieval society, it is not surprising that many fourteenth- and fifteenth-century people perceived God as being more distant—and sometimes less benevolent—than their twelfth- and thirteenth-century counterparts did. Some Renaissance thinkers even contended that there were areas of human activity in which conventional Christian morality had little or no relevance; the political vision articulated in Machiavelli's *The Prince* is the most famous example. Renaissance secularism sometimes conditioned a moral relativism which seems jarringly inconsistent with Christian teachings: a number of prominent Renaissance scholars, artists, politicians, and more than a few popes, led unabashedly scandalous lives. Nevertheless, the secularism of the Italian Renaissance was neither a repudiation of religious faith nor incompatible with Christian belief.

Aside from literature and scholarship, two other important aspects of Renaissance culture were significantly transformed by humanist ideas: art and architecture; and politics. The artistic revolution, which produced the most enduring images of Renaissance civilization, developed almost side-by-side with humanism. Already in thirteenth-century Italy, the same impulses that inspired literary humanism were conspiring to transform the representational arts. The sculptor Nicola Pisano (c.1220–1284) and the painters Giotto (c.1266–1337) and Simone Martini (1284–1344) abandoned the stylization of Gothic and Byzantine art, depicting human forms with a greater sense of anatomical accuracy. As humanism developed during the fourteenth and fifteenth centuries, artists continued to adopt classical techniques and began exploring secular themes, including classical mythology and history. The paintings of Uccello (c. 1396–1475), Fra Angelico (c. 1400–1455), Masaccio (1401–1428), Fra Filippo Lippi (1406–1469), and Botticelli (c. 1444–1510), and the sculpture of Donatello (1386–1466) exemplify the experimentation characteristic of the "Middle Renaissance." By the time of the High Renaissance (c. 1490–1530), Italian artists had not only revived the principles of classical art—balanced and orderly presentation; the synthesis of realism and idealism in the depiction of the human form—but, in the work of artistic titans like Leonardo da Vinci, Michelangelo (1475–1564), and Raphael (1483–1520), transcended it to create some of the greatest artworks in all of human history.

Renaissance architecture likewise bespeaks the humanist obsession with classical influences. The work of Vitruvius Pollio (fl. first century C.E.) exerted a profound influence on Filippo Brunelleschi (1377–1446) and Leon Battista Alberti, who were instrumental in devising the neoclassical style that typifies Renaissance architecture. Brunelleschi and Alberti were also artists whose architects' sense of tridimensionality led both men to pioneer the use of precise mathematical perspective in painting. With the support of their princely patrons, the artists and architects of the Renaissance quite literally transformed cities like Florence, Rome, and Venice. Analogous traditions, inspired by but distinct from those of Italy, quickly developed in other parts of Europe—some of the Renaissance artists of France and especially the Netherlands very nearly equaled the Italian masters in the brilliance of their own work. By 1600 there was scarcely an urban center in Europe that remained untouched by the transformative effects of neoclassical art and architecture.

Humanism also exercised a considerable influence on politics. The political history of Italy between 1350 and 1550 is enormously complicated. Within the Italian cities, the communal governments of the twelfth and thirteenth centuries gave way to the more static and exclusive regimes of oligarchy, in which cartels of wealthy families monopolized government, and despotism, which concentrated power in the hands of one autocratic ruler. Most oligarchs and some despots took pains to obscure political realities by preserving the rhetoric and institutions of communal government. The most famous of Renaissance rulers is probably Lorenzo *"il Magnifico"* dei Medici (1449–1492), who presided over the most brilliant phase of Renaissance cultural achievement in Florence. The Medici were the richest and most powerful of the dozen or so families who came to dominate Florence earlier in the fifteenth century; by Lorenzo's time the Medici were so powerful that Lorenzo could exercise almost absolute control over the city between 1469 and his death in 1492. Yet he never held any public office and refused formal titles, calling himself simply *reggitore della republica* (regent of the Republic). Lorenzo's government could thus be regarded as despotism masquerading as oligarchy masquerading as republicanism, an extreme, if not entirely atypical, example of the rhetorical shapeshifting that characterized many Italian regimes after 1350.

On a larger scale, Renaissance Italy witnessed dramatic territorial expansion by larger cities at the expense of their smaller, weaker neighbors. The competing ambitions of five cities, especially Florence; Venice, under its commercial oligarchy; Milan, under the despotic Visconti family; papal Rome; and the royal seat of Naples, precipitated a series of wars and constantly shifting alliances. In the Peace of Lodi (1454), the five cities attempted to orchestrate a balance of power in Italy. Conflict and intrigue continued, however, and ultimately brought about the fateful intervention of the Valois kings of France and the Austrian Habsburgs in the 1490s, which inaugurated a long period of foreign domination in Italy.

By the later fourteenth century, some humanists, especially in Florence, were coming to appreciate the potential value of humanism in negotiating the complex inter- and intra-urban politics of later medieval Italy. These so-called "civic humanists" emulated the activities and ideals of classical statesmen, in particular Cicero, in their own political careers. The first civic humanist was Coluccio Salutati (1333–1406), who served as chancellor (chief secretary) of Florence from 1375 until his death. Salutati was a superb writer, widely praised for the quality of his Latin, who used his persuasive eloquence to great diplomatic effect. Indeed, Salutati was so effective in shaping alliances that, during the course of a war between Florence and Milan in the 1390s, the Milanese despot Gian Galeazzo Visconti (1351–1402) complained famously, "a single letter of Salutati's is worth a thousand horsemen." Salutati's three successors were also talented humanists who continued to develop the new techniques that came to dominate fifteenth-century diplomacy.

Others applied humanist thought to political manners and morals. Baldassare Castiglione standardized courtly etiquette in his *Libro del corregggiano (Book of the Courtier)*, a work that was nearly as influential in courtly society beyond the Alps as it was in Italy. The most famous political treatise of the Italian Renaissance was Niccolo Machiavelli's *Il Principe (The Prince)*, which proposed political pragmatism and sometimes ruthlessness as the best means of preserving power and serving the general good. Reviled in its own time for its rejection of Christian morality in the sphere of politics and frequently misunderstood by subsequent generations, it nevertheless remains one of the most influential political writings in the western tradition.

It is vital to understand, however, that Machiavelli was not an innovator. He did not articulate a new approach to politics, but rather provided a written justification for political practices that had been used in Italy for centuries. The hero of *Il Principe*, Cesare Borgia (1475–1507), illegitimate son of Pope Alexander VI (1492–1503) and architect of the extended Borgia patrimony in Italy, was not a new political type, but part of a political tradition that went back to at least the time of the thirteenth-century tyrant Ezzelino da Romano (1194–1259). Machiavelli's importance lay in his willingness to articulate and justify modes of political conduct that were long established but rarely discussed before his time. Even the activities of the civic humanists in Florence were more responsive than innovative: Salutati and his successors did not create a complex new diplomatic situation so much as devise an effective response, based on humanist ideas and language, to one that already existed. The claim that the Renaissance extricated statecraft from religious morality to create the political pragmatism of the modem age is thus misleading. Rather, Renaissance political writers were the first to acknowledge and accept a political pragmatism whose origins extend much farther back into medieval history.

By the later fifteenth century, the Renaissance was spreading from its Italian centers to other parts of Europe. The first great Renaissance center outside of Italy was the court of the dukes of Burgundy, which played a vital role in transmitting Renaissance culture into France and the Low Countries, especially in the time of Duke Philip III [Philip the Good] (1396–1467). By the later fifteenth century, the princely courts of trans-Alpine Europe were sowing the seeds of a "Northern Renaissance" that transformed European thought, art and politics during the sixteenth century. Ferdinand V of Aragon (r. 1479–1516), the Holy Roman Emperor Maximilian I (r. 1493–1519), Francis I of France (r. 1515–1547), and, to a lesser extent, Henry VIII of England (r. 1509–1547) were all prominent patrons of humanist scholars and Renaissance artists. Royal patronage extended Renaissance culture into even the more remote parts of Europe. One of the leading Renaissance courts of the sixteenth century was that of Sigismund II "Augustus," Grand Duke of Lithuania (r. 1544–1572) and King of Poland (r. 1548–1572), whose mother was, not coincidentally, a daughter of the Duke of Milan.

In no place, however, was the Renaissance simply an Italian import. Wherever the Renaissance went, it generated distinctively "national" forms and expressions. Only in Italy could artists and scholars celebrate a direct descent from Roman antiquity—in other places, different pasts were studied and celebrated. The emblems and attitudes of medieval chivalry were prominent in French Renaissance culture, while the German Renaissance glorified a distant Teutonic past which Italians, like their Roman forebears, dismissed as barbarous. Moreover, the human activity that attracted the attention of writers and artists naturally assumed different characteristics in different places. Jan van Eyck (c. 1390–1444), Pieter Breughel (c. 1525–1569) and the latter's sons, Pieter the Younger (1564–1637) and Jan (1568–1625), are the greatest exponents of a distinctive Dutch and Flemish Renaissance art that often depicted daily life in the cities and countryside of the Low Countries. Albrecht Durer (1471–1528) and Lucas Cranach (1472–1553) developed an iconography peculiar to German Protestant art, and helped to establish the woodcut as a quintessentially German artistic medium.

If the "Northern Renaissance" defies a monolithic definition, it did have some general characteristics that set it apart from the Renaissance in Italy. Above all, it was far less secular in its focus. The antiquity that fascinated trans-Alpine humanists was the age of the early Church. Northern humanists studied Greek and even Hebrew, as well as classical Latin, in order to read the Bible in its original languages. The French priest Jacques LeFevre d'Etaples (1450–1537) and the Dutch cleric Desiderius Erasmus (c. 1466–1536) were outstanding biblical scholars whose humanist readings of scripture generated new scriptural interpretations; humanist studies of the apostolic Church underscored the extent to which the contemporary Church had "strayed" from its pure and primitive standards. Northern humanism became associated with a growing demand for religious reform and spiritual renewal. While some Northern humanists, most notably Erasmus and the great English humanist, Sir Thomas More (1478–1535), believed that change could be effected within the Catholic Church, many Northern reformers came to believe that a more radical break with Rome was necessary for any true reform of the Christian Church. Martin Luther (1483–1546) was not trained as a humanist, but humanist ideas and approaches to scripture directly inspired many leading figures in the Protestant Reformation, including Huldrych Zwingli (1484–1531), Philip Melanchthon (1497–1560), and John Calvin (1509–1564). Thus, Northern humanism played an absolutely central role in generating the Protestant Reformation of the sixteenth century.

While the Renaissance transformed many aspects of European thought, art, and belief, it must be stressed that its influence was not complete. The fact that the Renaissance was coterminous with some important developments should not be misconstrued as evidence of a necessary connection. It is often held, for example, that the great voyages of discovery were motivated by "Renaissance curiosity." In reality, the Crusades and the thirteenth-century mendicant missions to Asia had awakened a European fascination with exotic lands long before the Renaissance. In any case, the voyages of the fifteenth, sixteenth, and seventeenth centuries were motivated chiefly by the desire to find maritime routes to Asian markets, to discover new silver and gold reserves, and to convert unbelievers to Christianity; "curiosity" ranked relatively low among the priorities of Christopher Columbus (1451–1506), Vasco da

Gama (c. 1469–1524), Francisco Pizarro (c. 1478–1541), and Hernán Cortés (1485–1547).

Nor did the Renaissance have much to do with the Scientific Revolution of the early modern period. Renaissance thinkers had little interest in science; they privileged artistic activities, such as literature, painting, and sculpture, and conceived of a wide range of human activities, including politics and war, as art forms. The astronomical researches of Nicholas Copernicus (1473–1543), Johannes Kepler (1571–1630), and Galileo Galelei (1564–1642) had nothing to do with humanism and its influence; they were rooted in a Scholastic scientism that Renaissance scholars despised. Artists like Leonardo da Vinci, whose interest in science was decidedly atypical, and Michelangelo advanced the science of anatomy through their rigorous studies of the human form, but for the most part, the Renaissance witnessed few important medical advances. The work of the Flemish anatomist Andreas Vesalius (1514–1564), for example, was little appreciated until a century or so after his death. Indeed, the Renaissance emphasis on art actually precluded scientific advances in most fields. The seventeenth- and eighteenth-century Enlightenment, with its revival of interest in scientific thinking, reacted as much against the Renaissance indifference to science as it did against the intense religious conflicts engendered by the Reformation. In many respects, the fifteenth- and sixteenth-century advances in astronomy and anatomy, which inaugurated the Scientific Revolution, occurred in spite of, not because of, prevailing Renaissance sensibilities.

By 1550, the attitudes, ideas, and artistic forms that distinguished the Renaissance were giving way to new ones, as the Renaissance fell victim to the modern order whose coming it had so eagerly awaited. The Reformation and Counter-Reformation generated religious passions and conflicts that rendered many elements of humanist culture obsolete. In politics, secularism was pushed aside by the renewed prominence of religious issues in affairs of state, and remained in eclipse until vindicated at Muenster and Osnabruck in 1648 at the end of the Thirty Years' War. In art and architecture, the balance and realism of Renaissance classicism surrendered to the dramatic tension of mannerism and the exuberance of the Baroque. Yet the Renaissance had an enduring impact. Its ideas about the human condition, its approaches to literary and historical scholarship, and its belief in the importance of worldly affairs, were crucial in shaping the sensibility of the modern western world. Even if it did not—*could* not—account for all of the changes once attributed to it, the Renaissance remains an important and fascinating part of the legacy which the Middle Ages left to modern Europe.

SELECTED BIBLIOGRAPHY

Baron, Hans. *The Crisis of the Early Italian Renaissance; Civic Humanism and Republican Liberty in an Age of Classicism and Tyranny*, 2 vols. Princeton, NJ: Princeton University Press, 1966. One of the best general discussions available in English of Renaissance politics and political theory, with particular but not exclusive attention to Florentine politics.

Bishop, Morris L. *Petrarch and His World*. Bloomington: Indiana University Press, 1963. More "student friendly" than Wilkins, this lively and readable work provides a fine introduction to Petrarch's life and to the social forces that helped to shape his thought.

Brucker, Gene A. *Renaissance Florence*. Berkeley: University of California Press, 1969. The single best one-volume work in English on politics, economics, thought, and culture in the cradle of the Italian Renaissance.

Burckhardt, Jacob. *The Civilization of the Renaissance in Italy*, 2 vols. New York: Harper & Row, 1958. The publication of Burckhardt's masterpiece in 1860 inaugurated modern historiography of the Renaissance; though in many respects outdated, it remains essential reading for any student of Renaissance culture. There are many available editions, but students might like this well-illustrated version, which provides photographs of many of the Renaissance's most vivid images.

Burke, Peter. *The European Renaissance: Centres and Peripheries*. Oxford: Blackwell, 1998. A good survey of the Renaissance, particularly useful for its discussion of the movement outside of Italy.

———. *The Fortunes of the Courtier: The European Reception of Castiglione's Corregiatio*. University Park: Pennsylvania State University Press, 1995. An often-fascinating study of the formation, transmission, and influence of the "manual" of Renaissance court-life; a fine examination of the ways in which ideas were disseminated during the Renaissance.

Cassirer, Ernst, Paul Oskar Kristeller, and J. H. Randall, Jr., eds. *The Renaissance Philosophy of Man*. Chicago: University of Chicago Press, 1953. A fine reader, with excerpts from major treatises on the human condition by some of the leading Renaissance thinkers, from Petrarch to Vives.

Cole, Bruce. *Italian Art, 1250–1550: The Relationship of Renaissance Art to Life and Society*. New York: Harper & Row, 1987. A nice introduction to Renaissance art, organized thematically rather than strictly chronologically and lavishly illustrated, though without color plates.

Godman, Peter. *From Poliziano to Machiavelli: Florentine Humanism in the High Renaissance*. Princeton, NJ: Princeton University Press, 1998. An interesting, somewhat challenging investigation of Florentine politics and thought around the time of Lorenzo de Medici.

Goldthwaite, Richard A. *The Building of Renaissance Florence: An Economic and*

Social History. Baltimore: Johns Hopkins University Press, 1980. An extremely thorough and often fascinating discussion of the social, political, and economic factors underlying architecture and public art in the "first city" of the Italian Renaissance; includes some illustrations.

Grendier, Paul F. *Schooling in Renaissance Italy: Literacy and Learning, 1300–1600*. Baltimore: Johns Hopkins University Press, 1989. A capable survey of Renaissance educational processes and their cultural implications; erudite but accessible to most students.

Gundersheimer, Wemer L., ed. *The Italian Renaissance*, Renaissance Society of America Reprint Texts 2. Toronto: University of Toronto Press, 1993. First published in 1965, this work contains lengthy excerpts from the works of 11 major Renaissance figures (including Coluccio Salutati, Lorenzo Valla, Pope Pius II, Machiavelli, Castiglione, and Leonardo da Vinci) and provides an excellent introduction to the ideas that drove Renaissance culture.

Hale, John. *The Civilization of Renaissance Europe*. New York: Atheneum, 1994. This comprehensive overview, by one of the masters of Renaissance history, credits the Renaissance with the creation of the concept of modern Europe and modern western thought—an outstanding and highly readable work.

Hay, Denys. *The Italian Renaissance in its Historical Background*. Cambridge, Eng.: Cambridge University Press, 1977. An important study locating the origins of Renaissance phenomena squarely in the context of later medieval history.

Holmes, George. *Florence, Rome and the Origins of the Renaissance*. New York: Oxford University Press, 1986. Examines thirteenth-century Florentine politics and the changing fortunes of the early fourteenth-century papacy as the source of Renaissance culture, with Dante as the link between the two places.

Hyde, J. K. *Padua in the Age of Dante*. Manchester, Eng.: Manchester University Press, 1966. A fine examination of the roots of Renaissance classicism in later thirteenth-century Padua, whose law school became one of the leading centers of the "pre-humanism" scholarship that anticipated the work of Petrarch and Boccaccio.

Kristeller, Paul Oskar. *Renaissance Thought and Its Sources*. New York: Columbia University Press, 1979. The definitive introduction to the origins of Renaissance thought in the ancient, medieval, and Byzantine traditions, by the greatest twentieth-century scholar of Renaissance intellectual history.

Levey, Michael. *Florence. A Portrait*. Cambridge, MA: Harvard University Press, 1996. With its greater emphasis on the fine arts, this thoughtful survey makes a nice companion piece to Brucker's rather more socially- and politically-oriented *Renaissance Florence*. Well-illustrated with black-and-white photographs and a few color plates.

Martines, Lauro. *Power and Imagination. City-States in Renaissance Italy*. Baltimore: Johns Hopkins University Press, 1979. A brilliant, if not always easy book; its convincing location of the Renaissance in an Italian urban history dating back to 1000 decisively supplants the older, Burckhardtian view of the Renaissance as a revolutionary development in fourteenth-century Italy.

Mattingly, Garrett. *Renaissance Diplomacy*. New York: Penguin Books, 1973. First published in 1955, this book explores the impact of Renaissance thought on early modern diplomatic practice, first in Italy and then in all of Europe. A masterpiece of modern historical writing.

Nauert, Charles G., Jr. *Humanism and the Culture of Renaissance Europe*. Cambridge, Eng.: Cambridge University Press, 1995. A thorough and accessible discussion of the formation of a humanist culture in later medieval and early modern Europe.

Partner, Peter. *Renaissance Rome, 1500–1559. A Portrait of a Society*. Berkeley: University of California Press, 1976. A very accessible social and cultural history of sixteenth-century Rome by one of the leading English-speaking historians of medieval and Renaissance Italy.

Rice, Eugene F., Jr. *The Foundations of Early Modern Europe, 1460–1559*. New York: W. W. Norton, 1970. This clear and thorough survey examines the principal phenomena associated with the advent of early modernity, including the age of exploration, the Renaissance, early modern politics, and the Reformation.

Stinger, Charles. *The Renaissance in Rome*. Bloomington: Indiana University Press, 1985. A lively history of the papal court and its influence on Roman society in the fifteenth and sixteenth centuries, with special attention to the development of Rome as a Renaissance concept.

Trinkaus, Charles E. *The Poet as Philosopher; Petrarch and the Formation of Renaissance Consciousness*. New Haven, CT: Yale University Press, 1979. Five interconnected essays on of the poetic values and ideas of Renaissance society as manifested in the work of the founder of humanism; a fascinating work, if at times conceptually difficult.

Waley, Daniel. *The Italian City-Republics*, 3rd ed. New York: Longman, 1988. A re-issue of the 1969 classic, this provides one of the most thorough and accessible discussions in English of Italian urban society from about 1000 to 1350; extremely useful in exploring the social and political context of the early Italian Renaissance.

Wilkins, Ernest Hatch. *Life of Petrarch*. Chicago: University of Chicago Press, 1961. Students may find it dense and a bit dry, but it remains one of the most complete biographies of the "Father of Humanism" available in English.

Joan of Arc at the coronation of Charles VII of France. Many painters have done portraits of Joan of Arc. This portrait suggests the awe in which her followers held her. (Reproduced from the Collections of the Library of Congress)

3

The Hundred Years' War, 1337–1453

INTRODUCTION

The origins of the Hundred Years' War are found in a complex mix of dynastic, political, economic, social, and international factors. Although the war's starting date is usually given as 1337, its belligerents—France and England—had been on uneasy terms for many years. Beginning in the twelfth century with the Plantagenet line of kings in England, English rulers had maintained extensive holdings in France. Although the Plantagenets held their French lands as vassals to the French king, the French monarchs distrusted their English cousins. Furthermore, they believed that the English presence prevented them from seizing these lands and thus furthering their policy of expansion and centralization.

In the late medieval world birthright meant everything, and the death of the French king Philip the Fair in 1314 touched off a major crisis. In rapid succession his three surviving sons took the throne and died without leaving a male heir. By 1328 the male line of the house of Capet—the French royal house since 987—was extinguished. Perhaps the French crown should have gone to Philip's grandson, whose mother was Isabella, Philip the Fair's daughter; however, this grandson was Edward III, the king of England. The French nobility detested the prospect of the French throne passing to the English king, and they rallied behind Philip's nephew who headed the house of Valois. In 1328 the nephew was crowned king of France as Philip VI. Edward reluctantly accepted this outcome.

Political problems complicated the dynastic ones. Philip resolved to continue the royal policy of expansion and consolidation. In particular, he wanted to extend his royal authority to Aquitaine, Edward's major holding in France. Edward, duke of Aquitaine and now Philip's vassal, was just as determined to maintain both his duchy and his independence of the French king. Neither side gave serious consideration to compromise and, in fact, as true medieval knights both Philip and Edward relished the prospect of chivalric warfare. In 1337 Philip attempted to confiscate Aquitaine from Edward, a step that touched off intermittent conflict between France and England that lasted for more than a century. After rebuffing Philip, Edward went on the offensive. In 1340 he declared himself king of France by virtue of his relationship to Philip the Fair, a claim made repeatedly, if only ceremonially, by subsequent English monarchs for the next 400 years.

However, additional issues help to explain the coming of war. For one thing, the French had for years given aid to the Scots, who caused major headaches for the English due to their crossborder raids and their unwillingness to subordinate themselves to England. More importantly, perhaps, economic concerns poisoned the atmosphere. England's economic life and certainly the health of the royal treasury depended in large measure upon the wool trade. During the late medieval period, Flanders was the center of the wool trade. English producers sold their wool there and much of the finished product (woolen cloth) made its way back to England. The king taxed both the export of the raw material and the import of the finished product. Naturally enough, Flanders' merchants and manufacturers sympathized with England; however, the count of Flanders was a vassal of the French king and the Flemish nobility linked themselves to France. For their part, the French kings hoped to capture the wealth of Flanders and, simultaneously, harm the economic interests of their English rivals.

The first consequential battle of the Hundred Years' War occurred in 1340 when an English fleet defeated the French navy at Sluys, thereby gaining control over the English Channel and opening France up to repeated invasions from England. Six years later, at the Battle of Crécy, the English relied on yeomen armed with longbows to destroy the mounted French nobility. In 1347 the English seized Calais, an important Channel port. In 1356 at the Battle of Poitiers England administered yet another crushing defeat to France's feudal army. The French knights were annihilated and the French king, John II, and his son and many of his retainers were captured and sent to England where they were held for ransom. This first phase of the Hundred Years' War came to a close in 1360 with the Treaty of Brétigny. By its terms, Edward received complete control over Aquitaine, Calais, and additional territory, and the French paid an indemnity amounting to 3 million gold coins. In return, Edward abandoned his claims to the French throne.

At the start of the war, few would have believed that the French would have fared so poorly. France's population was three to four times that of England and it was a much richer country. Furthermore, the military campaigns were to take place on familiar French soil. However, France faced numerous obstacles beyond a misguided reliance on obsolete formations of mounted knights that led to the disasters at Crécy and Poitiers, and incompetent kings in Philip VI and John II.

Wars are expensive, and the French monarchy lacked the means to raise adequate funds in a coherent, systematic manner. Consequently, a dearth of money hobbled the French cause. Moreover, feudal kings were not absolute; rather, they had to share power with a variety of interest groups including the nobility. The tension between crown and noble was always fairly high, and at time of war many noblemen took the opportunity to increase their independence at the expense of the monarch. The small but important middle class—the merchants and artisans—also used the war to raise objections to royal prerogative and to demand favorable reforms. Peasants, almost always disgruntled in any case and strapped now with the additional burden of paying for the war, rebelled. Jacqueries, or peasant uprisings, spread across the face of France. Finally, the first years of the Hundred Years' War corresponded to the years of the Black Plague. This horrible disease first devastated Europe, including France, in 1348 and 1349. It killed a significant percentage of the population, disrupted trade and commerce, and created such a labor shortage that rich land was left uncultivated. The almost total breakdown of authority that permitted bands of soldiers to roam at will through the land after the devastating defeat at Poitiers aggravated the effects of the Black Plague.

Despite their apparent success, the war also brought difficulties for the English kings. The chief problem for Edward and his successors was finding enough money. The solution hit upon was not only a novel one, but also one that held monumental consequences for the future. Gradually, the English monarchs surrendered the right to levy taxes to the English Parliament, a sort of national assembly that now began to meet regularly and represented the interests of the merchants and petty nobles as well as the great magnates.

Not unexpectedly, the English search for money led to those least able to defend their economic interests, the lower classes. Taxes and additional restrictive measures fell on the downtrodden, chiefly the peasantry, who had already been ravaged by the Black Plague. As was the case in France, violence resulted. In 1381 a serious rebellion swept parts of England. It was savagely put down, but it fractured English society.

Baronial unrest was also evident in England. Edward III's successor, his grandson Richard II, tried in a highhanded manner to bring the nobility under control and was deposed in 1399 for his pains. His replacement, his cousin Henry Bolingbroke, the duke of Lancaster, reigned as Henry IV until 1413. He spent most of his time unsuccessfully trying to satisfy his aristocratic allies who hungered for even more authority. The result was anarchy sometimes verging on civil war.

While domestic strife consumed both France and England, the war between the two countries proceeded by fits and starts. Charles V, who followed John II to the French throne in 1364, proved fairly adept at dealing with the English. Renewing hostilities in 1367, Charles engaged in a primitive form of guerrilla warfare, gradually pushing the enemy out until, by the time of his death in 1380, the English held only Bordeaux and Calais.

From about 1380 until 1415, stalemate ensued as domestic unrest engulfed both countries. Perhaps France benefitted the most from this dismal situation since its new king, Charles VI, was not only hopelessly incompetent but also suffered from periodic bouts of insanity. Nevertheless, the third and final phase of the Hundred Years' War opened in 1415 when the new English king, Henry V (Prince Hal of Shakespeare fame), invaded France, at least in part to keep his restless nobles occupied. In that year's Battle of Agincourt, English bowmen once again destroyed the flower of the French nobility. About 4,500 French died at Agincourt; English casualties totaled about 100. England now held much of northern France.

Feuds among the French nobility, which had already reduced France to a state of virtual civil war, greatly aided English progress. Chief among the warring French nobility were the Armagnac faction, who for their own selfish interests supported the monarchy, and the Burgundians. In 1361 John II had given the duchy of Burgundy to one of his younger sons. Subsequently, the duchy served as a power base for that collateral branch of the royal family that wanted to rule independently;

it also attracted numerous French knights who concluded that support for the Burgundians would weaken the French crown and, thus, bring greater freedom for themselves.

In the years after Agincourt, the Burgundians as well as other French noblemen allied themselves with the English. This alliance, coupled with further battlefield losses, forced Charles VI to conclude the humiliating Treaty of Troyes in 1420. By the terms of the treaty, Henry became regent of France with the right to inherit the throne upon Charles' death. He also married Charles' daughter, Catherine, with the understanding that their children would inherit both the French and English thrones. To facilitate this, Charles' son, who, in fact, would become Charles VII, was declared illegitimate. With the Treaty of Troyes, French fortunes reached their low point.

Charles VI died in 1422; surprisingly, so did the 35-year old Henry V. In theory at least, the crown of both kingdoms should have passed to Henry and Catherine's baby son, Henry, who will rule in England as Henry VI. However, in France there was a rival claimant to the throne. After the Treaty of Troyes was signed, Charles VI's son had slipped away to Bourges in central France. Charles was a weak man lacking both courage and ambition. Ironically, however, he soon attracted the support of a growing number of French patriots who wished to rid themselves of the English invaders. Foremost among these was the peasant maid, Joan of Arc, who worked long and hard to convince Charles that he should take the crown of France.

Joan was born in 1412 in Domremy, a village located east of Paris. Although her family were peasants, they were fairly prosperous. At an early age Joan began to hear voices, which she attributed to several saints. Commanded by these voices to seek out Charles and to persuade him to allow her to lead an expedition to relieve the city of Orléans, she arrived at his court in 1429. Miraculously enough, the desperate Charles not only received her but also agreed to her request. Joan succeeded and the siege was raised. Subsequently, in May 1429 Charles was crowned king of France in the cathedral at Reims.

After that, Joan's luck turned bad. In 1430 the Burgundians captured her and sold her to the English, who then had her tried for heresy. Condemned by the Inquisition, Joan was burned at the stake in 1431. However, Joan had reversed France's fortunes. A new spirit and determination gripped France, while at the same time discontent with both the monetary and the human expense of the French adventure grew in England. In 1435 the Burgundians reconciled with the French monarchy and slowly but surely the English were ousted. By the time the war petered out in 1453, England had relinquished all its gains and had surrendered Aquitaine as well. Only Calais remainded under English rule.

INTERPRETIVE ESSAY
Daniel Webster Hollis III

The early Renaissance was often a time of tumultuous transition from the feudal to the modern era, and the Hundred Years' War contributed to the transformation in several areas—political, military, economic, and social. Historians love period labels and the term "Hundred Years' War" originated in post-Napoleonic France at a time when jingoistic nationalism reached a peak of intensity. Although the traditional time span for the Anglo-French conflict is 1337–1453, many recent historians have extended its origins to well before 1337 and its final resolution to well past 1453. Since the twelfth century, the monarchs of England and France had been engaged in a process of acquiring greater authority within their kingdoms by representing themselves as the guarantors of justice and security, both internal and external. The monarchical agenda jeopardized the political power and legal jurisdiction of local feudal lords who resisted the monarchs whenever practical. Looking beyond securing mere feudal privileges, the monarchs advanced a novel political system framed around the ingenious legal-constitutional dictum of the royal prerogative. Its salient feature stated that the royal executive could assume whatever powers it needed in order to carry out governing responsibilities. In seeking nearly absolute political power, monarchs not only tried to extinguish the authority and jurisdictions of feudal entities but also created permanent state institutions to effect their control in the localities. Thus, at the same time that English and French monarchs competed for power and territory in France, they were striving for the same ends within their kingdoms, i.e., the creation of a centralized, dynastic nation-state.

What were the dynamics and consequences of the great Anglo-French war upon the transfer of political power from local to central government? The implementation of a centralized regime to ensure justice and security for subjects proved to be, at the least, very expensive. Thus, the erection of a central state apparatus created a necessity for new taxes, in any age an unpopular byproduct of bigger government. The primary concern of late medieval English monarchs, even greater than the potential revival by the barons of a decentralized system of feudal government, was the security of the realm, both territorial and economic, in the face of an aggressive French expansionism. Because the early French Valois kings, seeking to secure their dynasty, proved that royal incompetence was a greater risk than an overly powerful monarch, France began a steady drift toward royal absolutism which would culminate in the seventeenth-century reign of Louis XIV. Thereby, the processes of centralization in both kingdoms led to different outcomes because of their experiences in the Hundred Years' War—victory and unity for the Valois versus defeat, disorder, and civil war in Lancastrian England. Thus, while the French gradually embraced absolutism as the appropriate solution to their need for national unity, the English lost confidence in a centralized system which failed to provide adequately for security and prosperity. Concurrent with French absolutism reaching its apogee in the seventeenth century, England threw off the last vestiges of absolutism and opted for a constitutional mixed form of government making Parliament an equal partner with the royal executive.

The Anglo-French territorial connection began in 1066 with the conquest of England by William, duke of Normandy, who became King William I (1066–1087). The Norman conquest of England established an essentially French ruling elite so that monarchs, nobility, and upper clergy in the two states reflected a cultural unity. In the case of the monarchs and nobles, their political relationships were further bonded through frequent intermarriage. In 1127 Matilda, daughter and heir of Henry I (1100–1135), married Geoffrey Plantagenet, count of Anjou. Their son, Henry II (1154–1189), added to his holdings of Normandy and Anjou the territories of Poitou, Touraine, and Maine, and most importantly, through his 1152 marriage to Eleanor of Aquitaine, the extensive holdings of her duchy in southwestern France. Meanwhile, the last Carolingian king of the West Franks had died in 987 and the count of Paris, Hugh Capet, claimed the title. Undoubtedly, because the Capetian monarchs saw themselves as the heirs of Carolingian sovereignty over a kingdom extending from the Rhine River to the Pyrenees Mountains, their priority was to establish direct authority over the duchies and counties which previously had asserted independence. Since the English monarchs held the greatest portion of those lands, England became the Capetians' main rival for territorial supremacy in France. Significantly, the legal rules which largely determined medieval territorial claims were based on feudal contract law which considered right of possession of the fief rather than title the essential element of property rights.

During the reign of Philip II (1180–1223), the King of France gained dominion over most of England's Angevin empire in France. By the time of the lengthy quarrel between England's Henry III (1216–1272) and France's Louis IX (1226–1270), English possessions had been reduced to the Gascon portions of Aquitaine. Nonetheless, the Plantagenet kings of England continued to claim suzerainty over former estates such as Normandy and Anjou. Thus, the Treaty of Paris (1259) was intended to settle permanently these territorial disputes. By the terms of the agreement, Henry III renounced English claims to former Angevin properties (Normandy, Anjou, Maine, Touraine, Poitou) in exchange for Louis IX recognizing Henry's possession of Aquitaine. In sealing the 1259 pact, Henry III did homage to Louis IX as his feudal lord, thereby making the English ruler, in his role as duke of Aquitaine, a vassal of the French king. Moreover, the royal heirs of Henry III would have to perform liege homage to each succeeding French king or suffer the penalty of having Aquitaine confiscated.

Henry III's son and successor, Edward I (1272–1307), recognized that maintenance of England's profitable commercial ties with the county of Flanders was jeopardized by the restrictions of the 1259 treaty tying the duke of Aquitaine, and hence the king of England, to French interests. Moreover, judicial appeals from court decisions in Aquitaine to the Parlement of Paris, under the authority of the king of France, undermined the duke's authority in the duchy. Edward I concluded that the Treaty of Paris needed to be revised.

The signal importance of the English possession of Aquitaine was evident in the fact that the duchy's revenues from customs duties on wine exports were as great as the English crown land revenues. From about 1290, Edward I's lawyers argued that despite Edward's acts of homage to two French kings, the Treaty of Paris was null and void since the French monarchs had not fulfilled its terms for ceding territory in Aquitaine. In 1294 Philip IV (1285–1314) of France confiscated the duchy of Aquitaine; however, in 1303 the duchy was returned to Edward who fulfilled homage to Philip.

A particularly weak and incompetent king, England's Edward II (1307–1327) postponed doing homage for the duchy of Aquitaine after Charles IV ascended the French throne in 1322. As a result, the French attempted to capture Aquitaine again in the War of Saint-Sardos (1323–1325). As it happened, 13-year-old Prince Edward, who had been awarded administration of England's continental lands, in 1325 did homage to Charles IV for Aquitaine and Ponthieu leading to a truce. A 1327 treaty required Edward III (1327–1377) to pay a large sum to recover control of Aquitaine. Edward III's determination to achieve a full restoration of sovereignty in Aquitaine caused another delay in performing homage to the first Valois king of France, Philip VI (1328–1350). Although Edward feared further French encroachments, he promised in 1331 to execute liege homage to Philip in order to recover Aquitaine revenues confiscated after 1328. Another crucial point of tension between England and France was Scotland. English kings demanded homage from rulers of Scotland much as French kings asserted their feudal rights in Aquitaine. However, in 1295 France's Philip IV pledged political and military aid to the Scots in their contest with England.

Although he had declared a willingness to perform liege homage to Philip VI for Aquitaine in 1331, Edward III was unable to resolve the issue of Aquitaine due to the Franco-Scottish alliance. In 1335, France's movement of its Mediterranean fleet to the Atlantic coast led to English fears of an invasion. Although no invasion ensued, Edward signed a peace with Scotland in 1338 after war with France had been declared.

Economics combined with provincial particularism to influence England's continental interests through the longstanding wool trade with Flanders. The French kings pressured the counts of Flanders to recognize feudal lordship which, if given, might jeopardize England's profitable commerce with Flanders. Even more important than economic considerations in the Low Countries, Edward sought to forestall a Franco-Scottish attack upon England which meant keeping Flemish Channel ports in friendly hands. Flanders could also supply mercenary soldiers to Edward and become a strategic base for military penetration into French territory. Thus, his efforts to solicit allies in the Low Countries after 1337 were motivated by national security and economics rather than problems in Aquitaine. While England gained no significant strategic advantage from extensive monetary and diplomatic efforts in the Low Countries between 1337 and 1340, it may not be accurate to conclude that money and time were wasted. Edward's endeavors at least forced Philip to divert attention away from plans to invade England in order to secure his northern frontier.

Traditional accounts of the Hundred Years' War cite the claim of Edward III to the French throne as a primary cause of the conflict. How serious was this claim? Was it merely a vehicle for protecting his French properties or was it a genuine assertion of a dynastic right? Many, but not all, scholars now think it was indeed part of a strategy to prevent a French invasion of England and to regain sovereignty in Aquitaine. Edward had a substantial basis to assert a right to the French throne through his mother Isabella, the daughter of Philip IV. Yet, French royalists argued that the claim was illegitimate since under Salic law a female supposedly could not inherit lands or titles, although there were several historical exceptions. After initially giving up his right to the French throne upon his accession, Edward affirmed his entitlement in 1340 after the war began in 1337 with Philip VI's attempt to confiscate Aquitaine. Certainly, Edward came to believe that claiming the French throne might be the best defense of his rights in Aquitaine. By asserting a right as king, Edward made the conflict a quarrel among equals instead of merely a feudal lord-vassal dispute. In the Middle Ages, theologians had made it necessary for monarchs to argue that any conflict was a "just war." Moreover, medieval wars also required sufficient justification in the eyes of the public to assure support. Thus, by positioning himself as king of France—a monarch deprived of his birthright—it was easier for Edward to demand sacrifices by the English for the cause.

As for the military balance of power at the onset of war, the French had a two to one advantage over the English in both manpower and resources. Thus, the ability of England to extend the war and dominate France for many decades with smaller forces was due to superior leadership, diplomacy, and what one scholar has called a "military revolution." The code of chivalric knighthood, which bred incessant local wars through the feudal legal concept of trial by combat, definitely was stronger in France than in England, thus retarding French acceptance of modern methods of warfare. Through regional wars, England, by contrast, advanced military innovations including archers with an improved six-foot longbow and men-at-arms equipped with pikes which helped infantry neutralize the advantage of mounted knights. One of the rationales for a strong centralized state was to eliminate the corrosive feudal warring. Yet, the monarch's added ability to marshal massive military resources actually increased rather than diminished the impact of war on society in the late Middle Ages. England's first important military success was a 1340 naval victory over a French fleet at the Battle of Sluys that significantly diminished the threat of a French invasion. Since England had the ability to land troops and supplies through Channel ports but lacked the needed financial resources to sustain a large armed force, it opted for a military campaign known as a *chevauchée*, which consisted of raiding and plundering to reduce an enemy's resources and support.

Edward used the *chevauchée* both to disable France's ability to prosecute war and to draw Philip into a decisive battle. A larger French force chasing the English across Picardy and Artois forced Edward to make a defensive stand at Crécy in 1346. English archers with their longbows decimated the charging French cavalry and pikemen finished off the survivors. It was a devastating defeat for the French, but Edward lacked the financial means to capitalize upon his advantage. The most significant result of Crécy was the English capture in 1347 of the strategic port of Calais. With sufficient revenues, at least Edward could have forced Philip to recognize his territorial independence in Aquitaine. Yet, the onset of the bubonic plague in 1348, moving through France from Mediterranean ports, effectively brought the war to a temporary and thus inconclusive halt. Plague mortality during 1348–1349 reduced the populations of France and England between 20 and 30 percent.

By the time Edward was able to renew military operations in France in the mid-1350s, France had a new king, John II (1350–1364). Edward opted to operate from Aquitaine where the English armies were led by perhaps the greatest soldier of the era, Prince Edward, known by his suit of armor as the "Black Prince." The Prince invaded the former Angevin territory of Poitou on the border with Aquitaine forcing King John to try and block the advance. At the battle of Poitiers (1356), the Black Prince's small force of 3,000–5,000 chased by John's army of 9,000 successfully defended itself against French assaults in a pattern reminiscent of Crécy. The French cavalry suffered 40 percent casualties, but the major dividend for England was the capture of King John who became a bargaining chip in negotiations for a settlement. Further campaigns followed until the two sides signed the Treaty of Brétigny (1360), negotiated in two fairly distinct sessions. Originally intended to be merely a "ransom treaty," Edward's failed 1359 offensive led him to withdraw his claim to the French crown and to the territories of Normandy, Anjou, and Maine upon the condition of France's recognition of Edward's independent, non-feudal possession of Aquitaine, Poitou, Ponthieu, Guines, and Calais. Further, King John would remain captive until France had paid the first installment of a ransom of 3 million *écus* (£500,000), which was more than five times the annual income of the English crown. About half the ransom remained unpaid at the time of John's death in 1364, and his successor, Charles V (1364–1380), declared the mutual renunciations of territory by Edward and John in the Treaty of Brétigny to be void. When Edward refused Charles' demand of homage, Charles declared Aquitaine confiscated. Edward then revived his claim to the French throne and hostilities resumed in 1369.

Charles V and his chief military advisor, Bertrand du Guesclin, decided to utilize a guerrilla-type warfare against the English and avoid the large confrontations such as at Crécy and Poitiers. In combination with growing hostility toward English rule in their possessions, the French strategy worked to halt English advances and to neutralize their prior military advantage. Warfare reverted to a garrison mode with small forces utilizing fortress cities to ravage the neighboring countryside. Artillery was still not designed to breach such fortifications. Though gunpowder was used in Chinese weapons as early as the ninth century, the development of artillery began only in the early fourteenth century. It was not until the 1420s that improvements in artillery—longer gun barrels and improved gunpowder—made it a decisive weapon in sieges.

The Black Prince contracted tuberculosis and had to retire from the war in 1371. He died in 1376 just a year before his father's death. England even lost its naval dominance in the Channel by the late 1370s. Meanwhile, an emboldened Parliament demanded accountability for misspent appropriations. The new king, Richard II (1377–1399), the eldest son of Prince Edward, was a minor and thus the helm of state was left to Richard's uncles. The French were not able to capitalize on the void in English leadership. Indeed, they faced a crisis of their own. Charles V died in 1380 bringing to the throne the perhaps mentally unstable Charles VI (1380–1422), also a minor. Richard II gained direct control of government from his uncles in 1389 and agreed to a truce with France, in part because the war's costs made the king unduly dependent on creditors and Parliament. Another truce with France in 1396 ended the fighting without resolving any key issues dividing the kings of England and France. The hope for a lasting peace was vested in the marriage by proxy of Charles VI's seven-year old daughter, Isabella, to Richard, accompanied by a £100,000 dowry.

Upon the deposition of Richard II by his cousin, Henry Bolingbroke who became Henry IV (1399–1413), the French conflict became secondary to the Lancastrian monarch's efforts to secure his throne and dynasty by suppressing domestic opposition. Nonetheless, it was Henry IV who conceived of returning to France to finish the task of recovering and safeguarding English lands. The reasons were because the French refused to recognize Henry as king of England and sought to use his distraction at home to sweep the English out of France altogether. Fortunately for Henry, the French were facing dangers of their own from an ambitious duke of Burgundy. In fact, peace seemed more likely when a proposed marriage between Prince Henry and Catherine, daughter of Charles VI, was negotiated. When the Prince became Henry V (1413–1422), he was both freed from concerns about dynastic security and led by his father to renewed interest in the French war, having served as duke of Aquitaine since 1399.

Henry V's political aims and thus his military policy in France were distinct from his predecessors in that he intended to conquer and hold as much French territory as possible, regardless of previous ownership. Conquest was primarily for its own rewards and not just to enhance the security of Aquitaine and Calais. Henry's singleminded determination quickly paid huge dividends. Because of Henry's excessive demands for full sovereignty over Aquitaine, Poitou, Normandy, Maine, Anjou, Touraine, and Ponthieu, negotiations begun earlier for a marriage contract and peace collapsed in 1415. Henry tried to invade through Normandy, but failed and moved his depleted force into Calais. Seeking to seize the opportunity, the French carried the war to Henry which led to the battle of Agincourt. The English victory resembled the great wins at Crécy and Poitiers, and the French seemed utterly demoralized and without effective leadership. A second English invasion force returned successfully to Normandy in 1417 and penetrated into much of northern France, capturing Paris in 1419. Henry's alliance with the duke of Burgundy confirmed the French fate. By the terms of the Treaty of Troyes (1420)—the first complete peace agreement since 1360—Henry became the heir to the French throne at Charles VI's death and sealed the agreement by finally concluding the much anticipated marriage to Catherine, Charles' daughter. Since he would be the next king of France, Henry did not feel it necessary to include a statement of his sovereignty over French territories such as Aquitaine and Normandy.

Yet, the apparently triumphant end to the conflict faded with the death of Henry V in 1422 some months prior to Charles VI's death. Henry and Catherine's son, Henry VI (1422–1461), was only nine months old which made it easy for the French nobility to refuse recognition of the child-king and promote the ambitions of Charles VI's disinherited son, the dauphin, as King Charles VII (1422–1461). France had for the moment two kings, yet Henry did not come of age to rule until 1436. Obviously, the royal regents, led by Henry's uncle, John, duke of Bedford, determined to enforce the terms of the Treaty of Troyes which meant resuming the war. Though the experienced English commanders seized the military initiative and had the dauphin's forces on the verge of defeat in 1429, a miraculous turn of events shifted the tide of war in favor of France. French disunity, which had prevented the concentration of their manpower and resource advantage over the English, finally ended through an unlikely sequence of events. The controversial English decision to attack Orléans instead of continuing the expansion from Normandy was fateful. The lifting of the siege of Orléans by the religiously inspired maid, Joan of Arc, gave new life to the French armies and led to the coronation of Charles at Reims.

The English suddenly shifted from an offensive to a defensive posture. Though England had resumed its Burgundian alliance after 1422, that arrangement ended in 1435—the same year as Bedford's death—with the Treaty of Arras whereby Philip, duke of Burgundy, agreed to recognize Charles VII as king and terminate the agreement with England. The English retreat continued with the loss of Paris in 1436. After the truce of 1444, Henry was prepared to yield his claim to the French throne in return for full sovereignty in Aquitaine and Normandy. Yet, by then the French already had captured half of Normandy and were launching an invasion of Aquitaine for the first time since the war began in 1337. Thus, the truce permitted Charles to strengthen his forces for a final military push, incorporating the skillful use of improved artillery. Charles pressed a full-scale assault on Normandy in 1449 which proved to be the climactic campaign leading to England's expulsion by 1453. Ultimately, as in the past, military advantage became the final determinant of legal claims. In both the 1350s and 1410s, French defeats leading to decisive treaties were due as much to internal problems as to English military superiority. England fought after 1369 to enforce the Treaty of Brétigny (1360), which settled a feudal dispute, and after 1422 to enforce the Treaty of Troyes (1420), intended to resolve a dynastic issue. Charles V's rather successful military strategy of the 1370s was not pursued during Charles VI's reign. After 1429, however, French internal unity combined with military successes led to an English defeat.

England faced domestic chaos after its loss in France. Another serious peasant rising in 1450, led by Jack Cade, was followed in 1455 by the outbreak of a dynastic struggle known as the War of the Roses. The duke of York claimed the throne usurped by the Lancastrians in 1399. The French boldly raided the southern English coast during 1457. The Yorkists deposed Henry VI in 1461 and crowned Edward IV (1461–1483) king. After defeating the Lancastrians by 1471, Edward reasserted the English claim to the French throne, fashioned a new alliance with the duke of Burgundy, and invaded France in 1475. Yet, Edward's effort seemed half-hearted and he quickly signed the Treaty of Picquigny (1475) relinquishing his French titles for an annual pension to be paid by France's Louis XI. The last episode of the French conflict played out during the Tudor era. Henry VIII (1509–1547) sent English soldiers to French soil on three occasions in 1513, 1523, and 1544, but without lasting achievement. England's last continental possession, Calais, was returned to France in 1558.

The social implications of the Hundred Years' War have been given more attention by scholars in recent decades. Following a stable era of European growth and prosperity in the thirteenth century, one disaster after another disrupted fourteenth-century life. Bad harvests which produced famines marked the periods 1315–1322 and the 1340s. Europeans also faced a recurring cycle of plague beginning in the 1340s. Together, the bubonic plague and famines took an incalculable demographic toll on medieval societies. Indeed, over the course of the Hundred Years' War, deaths from plague and famine were much greater than those from battle wounds. The coincidence of famine and plague also brought the first serious wage and price inflation since the fifth century. Contemporary chroniclers such as Jean Froissart, with their biased though not necessarily inaccurate accounts, tended to write the story of war almost entirely through the roles of royalty and nobility. Yet, clearly war affected all social classes and economic activities in both France and England.

The demands of war were constant throughout the Middle Ages. Thus, the social conditions, especially for the aristocracy, of the Hundred Years' War were more nearly normal than extraordinary. Indeed, the conflict might be described with some accuracy as periods of peace punctuated by episodes of fighting which were few and brief. Medieval warfare was accompanied by problems of economic transformation from a feudal agrarian to a capitalist commercial economy and the resulting social changes caused by the breakdown of manorialism and the emergence of a non-feudal urban middle class. Disrupted trade impacted some cities, especially seaports, so that famine and plague merely compounded urban economic troubles. Because war profits represented the transfer of property from losers to winners, there were unique occasions for both enhancing personal wealth and creating financial distress. Notable fortunes in the fifteenth century were made by a few such as England's Sir John Fastolf and France's Jacques Coeur, though there were more losers than winners in the redistribution of wealth. War often undermined traditional social and economic barriers so that a commoner such as Bertrand du Guesclin could rise to the pinnacle of office and wealth in France. Thus, the combination of war, socio-economic upheaval, famine, and disease directly affected commodity prices, laborers' wages, and tax increases. This combination also helped to determine which parts of society were wealthy and which were not. There also was much greater population mobility—especially among the younger generation—than normal, often to far distant provinces seeking to escape the destruction. The population loss caused reductions in crop production and fewer tax revenues, while those provinces which received immigrants enhanced the resources of local princes.

Peasant rebellions, especially the large-scale ones such as the French *Jacquerie* in 1358 and the English risings of 1381 and 1450, were caused first and foremost by the breakdown of feudalism which forced laborers to seek employment beyond the manor. Yet, the war added fuel to the economic fire by contributing to shortages of necessities. In the case of the Jacquerie, it was certainly no mere coincidence that violence occurred in the aftermath of the most devastating French defeat at Poitiers (1356) accompanied by the capture of King John II. In both the French and English episodes, heavier than usual taxation of the peasants was a direct outgrowth of war. The enactment of eight new tax subsidies by England's Parliament, including the hated poll tax, between 1371 and 1380 fueled the Peasants' Revolt of 1381. The failure of the central governments to provide security from military assaults, especially for coastal towns, also led to widespread anti-government feeling. Though each peasant rising evidenced a strong anti-noble sentiment, the main concern of the vulnerable classes was simply to survive the threats to their existence.

Political changes wrought by the Hundred Years' War tended to strengthen royal authority, though England's situation was unique. Although the costs of financing the Hundred Years' War may have been little more than the costs of ordinary wars, monarchs took advantage of the conflict to seek new revenue measures. The royal executives used their representative assemblies—France's Estates-General and England's Parliament—to impose direct royal taxes. Since ordinary crown revenues supplemented by loans were often insufficient to maintain military forces, English kings frequently convened Parliaments to appropriate fresh taxes. Thus, Parliament's role in statecraft became augmented and helping to finance the war made its legislative function appear as indispensable as the executive power of the monarch. Military setbacks caused the Good Parliament of 1376 to question royal fiscal management and political corruption, thereby setting records for the length of meetings and the number of petitions. It was also the first Parliament to name a speaker of the Commons.

In both England and France, the Hundred Years' War aided the monarchy in establishing the principle of permanent national taxes. Indirect assessments such as the salt tax in France and customs duties on trade raised the greatest amount of income and were the least unpopular. Needing cash quickly forced the crown to employ a series of financial devices including subsidies, loans, and even debasement of the coinage. From the 1340s onward, raising somewhat larger than normal military forces required supplements to the traditional feudal resources which had been based on a vassal's military obligation to his lord in the feudal contract. Both kings and nobles supplemented their manpower needs by making limited agreements—indentures—for cash payments to soldiers who served under them without the trappings of feudalism such as ceremonial homage. This growth of "bastard feudalism" was yet another sign of a weakening feudalism in late medieval Europe. The next step would be the establishment by monarchs of permanent standing armies. Although some scholars have attempted to argue that nationalism was a cause of the conflict, most conclude that increased national consciousness was a result rather than a cause of the Hundred Years' War.

Much can be learned about the Hundred Years' War from contemporary literary accounts. Because of an obvious popular fascination with combat, most chroniclers tended to glorify war by upholding medieval notions of chivalry. Yet, other accounts revealed the downside of war for the population. Though most writers on both sides of the Channel remained patriotic in support of the respectable goals of the war, some such as Philippe de Mézières offered political and moral criticism of mismanagement and corruption in the conflict. Even notable authors such as Geoffrey Chaucer cited the importance of responsible actions by kings and nobles to promote the common good. Less concerned with historical accuracy, William Shakespeare's postwar hindsight in his plays nonetheless fixed the popular modern stereotype of the royal participants.

In sum, although it cannot be said that the Hundred Years' War initiated any profound changes, it clearly influenced several important ongoing trends which heralded the end of the feudal era and the beginning of modern times. The most important development, already underway in France and England before the war, was the replacement of local feudal government by a centralized, dynastic nation-state. The maturity and credibility of representative assemblies, especially England's Parliament, was accelerated because of their roles in the conflict. The war forced all European states to consider the professionalization of their diplomatic structures, thereby recognizing the significant role of diplomacy in international affairs. Obviously, the advance of technological innovations such as artillery benefitted from the demands of war, but as national armies and navies became commonplace so too did the popular makeup of those forces. War was no longer just an affair of the noble class. The demands of war spurred the growth of commercial capitalism while also contributing to the decline of subsistence farming characterized by the manor. War promoted an increase in social mobility and the continuing rise of the middle class. Finally, the Hundred Years' War produced a marked increase in national consciousness and the popular identification with the nation instead of just localities.

SELECTED BIBLIOGRAPHY

Allmand, Christopher. *The Hundred Years' War: England and France at War, c. 1300–c.1450*. Cambridge, Eng.: Cambridge University Press, 1988. Incorporates the best scholarship; especially good on diplomatic, political, and military aspects.

Bridbury, A. R. "The Hundred Years' War: Costs and Profits." In *Trade, Government and Economy in Pre-Industrial England*, pp. 80–95. Edited by D. C. Coleman and A. H. John. London: Weidenfeld and Nicolson, 1976. Argues that notwithstanding scholarly debates about the war being either a burden or a windfall economically, its financial consequences were not much different than other periods of the Middle Ages.

Campbell, James. "Scotland and the Hundred Years' War in the 14th Century." In *Europe in the Late Middle Ages*, pp. 184–216. Edited by John R. Hale, R. Highfield, and B. Smalley. Evanston, IL: Northwestern University Press, 1965. Shows how fears of a Franco-Scottish invasion delayed Edward III's attack on France.

Chaplais, Pierre. "The Making of the Treaty of Paris (1259) and the Royal Style." *English Historical Review* 67 (1952): 235–53. Emphasis on the treaty as the key underlying cause of Anglo-French conflicts which led to the outbreak of war in 1337.

Contamine, Philippe. *War in the Middle Ages*. Translated by Michael Jones. Oxford: Basil Blackwell, 1984. Principal military authority for all technical aspects relating to the art of war.

Curry, Anne. *The Hundred Years' War*. London: Macmillan, 1993. The best short study from the English perspective; includes a historiographical analysis.

Curry, Anne, and Michael Hughes, eds. *Arms, Armies and Fortifications in the Hundred Years' War*. Woodbridge, Eng.: Boydell and Brewer, 1994. Detailed analytical essays reviewing various aspects of war including strategy, tactics, weapons, and fortifications.

Cuttino, G. P. "Historical Revision: the Causes of the Hundred Years' War." *Speculum* 31 (1956): 463–77. A diplomatic historian who tends to place more blame on France for the outbreak of war.

Fowler, Kenneth. *The Age of Plantagenet and Valois: The Struggle for Supremacy, 1328–1498.* London: Elek Books, 1967. A well-balanced general treatment with superb illustrations, many in color.

———, ed. *The Hundred Years' War.* London: Macmillan, 1971. Wide-ranging collection of essays by leading scholars on various aspects of the conflict.

Hewitt, Herbert James. *The Organization of War under Edward III, 1338–62.* Manchester: Manchester University Press, 1966. Contends that Edward's *chevauchée* strategy both destabilized the French regime and revealed France's military vulnerabilities.

Hilton, R. H., and T. H. Aston, eds. *The English Rising of 1381.* New York: Cambridge University Press, 1987. Details the causes and consequences of peasant uprisings and their relationship to war.

Kaeuper, Richard W. *War, Justice and Public Order: England and France in the Later Middle Ages.* Oxford: Clarendon Press, 1988. Suggests that war aims had different outcomes: strengthening royal absolutism in France but generating constitutional trends in England.

Le Patourel, John. "Edward III and the Kingdom of France." *History* 43 (1958): 173–89. Believes Edward III's claim of the French throne was sincere and not an ulterior motive for war.

Maddicott, J. R. "The Origins of the Hundred Years' War." *History Today* 36 (May 1986): 31–37. A careful analysis of events leading up to the outbreak of war.

Perroy, Edouard. *The Hundred Years' War.* Bloomington: Indiana University Press, 1959. The standard scholarly account by a French historian concentrating on military aspects.

Prestwich, Michael. *The Three Edwards: War and State in England, 1272–1377.* London: Weidenfeld and Nicolson, 1980. Readable general account of England's role in the early war era.

Rogers, Clifford J. "The Military Revolutions of the Hundred Years' War." *Journal of Military History* 57 (1993): 241–78. Informed thesis that the early modern "military revolution" actually began in the era of the Hundred Years' War.

Sumption, Jonathan. *The Hundred Years' War: Trial by Battle.* Philadelphia: University of Pennsylvania Press, 1991. The most detailed account to 1360; first of a promised multivolume treatment.

Vale, Malcolm. *The Origins of the Hundred Years' War: The Angevin Legacy, 1250–1340.* New York: Oxford University Press, 1996. Carefully-researched conclusion that the quarrel over Aquitaine, especially the 1290s war, was the most important cause of the 1337 conflict.

Wright, Nicholas. *Knights and Peasants: The Hundred Years' War in the French Countryside.* Woodbridge, Eng.: Boydell Press, 1998. An important, unique view of the war through the experience of the peasants seeking merely to survive.

A section of the Great Wall of China. The early Ming rulers constructed one of the world's most spectacular engineering feats in order to protect their empire from threatened Mongol raids. (Reproduced from the Collections of the Library of Congress)

4

The Ming Dynasty Comes to Power, 1368–1431

INTRODUCTION

During the latter half of the fourteenth century, China underwent a change in leadership as the Ming dynasty replaced the Mongols. Little more than a century earlier, the Mongols had swept out of central Asia to establish their hold over China. These fierce, nomadic warriors, whose horsemanship and endurance were legendary, constructed a huge empire that stretched from the China Sea to the plains of eastern Europe and also included much of the Middle East. The Mongol chieftain Genghis Khan attacked northern China and conquered the important city of Beijing in 1215. Although Genghis Khan died in 1227, the Mongol onslaught continued and by 1234 the Mongols controlled all of northern China. Next they turned to southern China, where Kublai Khan, the grandson of Genghis, led the Mongol hordes to victory. By 1279 they had conquered the south. The Mongols, styling themselves in the Chinese fashion the Yuan ("Origin") dynasty, now ruled all of China.

However, the Mongol grip on power was not as firm as it might have appeared. Like many other would-be empire builders, the Mongols soon discovered that their economic, administrative, and political infrastructure was inadequate. In the case of China, the conquerors adopted many of the forms and institutions of the conquered; but this proved futile as Chinese discontent with the Mongols grew steadily. Several specific issues fed Chinese dissatisfaction. To begin with, ethnic Chinese never fully reconciled themselves to Mongol suzerainty, especially as the Mongols implemented a number of discriminatory practices harmful to the Chinese. Moreover, the Mongols greedily exploited China's wealth for their own purposes. As a consequence, economic productivity declined and tens of millions of Chinese peasants—whose existence was marginal in the best of times—found themselves facing utter disaster. Corruption was rampant and confusion in the administration of sometimes contradictory regulations led to growing chaos. The Mongol decision to favor a clique of corrupt Tibetan monks over all other religious figures also offended the Chinese, as did perceived Mongol arrogance. It is not surprising then to find open resistance to Mongol rule appearing in the mid-fifteenth century.

The rebellion's rapid spread revealed the weakness of the Yuan dynasty; however, the rebels were not unified and a sorting out process among the rebel forces occurred at the same time that they were driving the Mongols from China. Out of this chaos emerged a strongman, Zhu Yuanzhang, who eventually defeated his Chinese rivals as well as the Mongols and founded the Ming dynasty that was to last until 1644. Zhu Yuanzhang was born about 1328 in humble circumstances. Zhu's father was a landless agricultural worker and at age 16 Zhu became a Buddhist monk in order to avoid starvation. Shortly thereafter he assumed command of a rebel band, and by 1368 had defeated both his Chinese rivals and the Mongols. Even though his armies captured the Mongol capital of Beijing in that year, Zhu decided to make his capital at the southern city of Nanking. There he established the Ming (Brilliant or Glorious) dynasty and took for himself the reign-name of Hongwu (Vast Military). After 1368, the Hongwu emperor continued his conquests until by 1387 he ruled all of traditional China. Moreover, the first Ming ruler extended his power beyond China proper to include much of Mongolia and Korea.

The Hongwu emperor died in 1398 and was succeeded by his teen-age grandson, Chu Yun-wen. However, Chu Yun-wen's rule was challenged by his uncle, Chu Ti, the so-called Prince of Yen who was a younger son of Zhu. In the ensuing struggle, the forces of Chu Ti triumphed and he came to the throne as the third Ming emperor in 1403. He chose Yongle as his reign-name and ruled until his death in 1424. Most experts consider the reign of the Yongle emperor to be the height of Ming power.

The China that the early Mings inherited was the largest, most populous, and most sophisticated country in the world. It was enormously wealthy, although the wealth was unequally distributed among the

country's 80 million people. A huge, well-educated bureaucracy that administered a complex body of law and regulations managed the country's day to day affairs. China's cultural life was unmatched and its
traditions were ancient and venerable. The ethical code developed by
Confucius in the fifth century B.C.E. continued to guide official Chinese
behavior and provided a firm foundation for Chinese life. The Chinese
were also technologically advanced as evidenced by their textile and iron
industries. Chinese armies traditionally dominated the region.

Although it is sometimes overlooked, early Ming China enjoyed a long
and successful maritime heritage dating back to at least the eleventh
century. A vast, modern merchant marine traded extensively with Japan,
Southeast Asia, and South Asia. Chinese goods, especially silks and porcelain, were in great demand. Large shipyards on the lower Yangtze
River turned out both commercial and naval vessels. The Mongols had
expanded the Chinese navy in order to coordinate it with their un-
equaled land forces; however, they suffered a crushing defeat when they
tried to invade Japan in 1281. Nevertheless, at the beginning of the fifteenth century China was the globe's most important naval power. In
terms of both size and technological achievement, the Chinese navy far
surpassed anything that contemporary Europeans knew.

China's impressive naval strength caught the attention of the Yongle
emperor, who had committed his realm to an active foreign policy on
both land and sea. In 1403 the emperor ordered preparations for the first
of seven voyages that over the next 30 years would take Chinese fleets
to Sri Lanka, India, the Persian Gulf, Arabia, the east coast of Africa,
and, perhaps, around the Cape of Good Hope.

To superintend these voyages, the emperor chose Zheng He, today
sometimes referred to as China's Christopher Columbus. Zheng was
born about 1371 in the southwestern province of Yunnan. His family
was Muslim and his father carried the honorary title of hadji, or one who
had made the obligatory Muslim journey to Mecca. Quite possibly Zheng
was selected to head the voyages because his Muslim background and
knowledge of Islamic customs would serve the Chinese fleet well as it
travelled west to stop at Muslim ports of call.

Zheng first made his mark at about the age of 20 when he helped to
suppress a rebellion in Yunnan against the Prince of Yen. When the
prince become the Yongle emperor, he named Zheng to the prestigious
post of Grand Eunuch of the Three Treasures and appointed him to head
the naval expeditions. This was the first time in Chinese history that a
eunuch had gained a command position over military forces.

To the western reader it might seem strange that in fifteenth-century China there was a class of people called eunuchs who were deemed important enough and competent enough to handle serious tasks. However, eunuchs fell well within ancient Chinese tradition. The ranks of the vast Chinese bureaucracy were filled with Confucian scholars who had passed a very rigorous civil service examination. While generally loyal to the emperor, the civil servants were virtually a class unto themselves and often acted in a fairly independent manner. Originally, eunuchs had been assigned menial tasks within the emperor's harem. Over the centuries, however, eunuchs had graduated to the role of keepers of the purity of the harem and then to the role of trusted personal advisors of the emperor. There was no love lost between the Confucian civil servants and the eunuchs.

Because the Yongle emperor never explained himself, his motives for undertaking the series of voyages remain open to speculation. Certainly the naval expeditions seem to have been a component part of the aggressive foreign policy pursued by the first Ming rulers. At the very time that the Yongle emperor ordered the voyages, he was sending military forces to conquer Mongolia and temporarily occupying Vietnam. Commercial considerations probably played a role as well. The seven expeditions included hundreds of ships laden with goods, or "gifts" that the emperor bestowed upon the foreigners his men encountered. In return, the foreigners were expected to offer an equal or greater amount of "tribute" to the emperor. In this manner, the emperor was able to carry on a lucrative, state-subsidized private trade that filled his coffers. Most likely, the Yongle emperor also authorized the expeditions for reasons of prestige. Not only would the expeditions boost China's reputation, but they would also enhance the name of the Ming dynasty, a new dynasty in search of glory and honor, and strengthen the position of the Yongle emperor who, after all, was a usurper. Some experts speculate that the expeditions reflected the Yongle emperor's fear that the nephew he had overthrown had not died in the fighting but, instead, had escaped abroad where his continued existence represented a challenge to the emperor's legitimacy. Because the Chinese made no territorial claims and because they blazed no new routes, one can probably eliminate both conquest and discovery as motives.

In 1405 the first expedition set sail for Vietnam, Indonesia, Sri Lanka, and India. In rapid succession there followed voyages to Sri Lanka and India (1407); Thailand, Sri Lanka, and India (1409); Indonesia, India, the Persian Gulf, and east Africa (1413); Indonesia, the Persian Gulf, Arabia, and east Africa (1417); Indonesia, the Persian Gulf, and east Africa (1421);

and Indonesia, India, the Persian Gulf, and Arabia, including Jeddah, the port of Mecca (1431). Sailing with the prevailing winds, each voyage took about two years to complete.

The expeditions were mammoth undertakings. The first voyage, which was not the largest one, included more than 300 vessels. By comparison, Columbus sailed decades later with only three vessels, and the great Spanish Armada of 1588 boasted only 132 vessels, or less than one-half the number that Zheng He commanded at the start of the fifteenth century. The pride of the Chinese fleet was 62 massive junks called treasure ships because they would return to China with "unnamed treasures of untold quantities." These ships measured 440 feet in length and 180 feet in breadth. They displaced more than 3,000 tons and featured nine masts up to 90 feet high, three decks, and watertight compartments. Each treasure ship carried 450 to 500 men. It is believed that the Chinese fleet at maximum strength had 250 such ships.

Thousands of men manned the fleet. More than 27,800 men sailed on the first voyage, including a slew of eunuch officials, military and naval officers, astrologers, medical personnel, secretaries, accountants, and common soldiers and sailors. Since these were not voyages of conquest, the soldiers served merely to intimidate and impress. However, on occasion they were used to make a point. For example, on the first voyage, Zheng He ordered his forces to subdue some stubborn pirates whose leader was subsequently captured and sent back to the emperor's court where he was executed. At the conclusion of the fourth voyage, the same fate awaited a certain Sekandar who had seized the throne of Semudera (a small Sumatran kingdom) from the emperor's vassal and was subsequently defeated and captured by Chinese troops attached to the fleet.

China's interest in the outside world seemed to end abruptly with the death of the Yongle emperor in 1424. His successor ordered an immediate halt to the expeditions, and while the next emperor, the Hsuan-te emperor, provided for one final voyage in 1431, China's glory days on the high seas had come to an end.

INTERPRETIVE ESSAY
Lung-kee Sun

The Ming Dynasty, established in the wake of the collapse of global Mongol domination, was a "nationalistic revival" by default. When Ming

China found itself seceding from the fragmented Mongol Empire, it entered the same category as other "successor" states such as Muscovite Russia and Shi'ite Persia. Understandably, modern "nations" only came into existence in the nineteenth century; but as "modern" itself is a relative concept, today's China, Russia, and Iran are certainly not pure inventions from the age of Western-style nationhood. They were fashioned out of pre-existing "identities" that reemerged after the breakup of the Mongol world.

The Mongolic Yuan Dynasty (1271–1368) largely restored the Chinese empire after a lengthy period of imperial ups and downs. The Chinese imperium originated in the Qin-Han empire (221 B.C.E.–220 C.E.) and was resuscitated as the second imperium during the Sui-Tang Dynasty (581–907). When the Tang empire broke down after 755 (before formally ending in 907), an interregnum ensued until 960 when the Song Dynasty arose. However, the Song failed to build a mighty third imperium. Rather, it coexisted precariously with powerful Sinified Khitan, Tangut, and Jurchid border-states. When the Song lost out to the last-mentioned, it relocated itself in the south where it became a commercialized polity with half of the state's revenues based on monopolies and excise taxes, and as much as 20 percent of its cash flow derived from maritime trade alone. Moreover, a quasi-modern nationalist sentiment also began to stir among the Song's populace due to its incessant conflicts with foreign states. Under the Song, a print culture, a precondition of modern nation-formation according to some theorists, also flourished. Finally, some scholars also discern in Song China an embryonic "industrial revolution."

All this seems tantalizingly "modern" from our perspective. Whatever the nature of the Song phenomenon—a foretaste of modernity or a failed imperium—the third version of the Chinese empire was achieved by the Yuan, which more than restored the Celestial Dynasty's hegemony over East and Inner Asia. The Yuan Dynasty's effect on China was paradoxical on the surface but in fact followed deep-seated historical patterns. One trend was increasing centralization, which was evident even under the weak Song state. The Song reclassified local officials as metropolitan officials who "knew" local affairs; the Yuan went a step further, turning provinces and districts into "itineraries" of the Central Secretariat. It was under the "alien" Yuan that the Beijing dialect, Mandarin, became the official language of the realm, thus laying the foundation of the future "national" language. Yet the Mongol rule was at the same time cosmopolitan. Genghis Khan's unified domain had broken up under Kublai

Khan, the lord of China who kept the nominal title of the Great Khan but had trouble controlling even the Asian heartland. Yet in their Chinese patrimony, the Mongol rulers used not only Confucian officials but also Central Asians or Europeans (like the Polo family) to rule the Chinese. The Yuan's Persian connection kept alive the Song's active international trade with West Asia.

In fact, a cosmopolitan streak persisted from the Tang Dynasty all the way to the early Ming Dynasty. Not only was the Tang capital Chang'an a world bazaar accommodating Nestorian chapels, Zoroastrian temples, Jewish synagogues, and Japanese students, but a sizable Arab colony also existed in the southern port city of Guangzhou. In the last days of the Song, the Maritime Superintendent Pu Sougeng was of Arab origin and his fleet and power base in the port city of Quanzhou was an important force after the fall of Lin'an, the Song capital. As for Zheng He, the central focus of this essay, his ancestors were Central Asians who came to China to serve in the newly conquered territory of Yunnan under their Mongol masters. When the Ming forces took Yunnan (1381–1382), the boy Zheng He was captured as an enemy element and castrated. Yet his Muslim background did not prevent him from rising to the highest rank of Grand Eunuch under Emperor Yongle and taking charge of the famous international voyages on behalf of the imperial court.

With good reason, this openness did not last beyond the early Ming. When the "alien" Mongol domination ended, the reign of Central Asians or other foreign elements perforce ended with it. The descendants of these people became Chinese and some would make it to officialdom, but the Yuan troika system—one Mongol, one Central Asian, and one Chinese—for governing at every level naturally came to an end under a native Chinese dynasty. The Yuan anomaly resulted from the fact that when Genghis Khan began his empire-building there were only around 1 million Mongols, so the ranks of the ruling class had to be augmented by Central Asians. China was the last country to be conquered by this mixed group.

Scholarly opinion on Ming xenophobia varies. One school sees the Ming as an effort to construct a "lesser China" of Han people from the very start, in contrast to the greater China built by the Mongols and Manchus within a "universal empire" framework. Others argue that the Yuan was not perceived as a foreign tyranny in early Ming, pointing to the fact that Kublai Khan continued to be venerated in the Ming's official pantheon of "Chinese" emperors. One thing is certain: the Ming Dynasty expelled the Mongols to the northern steppes without eliminating their constant threat from that quarter. After mid-Ming, the nomads and border peoples definitely put the empire on the defensive, and xenophobic sentiments against "foreigners" became virulent. The Ming's paradox lies in the fact that it inherited a revitalized empire from the Mongols yet became a "Chinese" state by more narrowly reinventing "Chineseness" as time went by. In this respect, by mid-Ming the Chinese had revived the Song "nationalist" sentiments against foreign invaders and conquerors, and the combined Song-Ming narratives of resisting the Khitans, the Jurchids, the Mongols, the "Japanese pirates," and eventually the Manchus came to inform the Han-centered "national" genealogy of twentieth-century Republican China.

In southeast China, political concerns initially motivated Emperor Hongwu (Zhu Yuanzhang) to seal off the coasts. During the general uprising against the Yuan Dynasty, Zhu, who operated from the Yangzi hinterland, had to contend with competitors based on the coastal regions—the former core of the Southern Song maritime state. After Zhu's victory, their remnants refused to submit and escaped overseas, probably even to Japan. It might explain the bizarre case of the "hired Japanese assassins" (1380) which Emperor Hongwu used as an excuse to eliminate China's last prime minister, Hu Weiyong, so that the despot could take over the office himself. In the eyes of the government, Chinese who traveled overseas were increasingly under suspicion of plotting subversion; consequently, they readily sank into the status of "abandoned subjects of the Celestial Dynasty."

Even after sealing off the coastal areas, the vibrant maritime trade with southeast, south, and west Asia was not discontinued; it simply became a state monopoly. Meanwhile, all foreign clients had to assume the guise of "tributary missions" to the Celestial Dynasty. Ming policy dictated that trade was open only to those who came to pay tribute in an official capacity and government agencies would receive their goods as "tribute." For that purpose, Hongwu set up the first maritime superintendency in Huangdu (near today's Shanghai) as early as 1367. In 1370 the same agency was established in three ports, with the specification that Ningbo trade only with Japan, Quanzhou with Liuqiu (Ryukyu), and Guangzhou with Champa, Siam, and the Indian Ocean states.

Zheng He's voyages reaffirmed the pre-existing overseas connections of the Chinese, which as early as Song times already included East Africa. With this in mind, the voyages do not appear as inexplicable aberrations. Even the phenomenal naval build-up of the Yongle reign was no anomaly. China's first national navy—as a distinct service branch—

began with the Song, and the Yuan Dynasty combined the Song fleet with that of Korea to make China the greatest naval power in the world. Inheriting this tradition, the Ming navy increased both the size of the individual ships and the total number of vessels.

This has led to the facile conclusion that the Chinese in Zheng He's age had the naval potential to conquer the whole world yet failed to seize the opportunity. A corollary is to blame conservative Confucian officials with a land-locked outlook for thwarting this prospect. The Confucians, it has been argued, had no stake in the maritime activities conducted by eunuchs who attained power through channels other than the civil service examinations. In their eyes, eunuchs, most of whom were illiterate and some even of non-Han origin, were an ignorant, greedy, and altogether worthless lot. As a result, after Zheng He they let the greatest fleet in the world rot in harbor. However, it can be argued that the first assumption is a pure myth, whereas the second assumption requires major revisions.

The Yuan dynasty, in its prime under Kublai, with the largest naval force in the world, had suffered catastrophic defeats in two attempts to conquer neighboring Japan (1274, 1281). Kublai's misadventure in Java (1292–1293) was also a fiasco. In the interval between Zheng He's sixth and seventh voyages, the Ming fleet sent to reinforce the army against Annamese separatism was cut to pieces in the Bay of Tongking (1426). The Chinese navy's efficacy as an attack force was in serious doubt.

The Confucian officialdom's power struggle with the eunuchs should be seen as an attempt to check unrestrained despotism. In Yongle's reign, the so-called state control of maritime trade was actually a court monopoly beyond the reach of the state bureaucracy. As it was the emperor's prerogative, he placed trusted servants such as eunuchs—not members of the formal bureaucracy—in charge of the whole operation. In the case of Zheng He's expeditions, the outcome was most positive in terms of linking up with the international community. But not all the emperor's private projects had such positive effect. In the Wanli reign (1573–1620), the emperor sent out eunuch commissioners to extort the provinces with ruinous socio-economic consequences.

Aside from the Confucian officialdom's mistrust of court initiatives that were deemed "irregular," practical reasons also led to the suspension of state-sponsored overseas voyages after Yongle. Some scholars argue that the "treasures" they brought back were mostly luxury items for the consumption of the court, and the Ming empire, posing as the Celestial Dynasty, conducted a deficit trade to show off China's prosperity and superior status. Others see the early Ming empire as mighty enough to dictate the prices of imported goods, often to the disadvantage of the client states. If that was the case, there must have been other incentives to lure foreign traders to China. One way or the other, official diplomacy strait-jacketed international trade.

Foreign diplomats and merchants were given a free ride on Zheng He's ships so that they could go to China to pay "tribute." Zheng He's first voyage (1405–1407) returned with envoys from Java, Malacca, and Sumatra; his sixth voyage returned in 1423 with diplomatic missions from six countries totaling more than 1,200 representatives. Each time, after meeting the official protocols and receiving handsome gifts, the "diplomats" were allowed to sell their private (non-tribute) goods in China duty free, which amounted to the sanctioning of smuggling. Then the envoys would wait, often for years, to be escorted home by a detachment from the Ming fleet. In the meantime, they were wined and dined at the host's expense as a gesture of the Celestial Dynasty's benevolence. After the suspension of Zheng He's voyages—which had become a shuttle service for China's overseas clients—the court began to discourage those "tributaries" who still wished to come and expected to be escorted home.

Yongle's active shuttle service for China's tributaries was an unprecedented experiment. Zheng He's seven voyages were simply the most spectacular ones—as he was China's highest ranking emissary—among the 62 official (mostly single destination) envoys Yongle sent to southeast Asian countries, not including Annam. Altogether the Yongle administration received 95 missions from the maritime states. Records also show that dethroned foreign heads of state occasionally came in person as supplicants for help to restore them. Since they did not have the means to make the trip, one must surmise they also took a free ride on Ming vessels. In fact, in 1408 Yongle restored the heir of Brunei to his throne and sent an envoy to escort him to his country. Although this sort of practice had occurred in the Tang Dynasty's dealings with Inner Asian client states, under the early Mings it was a radical departure in its sheer scale.

Yongle departed from conventional practice in much the same way as Kublai Khan had. Kublai had demanded that the heads of tributary states visit his court personally, and when they refused he launched very expensive expeditions against them, all of which ended in failure. Yongle's more client-friendly shuttle service ended because its cost also proved to be exorbitant. So, it was not simply the Confucian bureaucrats' jealousy of eunuch power which led to the end of the voyages. Post-Yongle administrations simply felt the need to retrench after his extravagant reign, which also included campaigns against the Mongols and Indochina, the construction of the Forbidden City, and 60-odd diplomatic missions (not counting the ones to Annam, Japan, and Inner Asia as far as Samarkand). After Yongle, even the mission to the "wild" Jurchids in northern Manchuria was discontinued, to say nothing of overseas missions.

At the very time that the Ming maritime ventures came to an end, the Indian Ocean's transformation into a Muslim lake was being completed. Long before the Ming, Muslim merchants and missionaries had fanned out from the Persian Gulf and the coastal communities in south India. During the early Ming Dynasty, Malacca in the east, and Mombasa and Kilwa on the African coast became centers for the further spread of Islam. By 1450 a vast new Muslim commercial and cultural network was in place and it was to function until the seventeenth century. Far from displacing the Muslims in the Indian Ocean, the Ming court sent a Muslim, Zheng He, to tap into the Islamic wealth evident there.

The Hindus and Buddhists had colonized southeast Asia long before the arrival of the Muslims, but at that early date the Chinese were still marching toward the subtropics. By the Ming period, China's nautical technology far surpassed that of the Muslims, but the state control of maritime trade restricted private Chinese activities in that quarter. Furthermore, the Confucians never had the kind of missionary zeal comparable to the Hindus and Buddhists before the Muslims and the Christian Westerners who would follow them.

This lack of Chinese assertiveness in the Indian Ocean may be explained by the Ming defeat in Annam in 1427. If the Ming empire had to retreat from Indochina, it would make no sense to pursue imperial interests laying further to the south. However, the same set of circumstances did not hold true for the Europeans. On the contrary, the Europeans, having tasted the fruits of the Far East, were desperate for more. Asia was far more advanced than Europe on the eve of the modern era, and within Asia post-Song China had surged ahead to lead the world economy. East Asia, together with insular southeast Asia, produced the most coveted products of the time—silk, tea, porcelain, printed books, pepper, and spices. The hunger for these products led the Europeans by early Ming time to make spectacular attempts to link up with the eastern Indian Ocean and the Far East—the hub of the pre-modern world economy. The European urgency was increased by the closing of the overland

Silk Road due to Timur Lang's (Tamerlane's) devastation of Inner Asia and the monopoly of rapacious Venetian middlemen in the eastern Mediterranean transit trade. However, there was no comparable yearning on the Chinese side. In fact, Ming China was hardly aware of Europe's existence.

Our modern perspective, biased by the conviction that economic development depends upon overseas expansion, sees Ming negligence of the ocean as folly. Yet, for China at the time, the maritime was not the most important sector of foreign trade. Especially under the Yuan Dynasty, land routes via Inner Asia carried a larger volume of international trade. During the Ming Dynasty, state-controlled foreign trade was also conducted at China's inland frontiers. "Horse markets," essential for acquiring horses for China's cavalry, were revived in northern Shanxi and southern Manchuria; "tea markets" were established in northwestern and southwestern border regions to trade with Inner Asia. Due to diplomatic considerations, the frontier trade incurred a deficit from time to time. It was a price the Ming empire had to pay to purchase peace along its border, and its function was not unlike the economic aid packages handed out by today's developed nations to the Third World. In comparison, the maritime tributary system was a greater drain on the empire's resources—not to mention that no serious threat came from that quarter before the revival of the raids by "Japanese pirates."

Ming relations with Japan were never cordial. Japan was not only suspected of harboring seditious elements from China—actually disgruntled elements under the Muromachi regime—it raided China's coast twice during the early Ming period. By mid-Ming, Japan itself had fragmented into "warring states," and it was hard to hold any central authority responsible for the disturbances. The Japanese trouble started again when different Japanese embassies competed to be the triennial "tributary mission" allowed to dock at China's Ningbo in 1523. Their dispute led to rioting that devastated the town. When the Jiajing Emperor (1522–1567) cut off trade with Japan, Japanese armed merchants launched raiding parties against the Chinese coast from Jiangsu to Guangdong. Meanwhile, powerful Chinese clans along the coasts, whose interests were badly hurt by the official maritime ban, allied themselves with Japanese and Portuguese privateers. As these Zhejiang and Fujian clans had powerful connections at the imperial court, all government measures against them failed. The collusion of certain court and local officials with illicit maritime interests belies the generalization that Confucian officialdom was staunchly opposed to profit-making through commerce.

As the Chinese pirate-smugglers built lairs on offshore islands, they became indistinguishable from the Japanese marauders. Some historians even speculate that they had bases in Japan as well. In any event, the official maritime ban also harmed those common Chinese who needed to eke out a living by the sea; consequently, they swarmed to join the ranks of the pirates. During the reign of Jiajing, half of the "Japanese pirates" were in fact Chinese from the ports of Zhangzhou and Quanzhou.

While England a few decades later would convert its "pirates" into the embryo of the Royal Navy, Ming China managed to turn its best seafaring subjects into "pirates" who attacked the mother country repeatedly. Expeditions sent against them greatly strained the imperial treasury. The pirates seemed to control the seas. In 1553 pirates assembled an armada of several hundred ships which put thousands of miles of the Chinese coast on alert. Sadly for Ming China, all major operations against the pirates occurred on land. General Qi Jiguang, who in the 1560s distinguished himself in quelling the "Japanese pirates," would make it to the twentieth-century Republican pantheon of "national heroes who resisted foreign invaders." An expert in the use of war-wagons and the siege of fortresses, he repeatedly vanquished the "Japanese pirates" on land *after* they had taken county seats and garrison outposts. The pathetic fact remained that an army general had to do the job of admirals. The once mighty Ming navy was nowhere to be seen; in fact, the records fail to disclose even effective coast guard operations.

Tragically, the Ming authorities repeatedly shrank the size of seafaring vessels until the technology to build superships of the Zheng He era was lost. Although these measures paralleled the downsizing of the imperial navy, the reduction of vessel size, thereby making them unfit for deep-sea voyages, could only be aimed at private shipbuilding. The imperial navy was nonetheless hurt by it. A school of thought actually shifted the blame for the ending of imperial voyages after Zheng He away from Confucian conservatism onto the powerful coastal clans who, fearful of a strong imperial navy, conducted lobbying activities at court designed to cripple their foe. Confucian officials likely catered to them, but it cannot be ruled out that certain eunuch factions were also on the take.

It might throw new light on the ruin of the Ming maritime enterprise by seeking its cause not in the Confucian-eunuch rivalry, but in the conflict of interest between the state and private sectors. Indeed, if the obstacle of Indochina halted southward imperial expansion, the same hindrance did not exist for the Chinese privateers. During Zheng He's first voyage, his fleet had a skirmish with a Chinese "pirate," Chen Zhuyi, who had established himself in Palembang on Sumatra, thereby posing a threat to the Straits of Malacca. Zheng had him captured and brought back to Nanjing to be beheaded. Indeed, the perennial official policy was to back the legitimate ruler of Malacca, using it as a naval base for all of Zheng He's expeditions. However, in 1511 the Chinese merchants in Malacca helped the Portuguese to capture the strategic city. Seeking protection from state power in their quarrel with its ruler, the Chinese looked toward the Europeans instead of the Mings, with the result that China's hegemony over Malacca ended. If the British privateers spearheaded that nation's maritime expansion, in China the state and private sectors did each other in.

In fact, this pattern had started under the Song Dynasty, thanks to the inexorable logic that China was a continental power with inland frontiers to defend. The Song had been a pro-maritime regime simply because it relied heavily on oceanic trade for revenue and also depended on the merchants for ships and contributions. State and private shipowners had a brief honeymoon after they combined their efforts to repel a Jin invasion in 1161; but when the Mongol menace began to loom large, the Song state had to requisition so many ships for its Yangzi River and coastal defense that it virtually crippled the merchant class and, by extension, China's maritime trade. Many shipowners defected to the Mongols, only to find their new masters even more relentless in pursuing state control.

With this background in mind, it becomes clear why the Ming fleet, once the mightiest in the world, did not undergo a revitalization in the face of the Japanese menace. Again, it is a matter of proportionately locating the "Japanese pirate" episode in the scheme of things. During the reign of Zhengtong (1436–1449), the Mongol threat in the north revived and in 1449 the Mongols even succeeded in capturing the emperor. A few decades later, in response to the Mongol threat, the Ming began to build the Great Wall. That project continued for over a century, with the construction shifting from the north to the northeast as the Mongol threat yielded to that of the Manchus. An American historian once compared this gargantuan defense system to the Reagan Administration's "Star Wars" project—an attempt to "spend the enemy out of existence." In the defense of the empire, the Ming had a clear set of priorities in budgetary terms. If the northern enemy is likened to the Soviet threat, then the "Japanese pirates" are at best comparable to the nuisance caused by Colombian drug lords.

Even before the "Japanese" disturbances, the Ming maritime hegemony was faltering: fewer and fewer tributary missions came from overseas. After the "Japanese" threat passed, the maritime tributary system remained in shambles. Meanwhile, illicit private trading between foreign privateers and Chinese smugglers thrived, bursting the official straitjacket. The Longqing emperor (1567–1572) had no choice but to partially lift the maritime ban, which also meant the loosening of the state monopoly on overseas trade by allowing a degree of "privitization." This new system, confined to the single port of Zhangzhou, still excluded Japan. In 1589 the Wanli emperor limited private Chinese trips to 88 ships per year, 44 each for the "eastern ocean" and the "western ocean." Since the "eastern ocean" quota easily filled up and most traders found the Indian Ocean route too daunting, many merchants applied for "western ocean" runs but, instead, headed illicitly for Japan. Despite these machinations, the Portuguese ended up reaping the largest profit by using Japanese silver to trade Chinese goods.

It was during the Ming period that the Portuguese rounded the Cape of Good Hope at the southern tip of Africa and the West annexed the New World, thereby bringing into place two of the modern world's key modules—the Atlantic Rim and the Pacific Rim. It seemed that Ming China withdrew from the ocean at the most inopportune moment—the birth of the Pacific Rim; when Japan repeated this folly after 1615 (making the two potential Pacific powers absentees in the region), the West enjoyed clear sailing. In 1511 the Portuguese seized Malacca, and by 1557 they would gain a foothold in Macao. The Spaniards and the Dutch followed in their footsteps. In 1565 the former began colonizing the Philippines; the latter moved to seize the Portuguese East Indies and also occupied Taiwan in 1623 when the Ming authorities virtually ceded the island to the Dutch.

The Ming overseas tributary system collapsed. Westerners not only destroyed the Ming Dynasty's client states but also came to control the sea routes in that part of the world. Ming "privatization" measures came too late and too little, for unprotected by their government Chinese traders fell easy prey to the Westerners. Chinese private trade withered because it could no longer compete with the more aggressive colonial powers. By the early Wanli reign, the Portuguese had reduced the China trade to a link in their Macao-Goa-Lisbon and Macao-Nagasaki routes. The Spaniards incorporated Ming China's official Zhangzhou outlet into their Zhangzhou-Manila-Acapulco run. This international trade poured large quantities of silver into China, effecting a currency revolution after the Jiaqing reign. Even more importantly, the import of New World crops such as the potato, yam, peanut, and maize at around the same time caused China's population to double by the eighteenth century.

Since the Spaniards failed to secure a foothold like Macao and, consequently, could not directly trade in China, they relied on Chinese merchants to service the Zhangzhou-Manila link. Better known as the "Manila Galleon," the Spanish transoceanic trade caused a large number of Chinese to settle in Manila. Like the Iberian Jews and Moors, these Chinese were economically useful but culturally unassimilable. As a result, two massacres erupted late in the Ming Dynasty. One in 1603 wiped out the entire Manila Chinese colony of 20,000; the other, in 1639, killed 20,000 or more out of the 30,000 Chinese who had migrated to Manila after the first massacre. While in 1639 the Ming Dynasty was on the verge of collapse and could generate no effective response, the 1603 outrage, occurring when Ming China was still fairly strong, also evoked no response from Beijing. The Manchu, or Qing, Dynasty that replaced the Ming displayed the same disinterest when the Dutch in Java massacred the Chinese there in 1740. This pattern of non-response seemed to set the norm regarding Chinese migration overseas. For example, massive molestation of Chinese women during 1998 riots in Indonesia only elicited a "serious concern" from Beijing, not even a "protest." Furthermore, lack of interest on the Chinese part may explain how the Dutch were able to dominate Batavia in 1700 with 6,000 men and why well-populated, nearby Chinese communities fell easy victim to outnumbered Western imperialists.

Whereas it was highly unlikely that a continental empire like China would turn into a maritime giant, a "maritime China" did develop from the embryo left behind by the Song Dynasty. Forces from this region resisted Ming founder Hongwu's unification of China and, having failed, moved their power bases overseas. A similar scenario occurred in late Ming, when anti-Qing loyalists controlled the southeast coasts and the new frontier province of Yunnan. For example, Zheng Chenggong kept the Ming banner flying on Taiwan until 1683. Zheng was born in Japan of a Chinese pirate and a Japanese mother. Known in the West as Koxinga, he had enough naval strength to take Taiwan from the Dutch and was on the verge of moving against the Spanish Philippines when he died in 1662. He and his descendants built a maritime state supported mainly by revenues from trade with southeast Asia. The Qing Dynasty, apparently threatened from the ocean, repeated the Ming policy of closing off the coast.

To answer the question whether the Ming Dynasty, which at its inception led the globe in nautical technology and seafaring capacity, could have acted otherwise to avert China's subsequent and unhappy fate, all we need to do is to look at China today. Those who accuse the Ming of missing the boat for global domination often cite the fact that by mid-Ming the output of one industrial town, Jingde Zheng with its 3,000 porcelain factories, alone exceeded the entire Gross Domestic Product of coeval England. The problem is that there were too few Jingde Zhengs and China never achieved a critical mass sufficient to effect a structural change. Likewise, although China today has an urbanized population the size of the American nation it is still the world's largest agrarian economy; and this economy remains based on labor-intensive small scale farming—the perennial foundation of the Chinese empire for the last two millennia. Moreover, the Chinese empire was also a "slow motion" one, most unlike the Alexandrine or Mongol or even the Russian. It took the Chinese two millennia to expand from their Yellow River "cradle" to the southwest—the distance between the American Midwest and the Deep South. Yunnan and Guizhou barely became part of the "interior" under the Ming, and China's boundary with southeast Asia became stabilized along that line under the Ming and has remained that way ever since. The major new accretion was Manchuria under the Qing in the north (thanks to Manchuria's joining China proper through "conquest"). In other words, from its inception China has been—and continues to be—a land empire with little or no interest in overseas expansion.

As for those Chinese who have migrated overseas, they have done so without official blessing from Ming times onward. During Communist China's most xenophobic phase—from the late 1950s to the early 1970s—these "abandoned subjects of the Celestial Dynasty" were under suspicion, and Chinese citizens who had "overseas connections" were treated as potential spies. Unlike the active colonialism of the West, Chinese settlers have had to "live under other people's roofs" and often at their mercy. China, unlike Japan, has not demonstrated much of a presence in the Pacific in the twentieth century. China's economy is still state-controlled with a smattering of privatization in a few "special economic zones" along the southeast coasts that actively interact with the new world market—a modern version of the maritime superintendencies of imperial China. And continental China today feels no less threatened by a maritime China based on Taiwan than during the Ming-Qing period. Before blaming the Ming Dynasty, which merely followed the *normal* Chinese pattern, for not becoming what "could have been otherwise," we need to ask why this "could have been" is not happening today.

SELECTED BIBLIOGRAPHY

Abu-Lughod, Janet L. *Before European Hegemony: The World System* A.D. *1250–1350.* New York: Oxford University Press, 1989. The author places the Ming phenomenon into her alternative "world system" theory. This premodern world system—safeguarded by the *Pax Mongolica*—was already fragmented and thus experiencing retrenchment when Zheng He ventured into the Indian Ocean. Instead of filling the vacuum, China retreated, thus opening the way for subsequent exploitation by the West.

Association for Asian Studies, Ming Biographical History Project Committee. *Dictionary of Ming Biography, 1368–1644.* 2 vols. New York: Columbia University Press, 1976. A useful and concise reference to important personages of the Ming Dynasty, dated in certain areas.

Boorstin, Daniel. *The Discoverers.* New York: Random House, 1983. Includes a chapter on Zheng He's voyages by a non-China specialist; helpful for the beginner.

Chan, Albert. *The Glory and Fall of the Ming Dynasty.* Norman: University of Oklahoma Press, 1982. A general history of the Ming Dynasty.

Crozier, Ralph C. *Koxinga and Chinese Nationalism: History, Myth, and the Hero.* Cambridge, MA: Harvard University Press, 1977. This study aims to demythologize the legend of Zheng Chenggong (Koxinga).

Dreyer, Edward L. *Early Ming China: A Political History, 1355–1435.* Stanford, CA: Stanford University Press, 1982. Dreyer asserts that Yuan-style practices actually persisted until the fifth reign of the Ming Dynasty, and Yongle's "attitude was nearly identical to that of the Yuan emperors, who eagerly sought relations with foreign countries and employed foreigners in their service."

Duyvendak, J. J. L. *China's Discovery of Africa.* London: A. Probsthain, 1949. A study of China's relationship with Africa up to the time of Zheng He.

Farmer, Edward. *Zhu Yuanzhang and early Ming Legislation: The Reordering of Chinese Society Following the Era of Mongol Rule.* Leiden: E. J. Brill, 1995. This study argues that the Ming empire was an attempt to reinvent Chineseness along more narrow Han ethnic lines.

Huang, Ray. *1587, A Year of No Significance: The Ming Dynasty in Decline.* New Haven, CT: Yale University Press, 1981. A study of the Wanli reign, this volume also includes a biography of Qi Jiguang and a description of his battles with the "Japanese pirates."

Levathes, Louise. *When China Ruled the Seas: The Treasure Fleet of the Dragon Throne, 1405–33.* New York: Simon & Schuster, 1994. The most recent study of Zheng He's voyages, thoroughly researched and well written. It maintains the conventional wisdom of court officials impeding the eunuchs' trade activities and stresses the dampening effect of the Ming's loss of shipbuilding technology on the development of guns and cannons.

Lo Jung-pang. "The Decline of the Ming Navy." *Oriens Extremus* 5 (1958): 149–68. Lo sees the early Ming tributary trade as highly exploitive of China's client states and a major source of revenue for the empire. He attributes the decline of this system to China's internal weakness and the shifting emphasis from coastal transportation to the Grand Canal.

———. "The Emergence of China as a Sea Power During the Late Sung and Early Yüan Period." *The Eastern Quarterly* 15 (1955): 489–503. Provides a background for the rise of Chinese sea power since the Song.

———. "Maritime Commerce and Its Relation to the Sung Navy." *Journal of the Economic and Social History of the Orient* 12 (1969): 57–101. Demonstrates how the Southern Song became the most pro-maritime regime in China's imperial history out of the need for survival; shows how the Southern Song in decline crippled China's merchant fleet and her maritime trade in order to survive.

Ma Huan. *Ying-yai Sheng-lan: The Overall Survey of the Ocean's Shores [1433].* Translated and edited by J. V. G. Mills. London: Cambridge University Press, 1970. A translation of the records of a Muslim interpreter who accompanied Zheng He on three voyages; includes his personal observations of 20 countries.

McPherson, Kenneth. *The Indian Ocean: A History of People and the Sea.* Delhi: Oxford University Press, 1993. Provides an overall picture of the development of the Indian Ocean as an economic region.

Mote, Frederick, and Denis Twitchett, eds. *The Cambridge History of China. Vol. 8: The Ming Dynasty, Part II.* Cambridge Eng.: Cambridge University Press, 1998. Sections on "The Ming and Inner Asia," "Ming Foreign Relations: Southeast Asia," "Relations with Maritime Europeans," "Ming China and the Emerging World Economy" represent the state of the art in Ming scholarship.

Risso, Patricia. *Merchants and Faith: Muslim Commerce and Culture in the Indian Ocean.* Boulder, CO: Westview Press, 1995. Studies the rise of Muslim domination in the Indian Ocean and its subsequent demise with the arrival of the Europeans; attempts to link the vicissitudes of the Indian Ocean with major changes on the Asian continent, including China.

Rossabi, Morris. "Cheng Ho and Timur: Any Relations?" *Oriens Extremus* 20 (1973): 129–136. Refutes a Taiwan scholar's thesis formulated in the Cold War era that Zheng He's voyages were Ming attempts at cementing political alliances halfway around the globe for the "containment" of Timur Lang's threat from Inner Asia.

So Kwan-wai. *Japanese Piracy in Ming China During the 16th Century.* East Lansing: Michigan State University Press, 1975. A thorough study of the "Japanese pirates," shows that almost all the ringleaders were Chinese.

Tsai, Shih-shan Henry. *The Eunuchs in the Ming Dynasty.* Albany, NY: SUNY Press, 1996. The only book-length study in English that focuses on Ming eunuch politics.

Wang, I-t'ung. *Official Relations Between China and Japan, 1368–1549.* Cambridge, MA: Harvard University Press, 1953. The only in-depth study in English of Sino-Japanese relations for the period under concern.

Wickberg, E. *The Chinese in Philippine Life, 1850–1891.* New Haven, CT: Yale University Press, 1965. Includes a chapter on the early history of the Chinese in the Philippines.

Wiens, Herold Jacob. *China's March Toward the Tropics*. Hamden, CT: Shoe String Press, 1954. A study of China's slow march toward the south from the earliest times to the twentieth century.

Willets, William. "The Maritime Adventures of Grand Eunuch Ho." *Journal of Southeast Asian History* 5 (1964): 25–42. Discusses the kidnaping of the king of Ceylon by the Chinese during Zheng He's second voyage, an act that seemed to deviate from normal policy.

Wills, John E., Jr. "Maritime China from Wang Chih to Shih Lang." In *From Ming to Ch'ing: Conquest, Region, and Continuity in Seventeenth-century China*. pp. 201–238. Edited by Jonathan D. Spence and John E. Wills. New Haven, CT: Yale University Press, 1979. This insightful article contends that a Maritime China existed alongside a Continental China and served as a middleman between the latter and the oceanic world. Wills recasts the Ming pirates in the role of "merchant-mediator-admiral."

5

The Age of European Expansion Begins, c. 1450–c. 1525

INTRODUCTION

The story is told of how the fifteenth-century Chinese Empire, the richest and most impressive state in the world at that time, dispatched several naval expeditions to the far corners of the world. These expeditions visited southeast Asia, India, the Persian Gulf, the Arabian lands, the east coast of Africa, and what is now Indonesia. Returning home, the Chinese sailors reported that these distant lands held nothing of value or interest for China. The emperors then suspended any further attempts to learn more about the rest of the world, a decision that apparently passed unchallenged. However, in a global context, the Europeans, who proved to be intensely interested in the world beyond Europe, balanced the Chinese disinterestedness.

With the collapse of the Roman Empire and the onset of the era known as the Middle Ages, Europe turned inward, beset with serious problems including the acquisition of such basic necessities as food, clothing, and shelter. Perhaps most critically, the Europeans sought protection from marauding barbarians and, later, marauding neighbors. Despite these hardships, Europeans evinced a lively interest in the non-European world that grew as stability replaced chaos and material conditions improved.

Ferdinand Magellan on his round-the-world voyage, 1519–1522. This illustration portrays Ferdinand Magellan encountering icebergs as he sailed past the southern tip of South America, through a body of water that would come to be known as the Straits of Magellan. Magellan's voyage was the first to circumnavigate the globe, although Magellan died before the expedition returned home to Spain. (Reproduced from the Collections of the Library of Congress)

As early as the ninth and tenth centuries, daring Norsemen sailed west from Scandinavia to discover Iceland, Greenland, and the extreme northeastern coast of North America. While no permanent settlements survived in North America, the Norsemen, or Vikings, clearly reflected an extraordinary spirit of adventure. So too did the Venetian merchant and adventurer Marco Polo, whose late thirteenth-century description of his travels throughout Asia as far as China stirred Europe's literate population.

The Crusades, the struggle of a militant western Christianity to expel non-Christians from Europe and to recover Christianity's holiest shrines in the Middle East, further sparked Europe's interest in the non-European world. Beginning in the eleventh century, crusading expeditions to the Middle East brought many Europeans into direct contact with the Arabs of that region. Even more importantly, by the end of the Middle Ages Europe had developed a virtual addiction for overseas products, especially spices from the Far East, or Indies. The commercial implications of this dependency greatly aroused Europe's interest in other parts of the world.

Fortuitously for Europe, its growing fascination with the globe coincided with certain technological improvements and innovations that enabled the Europeans to move confidently beyond their rather small share of the huge Eurasian land mass. The magnetic compass and the astrolabe helped the seafarer to better chart a course. More accurate maps and charts, called portolani, also played an important role. In the fifteenth century, the Portuguese combined Arab naval designs with already existing European ones to produce the Portuguese caraval, a superior sailing ship. The caraval featured both the square rigging traditionally used by the Europeans and the Arab lateen rigging. It proved faster and more maneuverable than other vessels. Moreover, European vessels were militarily indomitable. Like their rivals, the Europeans equipped their vessels with cannon; but the Europeans' cannons were more numerous and better made than those of the Arabs and the Turks, and European crews employed their advantage in firepower to sweep their opponents from the sea.

By the start of the fifteenth century, western man possessed the necessary technology to begin a long period of global exploration. He also had the motives. Sometimes referred to as "the three Gs," God, gold, and glory drove the Europeans forward. From its inception, Christianity had been an aggressive religion in the sense that it actively sought converts. Exploration now offered the possibility of bringing Christ's message to hundreds of thousands if not millions of non-Christians. More to the point, Christians, but especially the Portuguese and Spanish, had spent centuries waging war against Islam. Inspired by victories that had driven the Moslems from the Iberian Peninsula, Christians now wanted to pursue their advantage. Some hoped to team up with the mythical Prester John, legendary ruler of an allegedly rich and powerful Christian kingdom located somewhere in Asia or Africa, in order to claim the Moslem world for Christianity.

As a reason for exploration, the profit motive proved just as strong if not stronger than the Christian desire to convert the heathen. Many Europeans envisioned the discovery of gold; other, more subtle minds, thought in terms of commercial profit. The latter, understanding Europe's hunger for imported goods, especially spices from the Indies, hoped to find a new trade route to the source. The old route, from the Middle Eastern terminals of the Asian trade routes to Europe itself, was dominated by the haughty Italians, who reaped huge profits. A new route would divert those profits into the pockets of those who discovered the route. This desire for a new arrangement intensified when the Mongols and the Turks, who were warriors rather than traders, conquered the Arabs of the Middle East and destroyed the Byzantine Empire.

Finally, the quest for personal glory motivated the European explorers. The concept of glory was already present in the European mind when it received a strong boost from the Renaissance, which placed a premium on boldness and individualism. The Renaissance also enshrined curiosity as a virtue, thereby stimulating the desire to know as much as possible about as many things as possible, including the world beyond Europe proper.

The age of European expansion began in earnest early in the fifteenth century when Portuguese sailors cautiously but systematically started to work their way down the west coast of Africa. Portugal, with a population of barely more than 1 million, seemed an unlikely candidate to initiate such a grand undertaking. However, the Portuguese were already a seafaring people due to their Atlantic location and the absence of good soil which discouraged agricultural pursuits. Furthermore, they were fired with religious zeal derived from their successful, centuries-long struggle to oust the North African Moslems from their homeland. They were also intoxicated with the prospect of finding the source of African gold, which they knew from their commercial contacts with the Moslems lay somewhere south of the Sahara Desert.

The driving force behind Portugal's initial voyages of discovery was

Prince Henry, a younger son of the Portuguese king, who earned the nickname "the Navigator." After participating in the 1415 conquest of Moslem Ceuta in north Africa, Prince Henry established a school for navigation in 1419 at the southwestern Portuguese town of Sagres. Here he brought together sailors, astronomers, geographers, map makers, shipwrights, scholars, and technicians. There were Moslems, Jews, and Christians; and there were Portuguese, Italians, Greeks, and Arabs. Under Prince Henry's direction (and with his generous funding), they worked to assemble the knowledge vital for the task of exploration.

Technological uncertainties still dictated that sailors keep land in sight, and thus it was in 1434 when the Portuguese mariner Gil Eannes sailed south of Cape Bojador on the west coast of Africa at about 25 degrees north latitude. This was farther south along the coast than any other European had ever sailed. In 1442 a Portuguese vessel reached Cape Blanco south of the Tropic of Cancer, and the successful captain sent back to Portugal several black Africans. Six years later, the Portuguese established a factory, or trading station, there. During this time, the Portuguese also settled the Azores, the Madeiras, and the Cape Verde Islands.

In 1460, the year Portuguese sailors reached Sierra Leone, Prince Henry died. A lull in Portuguese exploration followed until the coronation of King John II in 1481. Less interested than Prince Henry in the scientific nature of the voyages, John saw them chiefly as a way to get rich.

A huge breakthrough occurred early in 1488 when Bartholomew Diaz sailed around what became known as the Cape of Good Hope and landed on Africa's east coast. His voyage provided conclusive evidence that an all-water route to the Indies existed. Nine years later, after extensive preparation, the new Portuguese king, Manuel the Fortunate, ordered Vasco da Gama to set sail for India. Da Gama, with his four commercial vessels, arrived at Calicut on the Malabar (southwestern) coast of India in May 1498. His subsequent return to Portugal, laden with spices from the east, meant instant wealth.

Da Gama's successful voyage opened the door to a flood of Portuguese traders, one of whom, Pedro Cabral, swung too wide in the south Atlantic, bumped into what was South America, and consequently laid the foundation for Portugal's claim to Brazil. However, neither the Arabs nor their Italian trading partners were inclined to surrender the lucrative trade route without a fight. Hostilities ensued, and the Portuguese, led by effective commanders such as Alfonso de Albuquerque, vanquished their Moslem religious and commercial rivals in a series of naval engagements. Thereafter, they established bases and trading centers such as Goa in India, Ormuz at the mouth of the Persian Gulf, and several sites along the east African coast. This allowed Portugal to control the Indian Ocean and to dominate the trade route to Europe.

For many, Christopher Columbus' voyage to the New World was the most spectacular and important event in the long history of Europe's expansion. Columbus was born in Genoa, Italy, in 1451, the son of a wool weaver. He soon took to the sea, making many voyages around the western Mediterranean before he was shipwrecked off Portugal in 1476. Columbus eventually made his way to Lisbon, where he worked as a cartographer. He also married a well-off Portuguese woman.

By the late fifteenth century, most educated people in Europe surmised that the world was round. Certainly Columbus did, and this served as the basis for his belief that one could reach the Indies, with all its fabulous wealth, by sailing west. What distinguished Columbus was not this conviction, but rather the determination and energy with which he championed it. In 1484 he tried to enlist the aid of John II, but the Portuguese rebuffed him. They thought that Columbus had badly underestimated the distance westward from Europe to the Indies and, besides, they clearly had a vested interest in promoting a water route to the East around Africa. If Columbus was correct, almost a century's worth of Portuguese efforts would have been wasted.

Turning from the Portuguese to the Spanish, Columbus convinced their royal majesties, Isabella of Castile and Ferdinand of Aragon, to fund his adventure. In 1492 he sailed from Palos, Spain, in three ships—the Niña, Pinta, and Santa María. Stopping first at the Canary Islands, he then proceeded westward. On October 12, 1492, after 33 days at sea, he made landfall at San Salvador, an island in the Bahamas. Columbus returned to Spain in glory.

Convinced that the islands he had found were off the eastern coast of Japan and that the Indies lay just over the horizon, he soon launched the second of what would be four expeditions. During the course of these later voyages, Columbus sailed to all the Caribbean's major islands as well as Central America and the mouth of the Orinoco River in South America. But, of course, this was the New World and not the Indies. Nevertheless, Columbus went to his death in 1506 a wealthy man but still clinging to the belief that he had sailed westward from Europe to Asia. In fact, this achievement belonged not to Columbus but to Ferdinand Magellan, a Portuguese nobleman who, like Columbus, sailed for

Spain. Departing in 1519, Magellan's little armada took three years to circumnavigate the globe by sailing west. In the process, Magellan became the first European to sail the Pacific Ocean. But he was killed en route in the Philippines, and only one of his original five vessels returned to port in 1522.

INTERPRETIVE ESSAY
Steven E. Siry

During the sixteenth and seventeenth centuries, Western Europe emerged as the greatest center of geographical expansionism within a new ocean-linked system of relationships among the major cultures of the world. Indeed, during this Age of Discovery, Western Europe rapidly achieved domination over much of the Western Hemisphere, southern Asia, and the African coastal regions. This unprecedented expansionism would continue until the end of the 1800s as European domination spread over nearly the entire globe. Thus it was the expansion and modernization of Europe after 1500 that initiated the unification and transformation of world history.

In the fifteenth century, the Portugese and Spanish began building larger ships, developing better maps, and compiling more information about winds and currents. These changes made distant travel on the world's oceans less dangerous. As a result, a number of European explorers, including Christopher Columbus in 1492, began to tie Western Europe to lands around the world. Until the end of the 1400s, Atlantic Europe had only been a peripheral part of Eurasia, but within less than half a century, Western Europe became an area of major power that influenced and was influenced by cultures around the globe. The Western Europeans' use of a complex military technology and their immunity from various diseases that proved lethal to non-Europeans led to the subjugation of many native populations and the establishing of trading posts or colonies in Asia, Africa, and the Americas.

As early as 1494, a rivalry between Portugal and Spain over claims in the New World threatened to develop into war. As a result, the Pope proclaimed a Line of Demarcation which was intended to divide the unexplored parts of the world by giving Spain the areas in the Western Hemisphere and by granting to Portugal the lands to the east of the line.

The two nations subsequently signed the Treaty of Tordesillas (1494) which accepted the Pope's dividing line but moved it further west. This change led to Portugese control of Brazil, though little else in the Americas. Nevertheless, in the late fifteenth century and the sixteenth century, Portugal controlled a large overseas empire including trading posts in China, Japan, Indonesia, Brazil, and Africa. Eventually tiny Portugal proved unable to control effectively its extensive maritime empire, and Spain gradually displaced it as the leader in exploration and colonization.

In the New World the Spanish conquistadors, noted for their greed and cruelty, quickly established an empire for themselves and Spain. The conquistadors, often the landless younger sons of Spanish nobles, wanted to gain a fortune in the Americas. The Spaniards led by Hernán Cortés gained control of the Aztecs' lands in Mexico, and other conquistadors led by Francisco Pizarro conquered the Incas' extensive lands in Peru and Ecuador. Soon Spain was reaping a vast fortune in gold, silver, and Indian slaves from its New World empire.

Eventually in the Americas, Spanish explorer-soldiers such as Francisco de Coronado, Hernando de Soto, and Juan Ponce de Leon, extended Spain's control over large territories. The Spanish government subsequently used viceroys to establish a powerful, centralized control. It divided vast amounts of the imperial land into *encomiendas*, a group of villages over which a Spanish ruler provided protection in exchange for a part of the villagers' labor.

In addition, the Roman Catholic Church, which viewed itself as the defender of the Crown's native subjects, became deeply involved in attempting to convert the Indian population. The result would be Roman Catholicism's domination of Central and South America.

Moreover, racially-mixed societies developed in Latin America. Nevertheless, they were divided along racial lines. The Spanish-born and the creoles, those of European ancestry born in the colonies, comprised the ruling classes. Below these, power and wealth declined among the mixed race population, and the Indians were at the bottom of the social and economic ladder. Furthermore, Spanish became the dominant language in Spain's American empire and this proved to be the most important influence in creating cultural unification.

Due to its New World empire, Spain experienced a "Golden Age" during the late fifteenth and sixteenth centuries. Wealth from the New World supported a number of creative individuals including Miguel de

Cervantes, who authored *Don Quixote de la Mancha*, and El Greco, who became the most outstanding Spanish painter of the era.

Although a vast fortune of gold and silver flowed from Latin America to Spain, the Spanish monarchs in the sixteenth century spent much of it on numerous wars. During his reign from 1516 to 1556, Habsburg Emperor Charles V defended the Holy Roman Empire against the Ottoman Turks, opposed the French over Italy, and fought the German Protestants. Then between 1556 and 1598, Philip II, the son of Charles V, embraced policies that resulted in a series of Spanish defeats. The Dutch Protestant revolt against Spain in 1568 and the English victory over the Spanish Armada in 1588 led to a significant change in the naval balance and signaled the end of Spain's domination overseas. Much as it had replaced Portugal, Spain was now forced to yield before the rising power of England, the Dutch Netherlands, and France. Indeed, increasingly after 1550 English, Dutch, and French explorers embarked on voyages throughout the world, and were soon establishing trading posts and colonies. The many rivalries of the European nations clearly fueled the transoceanic expansionism.

As with Spain, all these countries experienced a dramatic increase of royal authority. Rulers profited from overseas expansion and gained power at the expense of the church and the nobility. This opened the way for significant imperial conflicts which were further fostered by confrontation between the Protestant and Catholic nations.

The Age of Discovery also dramatically altered Europe in numerous other ways. For example, the introduction of many new plants from America played a significant role in adding more diversity to the European diet. Moreover, in some areas the new plants provided enough increased nutrition to help bring about an increase in the population. Among the new food products were potatoes, tomatoes, sweet potatoes, squash, pumpkin, maize, various legumes, cocoa, and vanilla. In addition, the importation of tobacco soon created a widespread addiction, and sugar was more available. Indeed, in Europe sugar replaced honey as the primary sweetener. Moreover, Europeans imported spices that were used for medicinal purposes or to preserve foodstuffs. And European clothing was substantially affected by the importation of silks, furs, and cotton. But there were also significant negative consequences, especially the spread of diseases to Europe, as seen in plagues that periodically struck London, Lisbon, and other cities.

Like Spain, other European countries would experience periods of major achievement throughout the Age of Discovery. In England during the Tudor Dynasty (1485–1603), the foundation of what would become the British Empire was laid as John Cabot, Francis Drake, and Walter Raleigh established English claims in the New World. During this era in England, there occurred a very creative period for Western literature known as the Elizabethan Renaissance. Many extraordinarily talented writers, led by Ben Jonson, Christopher Marlowe, Edmund Spenser, and especially William Shakespeare, provided a literature characterized by a great zest for life, enthusiastic self-confidence, and exuberant patriotism.

The Dutch Netherlands' extensive commercial empire also led to Dutch merchants controlling a huge amount of wealth. This vast increase in capital allowed them to become the primary moneylenders in Europe. As Amsterdam became the world's major commercial and financial center, the Bank of Amsterdam, established in 1609, emerged as a model for national banks set up in other Western European countries. As in Spain and England, the increase in national wealth became the foundation for funding widespread cultural activities. Indeed, there developed a golden age for Dutch painters such as Jan Vermeer, Franz Hals, and Rembrandt Van Rijn, who celebrated the middle and lower classes in Dutch society. In addition, the Dutch Netherlands became the center of European book publishing and Dutch scientists made significant contributions, including the invention of the telescope and the microscope. Furthermore, the nation's freedom attracted some of Europe's leading intellectuals such as René Descartes of France and Baruch Spinoza from Portugal, who were refugees from persecution in their home countries.

The invention of the movable-type printing press in the fifteenth century allowed for the more rapid diffusion of knowledge during the Age of Discovery. And the much more accessible European literature was filled with new themes. For example, writers described distant lands and cultures. Moreover, European expansionism overseas led to the rapid spread of scientific knowledge, including new discoveries in astronomy, botany, geography, mathematics, and medicine. In the latter discipline, numerous works informed Europeans about plants used for medicinal purposes by Asians and Native Americans. Moreover, scientific ideas, including those of Nicholas Copernicus and Galilei Galileo, reached Japan in books printed by Jesuit missionaries in China.

As geographical knowledge dramatically increased during the Age of Discovery, Europeans began to make new maps to indicate the territorial discoveries. The most important initial map from around 1500 was drawn by Juan de la Cosa, who, as pilot, had made voyages with Columbus in 1492 and 1498. His map is probably the first to doubt that the newly discovered lands were a part of Asia. But the most original and most influential map-maker of the sixteenth century was Gerardus Mercator. His "Mercator projection" presented the earth's entire spherical surface as a flat rectangle divided into a grid consisting of the parallel lines of longitude and latitude. This allowed a navigator with drawing instruments to mark off a course with a constant compass bearing as a straight line crossing all meridians at the same angle.

But probably the most dramatic initial effect of exploration was the development of a major and chronic inflation. Between 1500 and 1650, prices tripled as Europe's economy rapidly changed. The inflation resulted from the expansion of trade, demand outpacing the supply of agricultural products, the development of industrialization in northern Europe, the rise of the standard of living, and especially the vast importation of gold, silver, precious stones, and other valuable products from the New World.

People in the general population on fixed incomes suffered greatly. In addition, many of the royalty, the nobility, and the landed gentry received most of their income from rents on lands that had long-term leases. Inflation thus greatly undermined their economic base which in turn diminished their political strength. Furthermore, almost everywhere rising prices outpaced wages, and many of the unemployed workers formed an underclass of vagrants. Nevertheless, the early modern period saw a very substantial increase in social and economic mobility. Those people who easily adjusted to the altered economic situation usually did extremely well.

Overall, the great increase in money for investing in industries and the opening of new markets around the world stimulated the expansion of capitalism. Indeed, there occurred what is often called the Commercial Revolution. In particular, entrepreneurs now developed new types of business organizations to handle the significant increase in trade. Medieval guilds had been unable to deal with the expanding commerce, therefore businessmen organized charter companies, especially joint-stock companies which proved to be the most efficient. Investors in a joint-stock company received profits in proportion to the amount of stock they owned. Moreover, they hired or elected the managers of the company. Greater corporate stability was thus achieved since the company remained while individuals bought or sold stock.

Colonies became a key aspect of this increased global trade. Leaders viewed colonies as potential markets for finished products produced in the mother country as well as the suppliers of raw materials. Western European nations embraced the economic concept known as mercantilism which called for a self-sufficient national economy that had a favorable balance of trade, a large national reserve of gold and silver, and exclusive access to trade with its colonies. To facilitate the development of a mercantilist system, governments enacted legislation that promoted new industries, forced poor people to work, and created tariff barriers to limit or to exclude various foreign imports. At the same time, governments negotiated treaties with other countries that promoted national self-sufficiency. Until the late 1700s, mercantilism would remain the primary economic philosophy in Europe. In addition to the economic aspects, colonies were also viewed as outlets to relieve religious tensions and social pressures within European nations.

The most important New World agricultural exports were those from the Caribbean islands, especially sugar which the Arabs had initially introduced into Sicily and Spain. The Europeans eventually took sugar to the New World where it economically transformed Brazil and the Caribbean islands. Moreover, Europeans further changed the agriculture of the New World by introducing rice, cereals, vines, olives, coffee, horses, sheep, and cattle.

To have a large, cheap labor force, the European colonists initiated the extensive use of African slaves on the Latin American plantations. Prince Henry the Navigator of Portugal had started the involvement of Europe in the modern slave trade, but the Spaniards subsequently expanded the trade to meet labor needs in the New World. The Native Americans had been decimated by European diseases, whereas the Africans proved more immune. Eventually Europeans purchased as many as 10 million Africans from local chieftains. Approximately 10 percent of the Africans died during the voyage to the Americas or soon after their arrival. The slave traders then auctioned off the survivors with approximately 70 percent of the African slaves ending up on Brazilian plantations.

The colonization of the New World also had a major and immediate impact on the Native Americans. The Europeans in Latin America were largely indifferent to the Native Americans' culture, and the decimation of Indian tribes by European diseases, such as smallpox and measles, dramatically undermined traditional cultures. Nevertheless, the Europeans, due to their insufficient population in the New World, did not completely destroy the Indians' culture. Family structure, agricultural techniques, and art motifs did survive, but the Native American survivors often had their descendants and their surviving culture intermixed with the emerging Hispanic culture. Moreover, Christianity replaced traditional religions, and the Europeans, who dominated all aspects of society, banned some Native American customs.

In North America, European diseases also often decimated the Indian tribes and contributed to their dislocation from traditional tribal lands. But interaction between the French and the Native Americans did not greatly disrupt Indian societies because the French were primarily interested in trade rather than the acquisition of territory. At times, Anglo-Indian relations involved friendship and assistance, as in Pennsylvania between 1681 and 1712. The English desire for land, however, often led to conflict as the Indians fought to protect their territory and way of life. Eventually the British government tried to establish a policy that would protect the Indian lands, but the land-hungry settlers successfully resisted the efforts to stop the displacement of the Indians.

At the same time that the Europeans were having such a negative impact on the New World, they also were dramatically affecting much of sub-Saharan Africa. The Europeans' contact with the west coast of Africa quickly resulted in a redirection of trade from the traditional, vigorous trans-Saharan and Indian Ocean routes that carried gold, slaves, ivory, and numerous other goods northward to Europe and the Moslem world, as well as eastward to India. The redirected commerce went to the African coastal areas and then to Western Europe and the European colonies around the world. But the Europeans made few efforts to establish settlements in sub-Saharan Africa since their primary interests were the slaves, gold, and other items that could be gained through trade.

While the Europeans established a slave trade, African kingdoms on the Gold Coast or with ties to it began to prosper as they controlled the trade with the Europeans. With European weapons, the Africans went to war with each other to acquire slaves. Gradually the Europeans, who were seeking more slaves and other trade, began to move farther south along the west coast causing even more disruption in West Africa. Furthermore, European actions on the east coast of Africa, particularly by the Portugese, undermined the Swahili society. Nevertheless, central Africa experienced little of the impact of European involvement, and the other sub-Saharan Africans still adhered to much of their traditional culture despite the disruptions caused by the European contacts.

In contrast to the New World and parts of sub-Saharan Africa, the Europeans' impact was minimal on the peoples of Asia. The few Europeans who went to Asia largely remained in trading posts and encountered well-established societies based on very ancient cultures. At the time of the Europeans' arrival, India was a politically unified country due to the rule of the Moguls, a Moslem branch of Timur Lang's (Tamerlane's) Mongols. India's upper class gained increased prosperity and the country experienced a period of brilliant cultural achievement. But during the 1600s Mogul power declined and local native princes increasingly gained political control. The French and English encouraged this decentralization of authority since it helped them to establish their trading interests in India. Whether under the Moguls or local princes, India remained basically unchanged by the Europeans. Based on deeply held religious beliefs, especially those of Hinduism, India's fundamental social institutions, including the family, the village, and the caste system, remained largely untouched. Hinduism's stress on the acceptance of the status quo as a part of the divine order and its disinterest in the pursuit of wealth and new things meant that Indians were not strongly interested in acquiring what the Europeans had to offer. However, the basic structure of Indian society did not prevent the Europeans from making immense profits from trade in India.

During the sixteenth and seventeenth centuries, the Europeans also had little effect on China and Japan, the other major Asian civilizations. As with India, this was due to their solidly established societies. By the 1700s many Europeans tremendously admired Chinese civilization, but in China the Qing (Manchu) Dynasty (1644–1911) closely regulated the activities of European traders, whom the Chinese called "Ocean Devils," and thus there was a very minimal Western impact on Chinese culture. Though concerned about Western influences, the Chinese did not care whether trade passed through Moslem hands, as it had for centuries, or through the hands of European merchants. Indeed, though the Moslems in Southeast Asia, Southeast Europe, India, and Africa continued to win major victories and to advance into new areas, they lost their central position in global commerce as ocean routes replaced overland trade.

Japan's first contact with Europeans occurred in 1542 with the arrival of Portugese traders. Merchants and missionaries from Portugal and other Catholic nations visited in the following years. As these Europeans dealt with leaders of the central government and with many local rulers, the Japanese quickly adopted the use of firearms, tobacco, and other imports.

But Christianity proved to be the most important aspect of Western culture introduced into Japan. By the end of the 1500s there may have been as many as 150,000 Japanese Christians. After 1597, however, Japanese leaders began a campaign of persecution against the Christians. The Japanese leaders did not want their subjects to have divided allegiances and they feared that European missionary work could set the stage for a political conquest as the Spanish had done in the Philippines. Thus in 1638 the Japanese government used technical advice and material from Dutch Protestants to put down a rebellion by the Catholic community in Kyushu. In the aftermath of this bloody victory, the Japanese government feared foreign Christians might assist Japanese dissidents. Therefore, the Tokugawa shogunate (1603–1867), which promoted stability based on strict adherence to ancient values and customs, established a policy that prohibited Japanese from traveling abroad and prohibited foreigners from visiting Japan. Japanese leaders adhered to this exclusion policy until the mid-1800s.

The voyages of discovery were one of mankind's greatest adventures. And this overseas expansion was a very nationalistic phenomenon, as strong central governments which emerged in Western Europe during the fifteenth century and the sixteenth century supported policies of exploration and colonization. But also, as a result of Europe's expansion, the civilizations of the earth became interconnected with many and varied consequences for Europe and the non-European world.

SELECTED BIBLIOGRAPHY

Boorstin, Daniel J. *The Discoverers*. New York: Random House, 1983. Covers some aspects of the Age of Discovery as a part of the author's chronicling mankind's continuing efforts at unraveling the world's mysteries.

Boxer, C. R. *The Dutch Seaborne Empire, 1600–1800*. New York: Knopf, 1965. Examines life in the Netherlands during the growth and decline of Dutch imperialism.

Braudel, Fernand. *Civilization and Capitalism, 15th–18th Century*, 3 vols. Translated by S. Reynolds. New York: Harper and Row, 1982–1984. A highly praised and sophisticated analysis that deals with the background and development of capitalism and the growth of Europe's global trade network in a primarily pre-industrial era.

Cipolla, Carlo M. *Before the Industrial Revolution: European Society and Economy, 1000–1700*. 3rd ed. New York: Norton, 1994. Gives an overview of economic changes in Europe before and during the Age of Discovery.

———. *Guns, Sails and Empires: Technological Innovation and the Early Phases of European Expansion, 1400–1700*. New York: Pantheon Books, 1965. Stresses the connection between technology and successful expansion, especially how sailing ships and gunpowder gave Europe a great advantage over the rest of the world.

Crosby, Alfred. *The Columbian Exchange: Biological and Cultural Consequences of*

1492. Westport, CT: Greenwood Publishing, 1972. Covers the movement of germs, humans, and other organisms between the Old World and the New since 1492.

Davis, Ralph. *The Rise of the Atlantic Economies.* Ithaca, NY: Cornell University Press, 1973. An economic history of Western European countries bordering on the Atlantic and their colonies in the New World from the 1400s to the end of the eighteenth century.

Delouche, Frederic, ed. *Illustrated History of Europe: A Unique Portrait of Europe's Common History.* New York: Henry Holt, 1992. Information on several aspects of the Age of Discovery.

Elliott, J. H. *The Old World and the New, 1492–1650.* Cambridge, Eng.: Cambridge University Press, 1970. Examines intellectual, political, and economic aspects of the European discovery of the New World.

Garraty, John A., and Peter Gay, eds. *The Columbia History of the World.* New York: Harper and Row, 1972. This wide-ranging study includes a very useful overview of America and Asia during the Age of Discovery.

Gibson, Charles. *Spain in America.* New York: Harper and Row, 1966. Offers a description of the institutions and culture of Spanish America from the first explorers to recent times.

Greenblatt, Stephen. *Marvelous Possessions: The Wonder of the New World.* Chicago: University of Chicago Press, 1991. A study of Europeans' travel accounts of the New World, especially regarding the relationship between Europeans and the native Americans.

Kennedy, Paul. *The Rise and Fall of the Great Powers: Economic Change and Military Conflict from 1500 to 2000.* New York: Random House, 1987. Offers significant insights on Europe's commercial and colonial rivalries in the early modern period.

Mannix, Daniel P., and Malcolm Cowley. *Black Cargoes: A History of the Atlantic Slave Trade, 1518–1865.* New York: Viking Press, 1962. A very detailed study of the origins and development of the Atlantic slave trade.

McAlister, Lyle N. *Spain and Portugal in the New World, 1492–1700.* Oxford, Eng.: Oxford University Press, 1984. This work, which is volume 3 in the series titled "Europe and the World in the Age of Expansion," provides a wide-ranging overview of Spanish and Portugese rule in the Americas, as well as giving an analysis of the cultural and economic impact of Hispanic America on Europe.

Morison, Samuel Eliot. *The European Discovery of America.* 2 vols. New York: Oxford University Press, 1971, 1974. Provides an extensive narrative of European voyages of discovery to the New World to 1616.

Pagden, Anthony. *European Encounters with the New World.* New Haven, CT: Yale University Press, 1993. Analyzes the types of thought that shaped Europeans' changing attitudes toward the New World and covers how European encounters with the Americas altered European culture.

Quinn, David Beers. *North America from Earliest Discovery to First Settlements: The Norse Voyages to 1612.* New York: Harper and Row, 1975. A volume in the "New American Nation Series" that provides a very detailed narrative of Europeans' voyages of discovery, attempts at exploration, and efforts at colonization in North America down to 1612.

Scammell, G. V. *The World Encompassed: The First European Maritime Empires.* Berkeley: University of California Press, 1981. A useful survey of the transformation of Western European countries into seafaring, world-oriented nations.

Johann Gutenberg examining his first printed page, c. 1455. No contemporary picture of Johann Gutenberg's first printing press is known to exist. (Reproduced from the Collections of the Library of Congress)

6

The Development of Movable Type, c. 1450

INTRODUCTION

No other invention contributed as much to the dissemination of knowledge during the Renaissance than the development of printing through the use of movable type. Historians credit Johann Gutenberg, of Mainz, now in Germany, with this invention and note that a Bible, called the Gutenberg Bible, was the first book published (in 1456) using movable type. There is some evidence that movable type was known in China as early as the eleventh century, Korea in the thirteenth century, and in Turkey sometime later, but it is unlikely that Gutenberg was aware of this. His invention came about when it did because of the need for a better method of written communication, spurred by the spread of literacy to laypeople, a rise in the interest in collecting fine manuscripts, and a desire for both secular and religious literature. Demand was high, and Gutenberg found a way to increase the supply.

The facts of Gutenberg's early life are shrouded in uncertainty. The year 1398 has long been accepted as Gutenberg's probable birth year, but Albert Kapr, in his 1996 biography, asserts that Gutenberg was born on June 24, 1400. His father, who was nearly 50 at the time of Johann's birth, was a prominent merchant in Mainz; his mother, much younger, came from a patrician family. Both parents would have been literate and would have recognized the value of a good education. It is not known whether Gutenberg attended school in Mainz or learned to read and write at home, but it is likely that he went to a church-run day school. To have produced the Bible he did, he would have had to have learned Latin very well somewhere, and quite possibly, he learned his Latin at Erfurt University between 1418 and 1420.

During the 1420s, he lived in Mainz, caring for his widowed mother and learning the goldsmith's trade. There was a good deal of civic turmoil in Mainz at this time, mainly concerning matters of town finances, taxes, and the interests of competing factions, and perhaps because of this Gutenberg left the city in 1430 and lived in Strasbourg for a number of years. It may have been in Strasbourg that he began to develop the concept of printing with movable type; at any rate, he was back in Mainz by the mid-1440s, and in 1450, he borrowed some money from a lawyer, Johannes Fust, and set about capitalizing his invention. Two years later, Fust loaned Gutenberg more money and became his partner. It seems not to have been a happy arrangement, however, for in 1455, Fust seized most of Gutenberg's printing equipment after the printer had fallen behind in his payments. This equipment was given to Peter Schoeffer, who worked for Fust and would soon marry his daughter. As for Gutenberg, he carried on with his printing work the best he could for a few more years, but by 1460, he had retired from the trade. The local archbishop gave him a pension in 1465, but he did not have much time to enjoy it. He died on February 3, 1468.

It is technically incorrect to say that Gutenberg invented printing or that he invented the printing of books. Rather, Gutenberg invented the means—movable type—by which books could be machine-made in large quantities. And even here, the use of the word "invent" is questionable, since, as mentioned above, movable type was known in Asia long before Gutenberg's time.

Prior to Gutenberg's work, books had been handwritten by scribes or printed from woodblocks. To have a professional scribe produce a book was highly labor-intensive, time-consuming, and expensive. Religious orders sometimes specialized in the copying of texts as a source of income, and individual booksellers employed as many as 50 scribes. The Chinese had developed the system of printing from woodblocks cut in negative relief so that the ideographs would be correctly printed, and they also invented paper, which turned out to be the cheapest and most readily available medium to receive printing. But cutting woodblocks was also labor-intensive and expensive, and if an error was discovered, it was difficult to correct it. Gutenberg's moveable metal type enabled publishers for the first time to edit and correct their work quickly and conveniently.

Gutenberg made two significant improvements on Chinese woodblock printing. First, he used metal rather than wood, borrowing, in a sense, the practice of goldsmiths or silversmiths who cut metal punches with their trademarks. Second, he made type by the letter rather than as a block, thus immensely increasing its flexibility and long-term usefulness. Gutenberg also adapted an older invention, the screw press, to make a device ideal for pressing the inked type onto paper.

To make multiple copies of each letter, number, and symbol used in printing, Gutenberg utilized the principle of replica cutting. He (or an assistant) would engrave a letter in relief on a piece of hard metal and use it to make an impression in a brass mold. This would create a negative (or reverse) impression of that letter. Another problem was finding a suitable metal alloy for the type, one that would have a low melting point for ease of casting yet be strong enough to be used thousands of times in printing. After much experimentation, Gutenberg found that an alloy of lead, tin, and antimony worked best. This was melted down and poured into the brass mold to make the actual piece of type, and he repeated the process until he had as many of each letter as he needed. A "handle" or shank was formed on the back of the piece of type to allow for easy arranging into the words and lines on the page. Most historians give Peter Schoeffer credit for developing the typecaster's mold, a two-part device into which the molten lead could be poured and from which letters of identical height could be formed. Still, Gutenberg probably devised some variation of that mold for his own letter casting.

Another technological problem Gutenberg solved was finding an ink that would adhere to the metal type and leave a clear impression on the paper after it had gone through the press. What worked for woodblocks would not work for the metal type. After some experimentation, Gutenberg developed an ink based on linseed oil varnish and colored with pigment. The availability of waste rag, from which paper could be made, was vital to the success of printing, since vellum, an important medium for handwritten manuscripts, was scarce and expensive. Vellum was a paper-like substance prepared from the intestines (and later, the skin) of young goats, lambs, or calves.

The screw press had been developed as early as the first century of the Christian era. Although legend has it that Gutenberg was inspired by a wine press he saw while attending a wine festival, most historians believe that he asked Konrad Saspach, a local carpenter, to make alterations on a simple domestic press that might have been used for extracting oil from olives or for pressing cloth. A pressing board, called a "platen," was hung by hooks in a box-like holder called a "hose," and a screw at the top was turned to lower the board onto a surface that held the type. Paper attached to the board would absorb the ink on the type and result in a printed page. By the end of the fifteenth century, when the first known pictures of a printing press were made, a projecting table was used to hold the type. This could be slid underneath the descending platen until it was properly placed to receive the paper attached to the platen. Although Gutenberg's press was heavy, bulky, hard to use, and unable to print a very large page in one pressing, the basic design remained unchanged until the late eighteenth century. It was immensely popular; by 1468, every country in Europe had at least one printing press.

S. H. Steinberg links the evolution of type design to Renaissance humanism, noting that in countries that embraced humanism, printers adopted "roman" and "italic" styles. In other countries, principally those on the periphery of Europe, non-Latin alphabets and distinctive type styles continued to be used, such as the Cyrillic type still used in Russia, many of the former Soviet republics, and Bulgaria.

The earliest printed books looked very much like the handwritten works of the professional scribes, since that was what a conservative reading public seemed to want. Printers even left blank spaces at the beginning of chapters and elsewhere, so illustrators could add elaborate initials or other pictorial material, just as they did with handwritten books. By 1480 or so, however, the importance of creating an accurate and readable text had become recognized, and printers began using type of different sizes on a page to indicate chapter headings or sub-headings, tables of contents, indexes, and other compositional devices. All of these made for a greater variety of texts that were easier to understand. Along with this came a reduction in the number of different letters, combinations of letters (called ligatures), and symbols that printers used. Gutenberg had an array of almost 300 different pieces of type; over time this was gradually reduced to about 40.

For the first 150 years of printing, illustrations were made by the use of woodblocks, but in the late 1500s, copper engravings, in which an artist could include much greater detail, began to replace the woodblocks. Ink was forced into the thin lines of the engraving cut into the copper and then transferred to paper through the use of an engraving press. One drawback that was not overcome until much later was that with either method of illustrating a book, the illustrations had to be printed separately from the text.

In the English-speaking world, William Caxton enjoys a reputation next to that of Gutenberg in the history of printing. Born in Kent around 1420, Caxton spent his early life in the business world of London, where he was a mercer, a merchant who dealt primarily in haberdashery, cloth, and silks. He was apprenticed to a prominent businessman, William Large, who later became Lord Mayor of London, and through this association, Caxton not only learned the intricacies of fifteenth century business but also acquired a circle of rich and powerful friends and business associates.

In the 1450s, Caxton was in Bruges, in what was then Flanders (and is now Belgium) where he served as a sort of consul, representing British commercial interests. Bruges was the site of an important international market, and Flanders was also the center of fancy manuscript production. Caxton was almost certainly involved in the business of exporting some of these manuscripts to England, a task that might well have piqued his interest in printing and publishing.

In the 1460s, he left his post at Bruges, perhaps not by his own choice, and spent his time translating a medieval French romance, *Recueil des histoires de Troye*. He dedicated the work to King Edward IV's sister Margaret and, in order to produce a special edition, he went to Cologne in 1470 and learned the printing trade. His edition of the French romance was so well received that he set up his own printing press in Bruges in 1473 and published several other popular works, including one on chess.

In 1476, he returned to London, setting up his press in Westminster. He printed his own books there, but he also imported books from the continent and became England's first native-born book retailer (there were Dutch, German, and French booksellers in London by this time). Part of Caxton's importance lies in his close ties to the English royalty of his era. Edward IV, Richard III, and Henry VII all patronized and befriended Caxton, and Edward IV's brother-in-law, the second Earl of Rivers, was an author whose work Caxton published. Caxton's lasting importance rests in the fact that he translated and printed the first English editions of many great works. He also published editions of some of the principal works of English literature, notably Geoffrey Chaucer's *Canterbury Tales*.

Printing presses spread rapidly throughout Europe after the 1450s. They were in use in Italy by 1465, where Renaissance literature was published and where the roman and italic type styles were popularized. In Italy, innovations such as title pages, page numbers, and small, portable editions were introduced. By 1490, Italian printers were busily distributing cheap editions of the works of ancient Greek and Roman authors.

Not long afterward, scientific books began to appear in significant numbers on topics as diverse as mining and distilling. The mid-sixteenth century saw the works of Nicholas Copernicus and other astronomers appear, and the mid-seventeenth century marked the beginning of scientific journals, such as the *Philosophical Transactions* of the Royal Society, based in London. Newspapers, in the form of one-page broadsides, began to appear sporadically as early as 1573 in England, although regularly published newspapers were not available until 1609 in Germany and 1620 in England. The first daily paper in London was the *Daily Courant* (1702).

INTERPRETIVE ESSAY
Alison Gulley

In the fall of 1999, Arts and Entertainment Television's *Biography* series named Johannes Gutenberg, inventor of the movable type press in the West, the most influential person of the millennium. Given the phenomenal developments of the last 1,000 years, such a distinction is remarkable. Although the movable type press first appeared in China in the eleventh century, the Chinese language—with approximately 40,000 ideographs—limited the development of this form of printing. In fact, this early kind of printing press had no influence over the invention of the printing press in the Western world, the beginning of which has long been symbolized by the appearance of the Gutenberg Bible in 1456. Although the full impact of printing—on education, religion, the political realm, and indeed on the development of Western-style democracy— was not fully realized until several centuries later, by the beginning of the sixteenth century the face of European society clearly was forever altered. In fact, it is frequently argued that the results of this revolutionary invention are still ongoing.

The nature of this change has been widely debated. For some historians and philosophers, the key to the change lies in the modes with which knowledge is represented and assimilated. That is, humankind changed from an audial culture in which knowledge was transmitted orally and learned by hearing to one in which knowledge was transmitted via the written word. Such a shift had tenable as well as symbolic meaning. For example, the art of rhetoric—the theory and practice of using language—lay with spoken discourse and its effect on the audience (notice that this common word, which now means simply a group of people who receive word through any means written or spoken, reflects the original method of receiving information by ear). A successful orator considered his or her audience carefully and noted the difference between addressing a large crowd in a public arena, such as a Roman forum, where forceful articulation and perhaps theatrical delivery were effective, and the more intimate needs of, for example, a courtroom, where success depended on a softly spoken, careful argument. By the same token, a teacher might have weighed the relative merits of the Socratic method of question and answer against straight lecture. Textbooks, today accepted as commonplace by student and teacher alike, simply were not an option. Likewise, when a religious congregation, lacking easy access to Bibles and written doctrinal explication, looked only to its priest for enlightenment, a good preacher relied on the rhetorical strategies most likely to clarify Christian teachings, and, perhaps more importantly, to keep his congregation awake!

With the advent of printing and increased availability of books and other printed material, people no longer needed to gather together to hear the news, and rhetorical art began to encompass the written presentation of ideas. Michel de Montaigne, using the personal essay form in which he frequently addressed his audience with the intimate "Reader," was one of the first writers to successfully meet the needs of a diverse and scattered audience who received information in a variety of settings. The difficulty of such a rhetorical shift is illustrated on a lesser level when one thinks of the difficulties produced by a perhaps less revolutionary but no less extraordinary invention: talking pictures. Even if not entirely accurate, the Hollywood stereotype persists of the famous stage actors who failed miserably because of a ridiculously over-projected voice and acting more appropriate to a large theater than the intimate screen.

Another tangible change in the way knowledge was transmitted can be seen in the gradual loss of mnemonic devices. Before written materials were broadly available, public speakers relied on their memory. Poems, stories, songs, speeches, and sermons were passed down orally and so poets, minstrels, orators, and preachers relied on intricate memory devices—rhymes, cadences, alliteration, and even physical symbols. It has been argued that the stone carvings and stained glass windows of Gothic cathedrals, for example, served as reminders and cues for orators. Of course, images and intricate architecture remain an important part of print culture but the fact remains that memory and memory devices became less important when writers could record their words for posterity.

Writers had always recorded their words but particular obstacles stood in the way of their preservation. First, much of the pre-printing writing still extant survived because of luck rather than design. *Beowulf*, that Anglo-Saxon epic masterpiece, exists in one copy preserved by a collector who, many have suggested, apparently liked monster stories. (The collection also includes a description of giant hairy women with 11 feet, tusks, donkey teeth, and ox tails, in a work called *The Wonders of the East*.) Another Anglo-Saxon manuscript, containing now frequently anthologized elegies such as "The Wanderer," survived despite evidence that it was used as a beer and cheese mat by monks. The second obstacle, simply put, was that written records crumbled, whether they were on papyrus or the hardy vellum used in the Middle Ages. Frequently used writings wore out, and stored writings succumbed to moisture, vermin, theft, and fire. As Thomas Jefferson's letter to statesman and lawyer George Wythe illustrates, this problem existed even in modern times:

> Very early in the course of my researches into the laws of Virginia, I observed that many of them were already lost, and many more on the point of being lost, as existing only in single copies in the hands of careful or curious individuals, on whose deaths they would probably be used for waste paper. ... [The] question is what means will be the most effectual for preserving these remains from future loss? All the care I can take of them, will not preserve them from the worm, from the natural decay of the paper, from the accident of fire, or those of removal when it is necessary for any public purpose.... Our experience has proved to us that a single copy, or a few, deposited in MS in the public offices cannot be relied on for any great length of time. [quoted in Boyd, Julian, "These Precious Moments of ... Our History," *The American Archivist* 2 (1959), pp. 175–76]

Another kind of human error or carelessness that contributed to the loss of written material was simply scribal error. Letters and words could be misread and so miscopied. Scribes also made the kinds of errors writers make today, such as missing or doubled words, particularly at the end or beginning of lines, or even entirely skipped lines. More disturbing—or amusing depending on how one looks at it—are scribal interjections. Stories or teachings might be changed to suit the scribe's individual taste or philosophy.

The easy duplication made possible by the printing press solved many of these problems. Although the paper used in printing was not as durable as vellum, quantity made up for quality. However, even on this point there was skepticism—at times, scribes were ordered to make handwritten copies of books for posterity. On the other hand, the presence of duplicates made book-owners lazy. As Elizabeth Eisenstein has pointed out, "When written messages are duplicated in such great abundance that they can be consigned to trash bins or converted into pulp, they are not apt to prompt thoughts about prolonged preservation." In contrast, expensive manuscripts (Latin: *manu-*, by hand, *scriptum*, written) were frequently guarded carefully; despite the great loss of early written material, a surprising and overwhelming amount survives today. It has been estimated that, for example, a higher percentage of works by the Venerable Bede, who lived and wrote in the late seventh and early eighth centuries, survives than of printed eighteenth-century novels.

Of course, despite duplication, human error still existed. A major difference was that whereas a scribal error might be corrected at the next copying, or at worst duplicated a few times for a relatively small audience, in printing, errors were mass-produced and often widely disseminated. Such was the case with the so-called "Wicked Bible" of 1631 in which the compositor inadvertently left off the word "not" from the Seventh Commandment and thus instructed that "thou *shalt* commit adultery."

The fact remains, however, that regardless of the difficulties that came along with printing, the ability to mass-produce words and images wrought immeasurable changes on western European society. These changes are perhaps nowhere more visible than in the areas of literacy and education. One must tread lightly in this area, however. The extent to which printing affected education and literacy has been overstated in the past and ignores the thriving medieval literary tradition as well as a cultural and societal shift toward widespread literacy and education already underway. This was particularly true among the new middle classes that had emerged from a changing European economy. What perhaps can be said is that printing led to an increased availability of books which eventually resulted in a lower cost book and in turn allowed more people easy access to texts, religious and popular as well as educational, thus encouraging or perhaps speeding up certain processes.

Estimating literacy rates is always a hard business but some generalizations can be made. In England after the Norman Conquest of 1066, both French and English aristocracy had a reading literacy in French and some Latin. By the thirteenth century, works such as Walter of Henley's French-language *Husbandry* and *Stewardship* show that stewards of estates read and wrote at the level needed to run a household and carry on business transactions. At any rate, in fourteenth-century England scribes catered to bakers and merchants as well as lawyers and knights, and as early as 1405 authorities were worried about the posting of seditious fliers, indicating that such political messages could be read and understood by many. By 1450, some parts of England showed a literacy rate of 30 to 40 percent, and in London the rate may have been even higher. By the late 1500s literacy rates in cities appears to have been above 50 percent. On the continent similar numbers existed. Overall, the trend started at the top of the social scale and the top of the church hierarchy and worked its way down the social ladder as the growth of a middle class made literacy both necessary and possible, yet in Italy, for example, literate merchants existed alongside illiterate aristocrats. The rate continued to increase slowly, to about 60 percent in the eighteenth century and 90 percent in our era.

A similar pattern exists in terms of the availability of and desire for reading material. Chaucer's Clerk in the late fourteenth-century *Canterbury Tales* would have preferred "twenty bookes" at his "beddes heed" to nice clothing or a fiddle and harp, yet as a poor scholar he would not have been able to afford the exorbitant price. At the same time, while several books was perhaps not the norm, many people, rich, middle class, and poor, owned some kind of written material. Like the Clerk, clerics had always desired and often owned books, and the practice spread, again with the growth of the merchant middle class. Not only do we find wills of the aristocracy bequeathing books to friends, churches, and family, but we find a London vintner (c. 1349) leaving a psalter, townsmen (c. 1420 and c. 1435) leaving copies of *The Canterbury Tales*, and a Joanna Hilton of Yorkshire in 1432 leaving copies of a "Romance with the ten commandments," a romance of the Seven Sages, and a copy of the French *Roman de la Rose.*

What effect, then, *did* the advent of printing have on literacy and learning? The simple answer is that in a society with an increasing need for literacy and education, the ability to produce large numbers of books brought them and new ways of learning into the hands of more people. Prior to the invention of the press more and more children were being educated. Wealthy families hired tutors or sent their children—both boys and girls—to grammar schools, while parish schools served poor families, even in small rural villages. However, the presence of a teacher with access to books was always a necessity. In contrast, while mass production of books did not render the lecturing teacher obsolete, it certainly made individual study possible. "Why should old men be preferred to their juniors," asked Tycho Brache, the author of a fifteenth-century history book, "now that it is possible for the young by diligent study to acquire the same knowledge?"

Young students were not the only ones to benefit. It was now possible to read more books in a few months than earlier scholars had read in a lifetime. The stereotypical "wandering scholar" could now consult several texts in one place rather than waste time traveling from library to library or monastery to monastery; meanwhile the medieval practice of spending a life time glossing and commenting on one text was supplanted by the practice of cross-referencing several texts. Of course, such new techniques of study exposed the often conflicting or confusing work of earlier scholars but, again, having the books in one place allowed scholars to begin the valuable sifting and sorting necessary for productive research.

As for what kinds of information became readily available, the quality and diversity of topics varied. At first, it must be said, printing had little effect on the reading habits of the public. As has been pointed out, the general public in the late medieval and early Renaissance era was relatively well educated. When printers set up business popular taste dictated their choices of what to print. William Caxton, who introduced Gutenberg's press to England in 1476 and dominated publishing there for the rest of the century, was typical. He began by producing in Latin sermons, histories, and grammar books for school but quickly moved to supply the middle class and courtly taste for poetry, romances, and popular saints' lives; in short, Caxton provided the same kinds of writings that scribes copied before the printing press and, interestingly, continued to copy well after Caxton set up shop. England can perhaps be set apart from continental countries by the large numbers of manuscripts made from printed books—not only to preserve works but also to meet the public's request for such books. As N. F. Blake has pointed out, the reading public did not necessarily distinguish in any substantive way between printed books or handwritten books any more than the average reader today distinguishes (except perhaps aesthetically) between photocopied or printed words.

Yet during and after this transitional age, called the incunabula period (Latin: *in-*, in, *cunabula*, cradle) a veritable revolution in book production occurred. In the pre-printing era, it was not unknown for a scribe to spend a year copying a manuscript and what was being copied frequently depended on one person's needs or desires. Libraries were scarce and typically held small collections: the libraries at Canterbury and Bury, England, which each housed about 2,000 volumes, were the largest with collections including mainly Bibles, psalms, and religious works; books from classical antiquity were also common. However, when the printing press suddenly made rapid book production possible, the number of volumes available multiplied. By 1500, the numbers alone were mind-boggling: 1,120 printing offices could be found in 260 towns in 17 different European countries, with a combined output of 40,000 titles appearing in over 10 million different books.

However, just as mass production did not change reading habits overnight, surprisingly, neither were its effects felt in law or science, disciplines which today require large libraries. Canon (church) and civil law were both upheld despite their sometimes contradictory statutes; likewise, local laws and customs varied from one town or county to the next. Clearly, duplication would not have helped much at this point. As such, only general texts and commentaries found a market niche and even then were superior to the handwritten texts only in price.

Originally, the exploitation of the press by the field of science was only a little better. At first, professional scientists withheld their work from print, and the field was flooded with mass-produced quackery or outdated ancient and medieval texts. If anything, printing slowed, if only briefly, the advances of science. Printed legitimate scientific work did not sell well, and some scientific historians have posited that the ready availability of medieval scientific texts hindered the acceptance of revolutionary ideas and theories. In an age of pseudo-science and superstition, or perhaps simply concerned about innovation in the face of traditional, accepted scientific knowledge, Giovanni Borelli, author of an important seventeenth-century work on Euclid, questioned whether new scientific discoveries were even appropriate for the masses: "You have to decide whether the writing is for the experts or for everybody in town," he argued. Much of the debate over printing, then, centered on the nature and rhetorical art of scientific discourse. That is, how and for whom should knowledge be recorded and transmitted? Furthermore, others—having witnessed the controversy generated by certain scientific theories and thus wary of censure and censorship by fickle church and civil authorities—favored a less public venue, cautioning: "Learn at Galileo's expense. He ran into so much trouble just because he picked fights." Such concerns slowed the acceptance of the new print medium, and it was not until the 1660s with the publication of the first scientific journals in Italy that the rapid documentation and dissemination of scientific results was established as the standard.

Yet even as the debate over scientific publication raged, scientists benefited from increased availability of texts just as other scholars did. For example, when Copernicus was a student at Krakow in the 1480s, access to an edition of Ptolemy's second-century *Almagest*, which proposed an earth-centered universe, was limited. By the time he died, Copernicus had three editions to choose from. Despite the outdated nature of the *Almagest*, knowledge of it allowed Copernicus and his contemporaries to move beyond accepted astronomic theory. Other areas of science likewise benefited. Maps, no matter how inaccurate, could be compared and contrasted and then cross-referenced with the mass produced logs and charters of many different ships and explorers so that geographers no longer needed to rely on first-hand knowledge. Botanists and zoologists likewise could compare and contrast the same information from their studies all over Europe and then easily add their own data to the pool or even collaborate in large data collection. From a time-saving standpoint, the appearance of dictionaries, encyclopedias, book lists, and other bibliographical guides allowed scientists to quickly identify necessary texts, which were themselves often readily available and so freed the researcher from the hours needed to copy a manuscript or wait for one to be copied.

Whereas the effects on learning, literacy, and scholarship were not necessarily immediately apparent, one component of western European culture that felt an immediate impact was religion. It has been generally accepted that the Protestant Reformation of the Christian Church in the sixteenth century was the first religious movement aided by the printing press. Some historians have even proposed that the printing press *caused* the Reformation. When in 1517, the German Reformer Martin Luther formulated and posted his 95 theses against papal indulgences, such discussion was not revolutionary *per se*. What was revolutionary is the fact that within two weeks of their appearance in Wittenburg his ideas were spread throughout Germany. By 1520, the theses and Luther's other publications had sold over 300,000 copies. Christian "heresies" had been introduced and disseminated since the dawn of Christianity but Lutheranism was from the beginning associated with the printed book, which allowed almost instantaneous widespread public debate. Even among less literate sections of the population, one literate person could convey new ideas to large groups of people. Luther himself realized the different nature of his protest: "It is a mystery to me how my theses, more so than other writings, indeed, those of other professors were spread to so many places. They were meant exclusively for our academic circle here."

Another form of radical protest that hardly seems revolutionary by today's standards was the mass production of Bibles in the vernacular (the language spoken by the common person). Again, Luther's work provides an example of the magnitude of the enterprise. Three thousand copies of the first edition of his translation of the New Testament appeared in September 1522. The book was in such demand that a new, emended edition appeared in December, to be followed by six more editions by 1524, not to mention the 87 vernacular New Testaments—based on Luther's version—printed outside Wittenberg between 1522 and 1546.

Until the Reformation, most Biblical translations were Latin and those vernacular translations that did exist were in the hands of the clergy. As such, Christian doctrine was controlled solely by the Church hierarchy. Protestantism called this whole practice into question. Mass produced Bibles in an increasingly literate society meant that where once religion had been a public venture, individuals and small groups were suddenly able to study Scripture without a mediary. The Roman Church had condemned the printing of Scripture in the vernacular even before Luther's translation citing concern about inaccuracies and accidental as well as intentional corruption of ecclesiastical "truth." Furthermore, many authorities feared that making sacred writing widely available might lead to confusion and disobedience. One papal directive warned against the "mechanical reproduction" of the Scripture in the vernacular, calling it an "evil" that must be suppressed before it became a "roaring fire." The political import of Biblical translation and printing becomes even clearer when we realize that the most prominent printers and publishers in Germany, Switzerland, and Holland were Protestant.

In England, Reformers took it one step further. Although Henry VIII had opposed the Reformation, and won the title "Defender of the Faith" from Rome for his efforts, political and personal pressures (he wanted to divorce Catherine of Aragon and marry Anne Boleyn) led him to break with Rome and establish the Church of England with himself as head. Thomas Cromwell, his Vicar-General, was the first to use the press to engage in a propaganda campaign, and Henry himself ordered that English Bibles be made available in any church. The English Reformation was consolidated under Henry's son Edward VI, who issued a series of official books, including the *Book of Common Prayer* of 1549. Other works made widely available were official sermons, collections with the Lord's Prayer, the Apostle's Creed, and prayers for special occasions, as well as how-to guides for reformed religious practice by individuals and families, with such titles as *A Werke for Householders* (1530) and *Godly Private Prayers for Householders to Meditate Upon and Say in Their Families* (1576).

Alongside such Protestant furor, the Roman Catholic Church also put the printing press to good use. Prior to printing, when priests throughout Christendom practiced the mass, they relied on often faulty manuscript versions. However, new printed editions provided uniform texts and rites so that Catholics everywhere heard the same words and witnessed the same ceremonies. An added benefit to the established Church was that the service became fixed, preventing further erosion of the liturgy. Other important theological writings, such as the thirteenth-century doctrines of St. Thomas Aquinas, experienced a revival because of increased access. As devotional works became available both to priests and laity, the lay devotion movement, previously local, became widespread.

Whatever the religious preference, however, the printing press was embraced as a positive force in religion. Gutenberg had early been hailed for his help in the fight against the "illiterate Turks" in the Crusades, and a century later John Foxe, English Reformer and author of the extremely popular sixteenth-century *Book of Martyrs*, wrote, "The Lord began to work for His Church not with sword and target to subdue His Exalted adversary, but with printing, writing, and reading."

Roman Catholic or Protestant, literate or illiterate, rich or poor, the residual effects of the Reformation and thus of the printing press led to a revolution in the way that Europeans viewed country, church, town, and family. We are so used to seeing an excellent likeness of public figures that it is difficult to grasp the significance of seeing what a national figure looks like. Of course, coins commonly featured rulers, but printing produced crisp representations that, it can be argued, led to new concepts of celebrity and national identity with a sovereign. At the same time that printing encouraged new kinds of nationalism, it also contributed to a changing sense of community. The local parish church had long been the hub of a town or city's social and political life, a place where news was dispersed from the pulpit and by friends and family. Slowly, the pulpit was displaced by the monthly gazette and pamphlet of the sixteenth and seventeenth centuries and eventually by the periodical and newspaper. By the nineteenth century, people could spend Sunday mornings at home with their newspapers and get essentially the same information about births, deaths, and politics.

In addition to contributing to what has been called the secularization of society, these same gazettes, pamphlets, periodicals, and newspapers allowed political participation of a different kind. Where once an audience had to come together to hear a public address, the members of a dispersed audience could read the same report on their own time in a variety of locations, with the consequence that community, once defined by church and home, encompassed a broader unit. Individuals could support causes whose advocates lived far away. Attendance was no longer necessary in order to experience civic and public events; one might read about the experience after the fact or even vicariously participate through the purchase of commemorative prints and programs. This fragmented audience and society can be illustrated at a smaller level. We have already seen that the community of learners had been dispersed when students no longer needed to sit at the feet of their professors to learn. Yet even within a lecture classroom the very act of individual reading fragments the community. When students individually read a handout, they read at different rates and thus obtain information at different times. When the professor calls the attention of the class back to the front of the room, the community fragmented by individual reading must be reassembled. As historian Elizabeth Eisenstein notes in her important study of the effects of the printing press, "The notion that society may be regarded as a bundle of discrete units or that the individual is prior to the social group seems to be more compatible with a reading public than with a hearing one."

Although on the surface this type of social fragmentation seems detrimental to community cohesiveness, in one area particularly a consolidating force can be seen. Language is widely recognized as a unifying, nationalistic element of a people, and printing played a determining role in preserving and codifying certain vernaculars. Eisenstein has argued that during the sixteenth century, in areas where printing did not exist, certain vernaculars of small linguistic groups were excluded—or even disappeared—from the realm of literature. At the same time, where printing did exist, the vernaculars of similarly small groups survived and even expanded. In the latter case, a national literary culture appeared; in the former, often only a spoken regional dialect remained.

Printing also affected language because, just as the Catholic liturgy stabilized from the effects of duplication, so too did language itself. Although the standardization of a language—and indeed its very survival—depends upon a number of political, social, and economic factors, printing certainly played a major role in how such languages evolved as is illustrated by the example of English. The history of the English language has been broken down into three convenient time periods: Old English, running from the Germanic invasions of 449 to the Norman invasion of 1066; Middle English, up to about 1500; and Modern English, which period still continues. During the Old and Middle English periods, the language changed at a relatively rapid pace and regional differences were great. Until the ninth century, England was fragmented into many different kingdoms and the English people spoke a variety of dialects. Even in Chaucer's time, 500 years later, major dialectical differences remained. Although the political dominance of London ensured that the English spoken there would become the dominant dialect and form the basis of the standard English spoken today, the fact that the center of the publishing trade in England began and remained in London in Caxton's shop meant that the mass produced writings were in the London dialect.

Yet the standardizing effect must not be overstated. Surely, printing slowed the shifting of languages, but other, nationalistic factors were also at work. The Italian *Accademia della Crusca* and the *Académie Française* both attempted to refine and standardize language—in effect to cleanse it of impure foreign and domestic elements. Following suit, English groups proposed similar academies with similar goals. Grammar, punctuation, and spelling all came under scrutiny. Nevertheless, languages continued and continue to evolve, albeit less dramatically and perceptibly. Spelling remained in many ways in a hodgepodge until the nineteenth and twentieth centuries, and even now acceptable variations remain.

Despite these attempts to show the printing press as one of the many interactive and interdependent social, political, cultural, and economic factors at work in the development of modern western civilization, one should not downplay its importance in this evolutionary process. While literacy and education movements, religious reform, and modern science by their very force would have eventually succeeded, mass production of written material and the concomitant availability of information changed the way people viewed themselves and their world. Yet the communications revolution begun with Gutenberg's invention of the movable type press in Germany still continues. Photocopiers and personal computers have given individuals access to duplication; magnetic strip cards record and transmit information with one swipe. Human inventiveness in the mass production and mass communication of information apparently knows no bounds, and thus the revolutionary import of the printed word continues.

SELECTED BIBLIOGRAPHY

Baugh, Albert C., and Thomas Cable *A History of the English Language*. 4th ed. Englewood Cliffs, NJ: Prentice Hall, 1993. A standard classroom text for historical linguistics, this work covers in minute detail the syntactic changes in the English language as well as important social, historical, and political influences.

Blake, N. F. *William Caxton and English Literary Culture*. London: Hambledon Press, 1991. Blake's work is a good introduction to Caxton's life and work and contains a useful discussion of the English incunabula period.

Boyd, Julian. "These Precious Monuments of . . . Our History." *The American Archivist* 2 (1959): 175–76. This article contains Thomas Jefferson's letter concerning the preservation of important legal documents.

Chambers, R. W. "The Lost Literature of Medieval England." *The Library* 5 (1925): 293–321. This article discusses the preservation and loss of early English texts.

Dooley, Brendan. "The Communications Revolution in Italian Science." *History of Science* 33 (1995): 469–96. Dooley examines the early diffidence on the part of Italian scientists, or virtuosi, toward printing scientific research as well as the development of scientific journalism in the seventeenth century.

Eisenstein, Elizabeth. *The Printing Press as an Agent of Change: Communications and Cultural Transformations in Early-Modern Europe*. 2 Vols. New York: Cambridge University Press, 1979. Eisenstein's work, considered the first comprehensive study of the cultural effects of the printing press on the literate elite of Western Europe, is essential for any student seeking further information. The work appears in abridged form (see below) but this edition contains full notes and references.

———. *The Printing Revolution in Early Modern Europe*. New York: Cambridge University Press, 1983. A useful abridgement of Eisenstein's full scale work.

Gingerich, Owen. "Copernicus's De Revolutionibus: An Example of Renaissance

Scientific Printing." In *Print and Culture in the Renaissance*, ed. Gerald P. Tyson and Sylvia S. Wagonheim. Newark: University of Delaware Press, 1986, pp. 55–73. Gingerich discusses the dissemination and availability of *De Revolutionibus*, along with its influence on the scientific revolution.

Kapr, Albert. *Johann Gutenberg: The Man and the Invention*. Aldershot, Eng.: Scolar, 1996. Recent biography of Gutenberg, examining the controversies of his life in painstaking detail.

Keen, Maurice. *English Society in the Later Middle Ages, 1348–1500*. New York: Penguin, 1990. Keen discusses an important transitional period in England, focusing on the three traditional estates—priests, knights, and laborers—and the influence of the spread of literacy, mercantilism, the Black Death, and the Hundred Years' War.

Kjaergaard, Thorkild. "Origins of Economic Growth in European Societies Since the XVIth Century: The Case of Agriculture." *The Journal of European Economic History* 15, no. 1: (1986): 591–98. Kjaergaard argues that printing led to an increase of agronomic literature between the sixteenth and eighteenth centuries and correlates with the time period of sustained agricultural growth in Europe.

Monfasani, John. "The First Call for Press Censorship: Niccolò Perotti, Giovanni Andrea Bussi, Antonio Moreto, and the Editing of Pliny's *Natural History*." *Renaissance Quarterly* 41 (1988): 1–22. Monfasani argues that Perotti's effort to protect classical texts from incompetent editors, occasioned by the publication of Bussi's edition of the *Natural History* in 1470, constituted the first attempt at censorship.

Newman, Jane O. "The Word Made Print: Luther's 1522 New Testament in an Age of Mechanical Reproduction." *Representations* 11 (1985): 95–133. Newman's article explores the early suspicion about reproduced printed texts and the printing industry in general and the controversy surrounding Luther's New Testament in particular.

Rowan, Steven. "Jurists and the Printing Press in Germany: The First Century." In *Print and Culture in the Renaissance*, ed. Gerald P. Tyson and Sylvia S. Wagonheim. Newark: University of Delaware Press, 1986, pp. 74–89. Rowan discusses the initially minimal effect of the printing press on the practice of law.

Sessions, Kyle C. "Song Pamphlets: Media Changeover in Sixteenth-Century Publicization." In *Print and Culture in the Renaissance*, ed. Gerald P. Tyson and Sylvia S. Wagonheim. Newark: University of Delaware Press, 1986, pp. 110–119. This essay focuses specifically on the role of hymn pamphlets in the Reformation.

Steinberg, S. H. *Five Hundred Years of Printing*. New York: Penguin, 1974. Standard survey history of the subject, with considerable information on Gutenberg and his times.

Thorpe, James. *The Gutenberg Bible: Landmark in Learning*. San Marino, CA: The Huntington Library, 1975. This work contains a good general introduction to Gutenberg's life and art, as well as facsimile pages of the Gutenberg Bible.

Tyson, Gerald P., and Sylvia S. Wagonheim, eds. *Print and Culture in the Renais-*

sance: Essays on the Advent of Printing in Europe. Newark: University of Delaware Press, 1986. Tyson and Wagonheim have compiled a very useful collection of essays covering topics such as law, the Reformation, and science and the results of printing.

Wall, John N., Jr. "The Reformation in England and the Typographical Revolution: "By this printing . . . the doctrine of the Gospel soundeth to all nations." In *Print and Culture in the Renaissance*, ed. Gerald P. Tyson and Sylvia S. Wagonheim. Newark: University of Delaware Press, 1986, pp. 208–21. An extremely useful and interesting discussion of the role of the press in the Protestant Reformation, Wall's study focuses primarily on England.

Winship, George Parker. *Gutenberg to Plantin: An Outline of the Early History of Printing.* New York: Burt Franklin, 1968. Systematic study of Gutenberg and other printers of the fifteenth century.

7

The Fall of
Constantinople, 1453

INTRODUCTION

By 1453 the Byzantine Empire had shrunk to a mere shadow of its former self. It had dwindled to little more than its capital city—the wealthy and sophisticated Constantinople—and its environs. However, it had not always been like this. The Byzantine Empire, sometimes referred to as the Eastern Roman Empire, was the direct lineal heir of Antiquity's fabled Roman Empire. For centuries it had continued many of the Roman Empire's traditions in a cosmopolitan, prosperous, energetic atmosphere. The Byzantine Empire at its height included most of the Balkans and Asia Minor (Anatolia), and it dominated the eastern Mediterranean Sea. Constantinople, named after the famous Roman emperor Constantine, sat astride several of the world's great commercial routes. From its location on the western shore of the Bosporus (the narrow strait along with the Sea of Marmara and the Dardanelles that separates Europe from Asia), Constantinople handled trade from China and the Far East, the Middle East, Western Europe, Egypt, and Russia.

In the thousand years prior to its fall, the Byzantine Empire had experienced several periods of decline followed by recovery. One of these periodic recoveries occurred under the auspices of a ruling dynasty called the Macedonians (867–1081). However, as the Macedonian dynasty grew weak, several problems arose that in the long run proved fatal to the Empire. In the Balkans, indigenous people such as the Bulgars

The cathedral of Hagia Sophia in Constantinople (now Istanbul). After the fall of Constantinople in 1453, Hagia Sophia (Holy Wisdom) was converted into a mosque; today it is a major tourist attraction. (Reproduced from the Collections of the Library of Congress)

and the Serbs resisted Byzantine overlordship. At the same time, the Empire's economic and military base also deteriorated. By the eleventh century, large, aristocratic estates were absorbing the free Anatolian peasantry (who provided the manpower for the Empire's army and the taxes for its treasury) and turning these peasants into serfs. Furthermore, energetic Italian city-states such as Genoa and, especially, Venice began to chip away at the Byzantine Empire's commercial domination of the eastern Mediterranean. Trade concessions followed, and a weakened Empire even devalued its currency for the first time in centuries.

A religious dispute also caused difficulties with western Europe. Nominally, the Christian religion was a unitary force. However, the differences between Latin Christianity, headquartered in Rome and led by the Pope, and Orthodox Christianity, headquartered in Constantinople and led by a Patriarch who was appointed by and beholden to the Byzantine emperor, had been growing for centuries. During the eleventh century, the differences intensified and provoked a major crisis in 1054. In that year Pope Leo IX and Patriarch Michael Cerularius formally excommunicated each other, thereby fracturing Christianity. Great suspicion and ill will now characterized relations between Christians in western Europe and those in the Byzantine Empire.

It was in this already weakened condition that the Byzantine Empire suffered a near fatal blow in 1071 when the Seljuk Turks, bands of marauding barbarians from central Asia who had drifted into Asia Minor and settled there, annihilated the Byzantine army at the Battle of Manzikert. Byzantium somehow survived, but the loss at Manzikert removed the Byzantines from their Anatolian heartland and its vital supplies of food and manpower.

After Manzikert a new dynasty, the Comnenian dynasty, came to power. Relying chiefly on their wits, the new rulers oversaw a revival; but the Empire's foundations had been seriously undermined and the revival could not survive. This was evident both when Byzantine attempts to retake Asia Minor failed and when Venice, the Empire's chief rival, extracted significant commercial concessions and seized a number of islands and coastal settlements belonging to the Empire. Venetian traders also took up residence at Constantinople, where their influence was not insignificant.

The defeat at Manzikert prompted the new emperor, Alexius I Comnenus, to ask the West for help. Western leaders, but especially the papacy, had already cast their eyes toward the eastern Mediterranean, and Byzantium's call for aid only strenghtened a growing western determination to play an active role there. The result was the complex event called the Crusades; and one of its unexpected consequences was the further weakening of the Byzantine Empire.

In 1095 Pope Urban II at Claremont in France preached the First Crusade to retake the Holy Land from the Infidels. The response was overwhelming, and for more than a century western European warriors and their entourages flocked to the Holy Land. During most of this period, the Byzantine Empire and the western crusaders cooperated successfully. However, there were plenty of lingering doubts on each side about the other's sincerity and purity of motive, and Venice—propelled by its own self-interests—worked hard to undermine any chances of permanent reconciliation between East and West.

In 1204 the warriors of the Fourth Crusade, short on funds and egged on by a malevolent Venice, became involved in a power struggle over who would succeed to the Byzantine throne. Eventually they turned their destructive force not on the infidels who held Jerusalem but on Constantinople, the capital and holy city of the Orthodox Christian Byzantine Empire. The crusaders seized Constantinople, replaced Byzantine rule with Latin rule, and sacked the city. They even went so far as to seat a local prostitute in the Patriarch's chair at St. Sophia, the magnificent cathedral that symbolized Orthodox Christianity.

Latin rule in Constantinople not only proved ineffective but it also angered its subjects by forcing them to accept alien Roman Catholic forms of Christianity. Meanwhile, a new dynasty, the Palaeologus, established a rump Byzantine state at Nicaea, one of the few towns in Asia Minor that the Byzantines had been able to retain. In 1261 Michael VIII Palaeologus recaptured Constantinople from the Latins and regained control of the Byzantine Empire. Although the Palaeologus dynasty sponsored a Byzantine cultural revival of some note and employed an effective diplomacy, the Empire was a bedraggled thing. Shrunken, defenseless, bankrupt, and robbed of its commercial vitality, Byzantium limped along.

During this long period of Byzantine decline, significant changes took place in Anatolia. During the ninth and tenth centuries, large numbers of Turks had drifted into the Middle East from their home in Central Asia. By the eleventh century, they were rapidly moving into Byzantine-controlled Anatolia. The Turks were warlike tribal people who had converted to Islam, the religion of the prophet Muhammad. The most important Turkish tribe was the Seljuks, and it was the Seljuk Turks who defeated the Byzantines at the Battle of Manzikert. The Seljuk Turks could not exploit this victory to the fullest because they lacked administration and organization. Moreover, they found themselves caught up in the internecine conflicts of the various Turkish tribes. Nevertheless, they created the sultanate of Rum (a corruption of "Rome") from which they dominated Asia Minor. At the least, the Seljuk Turks possessed the potential to destroy the Byzantine Empire.

Fortunately for the Byzantines, the Seljuks themselves were destroyed in 1243 by Genghis Khan and his Mongol warriors who swept out of Central Asia and overwhelmed all before them. With Seljuk power broken, other Turkish tribes in Anatolia established petty administrative units. These included the Ottoman Turks, ultimately the most successful of the Turkish tribes, who had settled in northwestern Anatolia where they established an emirate. Led by Othman, who lived at the end of the thirteenth century and who lent his name to the tribe, the Ottoman Turks slowly expanded their power. By 1326 they had taken the important town of Bursa and made it their capital; Nicaea fell to the Ottomans a few years later.

The Byzantine emperors of the fourteenth century, playing a weak hand and torn by frequent internal disputes, dealt carefully with the Ottomans. At times Byzantine princesses were married to Ottoman sultans, and as the century wore on the emperors were more inclined to play the role of vassal to the Turkish lord. However, the Byzantines had their hands full containing the Balkan peoples, especially the Serbs and Bulgars. On several occasions the threat from the Balkans prompted the emperors to call upon the Ottomans for help, and in 1354 the Ottomans took up permanent residence in Europe when they established themselves on the Gallipoli Peninsula (the western shore of the Dardanelles). In 1365 Sultan Murad I moved the Ottoman capital from Bursa to Adrianople (Edirne), less than 150 miles west of Constantinople.

In the latter part of the fourteenth century the Ottomans conquered the Balkan peoples who had threatened Byzantium. The Ottomans crushed a Serb-led coalition in 1389 at the famous Battle of Kossovo, and a few years later they vanquished the Bulgars. Constantinople's situation appeared hopeless, but early in the fifteenth century fate intervened to give the Byzantine capital one final reprieve. As had happened before, Mongol hordes swept westward out of central Asia. The Mongols, led by Timur Lang (Tamerlane), threatened the Ottoman hold over Anatolia, and in 1402 they defeated the Turks and captured the sultan, Bayazid I, at the Battle of Ankara. After their victory, the Mongols turned their attention elsewhere; however, for several years Bayazid's sons fought among themselves for their father's mantle.

Growing ever more desperate, Byzantium frantically sought to break the Turkish grip. Cut off and surrounded by the Turks, the Byzantine emperors repeatedly appealed to the West for help and gave evidence of their willingness to concede major points in the acrimonious dispute between the two Christian camps in order to receive it. As early as the Council of Lyons (1274), Byzantine leaders pledged a religious union between Constantinople and Rome; tellingly, this concession was so unpopular with Orthodox Christians that the emperor dared not try to implement it. In any event, Byzantium received no real help from the West until the last decade of the fourteenth century when Ottoman advances galvanized the Hungarians and their western allies who feared further Ottoman encroachments into the Danube River valley more than they worried about Byzantium's survival. The result was a disaster for the West and Byzantium as the Ottomans wiped out a large Christian force in 1396 at the Battle of Nicopolis.

In 1400 Emperor Manuel II Palaeologus travelled to France and England where he pleaded in vain for support. Then, in 1439, a desperate Emperor John VIII attended the Council of Florence where he formally accepted the primacy of the papacy in religious matters and gave his blessing to a union of Latin and Orthodox Christianity in which the former would dominate the latter. Interestingly, many Orthodox clergy and laymen rejected this agreement, preferring instead to live under Muslim rule. A final western attempt to save Byzantium was mounted in 1444, at least in part due to the agreement reached at the Council of Florence. However the Hungarians, Poles, and Romanians who rallied to the pope's call for a crusade against the Turks perished at the Battle of Varna.

Surrounded and abandoned, Constantinople prepared to meet its fate. In April 1453 the Ottomans began their siege. The Byzantines were greatly outnumbered (80,000 Turks versus 7,000 Byzantines), but as in the past they relied upon their capital's stout walls for defense. However, to batter the walls the Turks employed siege guns, including a massive piece that could hurl stone balls weighing up to 1,200 pounds. The guns took their toll and the walls were breached. On the evening of May 28, 1453, Constantinople's defenders—Latin and Orthodox Christian alike— gathered in St. Sophia for Holy Communion. On the following morning they went out to meet the Turks in the final battle for the city. Virtually all the defenders, including Emperor Constantine XI, died in battle as the Turks overran the city. The victorious Ottoman sultan, Mehmet II, the Conqueror, almost immediately converted St. Sophia, the symbolic center of Orthodox Christianity, into a mosque. The Byzantine Empire had passed into history as a surging Ottoman Empire made ready for further expansion.

INTERPRETIVE ESSAY
John K. Cox

The fall of the Byzantine capital city of Constantinople in 1453 ushered in an entirely new era of history in both southeastern Europe and in the Middle East. This conquest did indeed signify the death of the Byzantine Empire, and by extension the end of the last direct descendant of the Roman Empire (the western portion of which collapsed about a thousand years earlier). It also reflects the increasing subjugation of much of the Balkans to Ottoman political control, although this rule was not as harsh as has been traditionally claimed. But the conquest also signifies the transformation of the Ottoman state—now resting partly on old Roman foundations—into a much different kind of empire and also into a major factor in European affairs. The fall of Constantinople occasioned six major changes: three more or less rapid and concrete, and three more long-term and composite in nature. The former include the end of the Byzantine Empire, the flight of Constantinople's scholarly community to the West where it gave support to the new cultural movement called the Renaissance, and the emergence in Russia of the belief that Moscow was the legatee of Constantinople's glory and mission; the latter include the symbolic beginning of Ottoman domination of southeastern Europe (a centuries-long period of rule which left a significant imprint on Balkan politics and cultures), the solidification of the position and the orientation of the Ottoman ruling family as a great power building on the foundations of other great powers before it, and a general European realization of the Turkish Empire's strength and danger.

From the European point of view, the first and most obvious change is simply that of the death of classical civilization's last remnant. The city of Byzantium, or Constantinople as it came to be called, was made co-capital of the Roman Empire by the Emperor Constantine. Thus it shared in the wealth and prestige of the city of Rome itself, which it in fact "outlived" by about 1000 years, since Rome fell to barbarian Germanic invaders in the fifth century C.E.

In fact, the Byzantine Empire fairly quickly lost most of its connection to Latin culture, except in the office of the Emperor and the official religion of Christianity; but the Empire's common language was Greek, which was an even older classical tongue than Latin. Byzantine art, architecture, and literature, while limited mostly to religious subjects and purposes, served to preserve classical—especially Roman—formulas and approaches. In terms of philosophy and scholarship, a great deal of Greek writing was also preserved in the Byzantine Empire's libraries and schools. This was especially important because Greek culture had gone out of fashion or become inaccessible in most of Western Europe, a condition that would change during the Renaissance.

The Byzantine Empire left its imprint on Eastern Europe and the Mediterranean world in terms of the architecture of its churches and monasteries (San Marco in Venice, Mount Athos in Greece), in the art of iconography and mosaics, and in the practice of writing hagiographies (stories of the lives of saints of the Christian church, often embellished or composed only from traditional sources), histories, and chronicles. But in the Balkans in particular, the Empire left other deep imprints.

One of the Byzantine legacies that survives in southeastern Europe to this day is the widespread adherence to Orthodox Christianity (as opposed to the Protestant or Roman Catholic Christianity common in Western Europe and North America). Orthodox Christianity has a number of important social and political differences from other forms of Christianity, in addition to the well-known theological differences. One such difference is that Orthodox Christians tend to take more of a collective than an individual approach to salvation, a trend that has been linked by some scholars to the rise of nationalism in the region. At any rate, the Orthodox Churches are organized on a national or ethnic basis, such that there are separate Greek, Russian, Bulgarian, Serbian, Romanian, Macedonian, and other Orthodox Churches. Also, the relationship of the patriarchs of these churches—their highest officials—with the governments of their countries has typically been much closer than the often adversarial church-state relations in the West. While most of the Orthodox churches have never been fully subjugated to the civil governments the way Peter the Great co-opted the Russian Church in the eighteenth century, the line of distinction between church and state has been blurry enough in Eastern Europe to allow critics to accuse the Orthodox churches of "caesaropapism," the supposed subordination of ecclesiastical to secular authority. In turn, some historians have this as limiting the growth of civil society in the region.

Another Byzantine legacy is simply the imperial idea. This has manifested itself in at least two different ways. For Balkan peoples such as the Serbs and Bulgarians, a massively important factor in their medieval histories was the attempt to rival Byzantium in greatness or even to eclipse it. They failed to conquer Byzantium, of course, but they did create large empires. When these peoples were re-emerging as independent states in the nineteenth and twentieth centuries, they often sought to conquer territory that had been part of these medieval empires. These "historic rights" to pieces of territory created great conflicts when they overlapped with another country's historic claims (perhaps from a different time period) or when the territories were inhabited mostly by other peoples, who can be said to have "ethnic rights" to the land in question. At any rate, the striving for imperial greatness has definitely left its mark on the region. For the modern Greek people, the impact was somewhat different, as it was specifically "their empire" that they feel was lost in 1453. The Greek national idea was known in the last several hundred years as the Megale Idea, the "Great Idea," and it called for the unification of all Greeks into one country, no matter how far-flung their lands might be. Thus the Greeks of the islands of the eastern Mediterranean, of southern Albania (northern Epirus), of eastern Thrace, of Macedonia, and of Ionia (southwestern Asia Minor) have all attempted *enosis* (unification with the motherland) at various times.

The Renaissance was an enormous artistic and intellectual movement in many parts of Europe that appeared at different times with different emphases. A skeptical attitude towards authority, praise for the potential of the individual, and an appreciation of the demands and rewards of the earthly—as opposed to heavenly—life are some of its general characteristics. Renaissance scholars and artists of the fourteenth to sixteenth centuries were eager to use the cultural legacy of Greece and Rome to broaden their horizons. In doing this, they sometimes ran afoul of the Roman Catholic Church, which was dominant in all of Central and Western Europe at the time. The Church considered much of classical civilization "pagan" because it was polytheistic instead of Christian and it endorsed a very different set of personal morals, especially with regard to sexuality. The Greek philosopher Aristotle had been partially "baptized" (approved for examination and use) by medieval Christian philosophers, but much of the rest of classical culture was still off limits.

Beyond this it is hard to generalize about the Renaissance, or at least to boil its causes down to a few simple factors. Its main figures are, of course, well known: poets like Dante and Petrarch; painters like Leonardo da Vinci, Raphael, Dürer, and Michelangelo; political writers like Machiavelli; philosophers like Pico della Mirandola and Erasmus, and architects like Brunelleschi. It might seem paradoxical that the fall of a city in Eastern Europe (Constantinople) could be linked in an important way to what was a mostly Western European cultural phenomenon, the Renaissance, yet that was the case. Why the Renaissance—or "rebirth," as the word means—began in Italy might be explained by the fact that the Italian city-states had grown extremely wealthy on trade in the Middle Ages and thus had money to spend on luxuries such as art. The growth of cities in this era of reviving trade and mercantile capitalism sparked interest in how the great cities of the past had been organized and governed. There were also many Roman and Greek ruins in Italy, and curious people noticed them and eventually asked questions about them and let themselves be inspired by them. In northern Europe the desire to combat corruption in the Church and the Europeans' discovery of the printing press made a boom in scholarship possible.

Unlike the Catholic countries of Western and Central Europe, however, the Byzantine Empire had lost neither access to nor appreciation of much of the combined Greco-Roman classical heritage. One should also note here that Arab Muslim and Jewish scholars—living in the various Arab empires which took over Rome's former Iberian and North African possessions—also preserved and spread classical knowledge. The West was re-exposed to some Greek and Roman works through contact with the Byzantine and Arab empires during the Middle Ages, but it was the political instability of the last decades of Constantinople's independent life that brought a flood of such knowledge to the West, especially to Italy. Some historians have compared the phenomenon of Constantinople's "refugee scholars" to that of the many intellectuals and artists who fled Nazi Germany in the 1930s and then greatly enriched the cultural life of the United States.

As the prospects for the survival of their country diminished, many Byzantine scholars—whose first language was Greek—fled Constantinople. Many of them, supported by the Medici princes in Florence, by other Italian leaders, and by the Popes in Rome, taught Greek to Italian students and scholars. A revival of classical learning, with its main emphasis on Latin, was already partially underway in Italy, but this flood of intellectual "refugees" added great emphasis to the reawakening enthusiasm for classical learning. Most of these Greek scholars were also fluent in the other great classical language, Latin, so they translated many Greek philosophical and literary works into that tongue for a wider readership in Italy. A final aspect of this westward flow of knowledge lay in the acquisition by Western scholars and libraries of whole collections of manuscripts, books, and documents from the Byzantine Empire. If the migrating scholars were the valuable human resource which Eastern Europe contributed to the Renaissance, then these manuscripts were an important material resource.

At the same time that the Ottoman Turks were making inroads in the Balkans, the Russian people were gradually freeing themselves from a different set of invaders, the Tatars. The Tatars (also known as the Mongols) had extended their control over most of Russia in the early thirteenth century, shortly after the death of their most famous ruler, Genghis Khan. Mongol rule was destructive in times of conflict, but was for the most part indirect; that is, the invasion little changed the lives (including the religion) of most Russians, as long as their Russian princes paid the proper tribute to the distant Mongol overlords.

One of the most important consequences of Mongol rule was found in how it ended. Before the Mongol occupation, the cities and regions in Russia had different political traditions. These ranged from strong monarchies to urban merchant oligarchies to feudal aristocratic systems. But in the late fifteenth century, the city of Moscow emerged as the leading political force among the various Russian polities fighting the Mongols, and the Muscovite rulers were strong princes who desired centralized control over the newly liberated areas.

It is against this background, then, that the news of the fall of Constantinople was received in Russia. Like the Byzantine Empire, Russia was an Eastern Orthodox country, so its rulers felt a great deal of affinity with Constantinople. In fact, Russia's ruling family (and then the Russian and Ukrainian people) had been converted to Christianity in the late 900s by missionaries from Byzantium (another name for Constantinople). In the Middle Ages, conversion to Christianity brought much more to a people than just a change of religion: it often brought cultural and economic relations, new forms of scholarship, and even literacy itself. This was certainly true in the Russian case, since even the Russian Cyrillic alphabet of today was based on Greek letters modified in the Middle Ages to fit Russian sounds.

Russian political and military rulers had always accepted Constantinople as the full and legitimate heir of the classical Roman Empire. Russia had, in turn, imbibed deeply of Byzantium's culture and religion. Now that Constantinople had fallen, just as Russia was emerging as a unified and ever stronger regional power, the Russians were eager to assume the mantle of authority that had rested with the Byzantine emperors in Constantinople. The Russians were the most numerous Orthodox Christian people, and sometimes they had even criticized the Greeks for endangering their common classical heritage by flirting too much with Catholic Europe in the search for allies against the Turks. Since Constantinople had been the "second Rome," or the Rome of the East, Moscow now portrayed itself as the "third" or "northern" Rome. Ironically, after 1453, many Greeks were favorably disposed to this, since the idea of having a powerful monarchy somewhere in Europe which would function as a protector and patron of the Orthodox faith appealed to them.

By 1500 Russian rulers were referring to themselves as "Tsars" ("Emperors") and "new Constantines" (an allusion to the Roman Emperor who made the city of Byzantium a co-capital, along with Rome). They had also married into the last royal family of fallen Constantinople. In 1511 came the first explicit reference to Moscow as Constantinople's successor. A Russian Orthodox churchman named Philotheus told Emperor Vassily: "For two Romes have fallen, but the third stands, and a fourth there will not be; for thy Christian Tsardom will not pass to any other, according to the mighty word of God." Thus a conception of messianic greatness came to be embodied in some aspects of Russia's official culture. The sense of importance and prestige attached to being a (self-perceived) imperial and cultural center with a neo-classical aura of greatness increased Russian self-confidence and made it easier for Russia to claim a leadership among Slavic peoples, including Poles, Czechs, Slovaks, Serbs, Croatians, Ukrainians, and Bulgarians.

The year 1453 marks the formal beginning of Ottoman political power in the Balkans. Of course, the Turks had already been active in Balkan political and military affairs since the 1350s, when they were first hired as allies by rival Byzantine factions involved in civil disputes. In addition, one of the most important battles in all of Ottoman and Balkan history occurred in 1389, well before the fall of Constantinople. This was the famous Battle of Kossovo, which many Serbs today believe marked the end of the medieval Serbian Empire and the confirmation of Serbia's role as "antemurale Christianitatis," the "Bulwark of Christendom," absorbing the blows of the Muslim invaders in defense of the rest of Europe. In fact, many of the supposed attributes of this battle are only myths; the point is that much of Constantinople's hinterland had already fallen to the invading Turks by 1453. In general, then, the Byzantine legacy is not the only one that has had a lasting effect on the Balkan peoples; the legacy of Ottoman rule in the region is at least as great if not greater.

The nature of Turkish rule in the Balkans remains a controversial topic. New scholarship in this area is constantly appearing, and the general picture of what life was like under the Turks has been considerably revised and updated in the past few decades. While it is true that the Christian communities of southeastern Europe suffered from discrimination, isolation, and occasional depredations under the Ottomans, the old image of the "Turkish yoke" of untrammeled and near-annihilatory oppression has been refuted.

The Ottomans respected Christianity and Judaism on theological grounds. All three are monotheistic faiths springing from the same geographic area, and Islam recognized the others' right to exist among subject peoples even while encouraging warfare against Christian governments. Knowing that a campaign of forcible conversions in the Balkans would yield fierce and unending resistance to Turkish rule, the Ottomans instituted policies that were, for the Middle Ages, very tolerant. All of the religious groups of the Empire (Muslims, Jews, and various kinds of Christians) were organized into *millets*, or communities of faith, which had important legal and financial functions. This was a kind of home rule based on religion rather than geography or ethnicity.

Forced conversion was against Muslim law, but it should be noted that significant portions of the populations of Bosnia, Albania, and Bulgaria switched over to Islam during this time. There were social and material advantages to doing so. The Ottomans also had a practice known as the *devshirme*, which is usually translated as "child levy" or "blood tax." This was the practice of sometimes taking Balkan children away from their parents and removing them to Istanbul, where they would be raised in Turkish and Muslim culture as intensely loyal and very well educated members of the Sultan's private entourage or government. Over the centuries, tens of thousands of babies were so "recruited," but it should be noted that they enjoyed a much more privileged life in Istanbul than would have been possible in the provinces, and in fact many of these "devshirme babies" grew up to be very powerful officials, sometimes even Grand Viziers of the Empire. They often used the power of their later offices to honor their original home towns. The sultans were fond of this practice because it gave them a body of soldiers and officials who were intensely loyal just to them and not beholden to any factions on the Turkish domestic scene.

There is also much historical bad feeling about the eras of warfare in which there was certainly blood shed between Muslim and Christian religious groups as well. If a city refused to surrender, Ottoman practice was to pillage it—and avenge themselves on its inhabitants—for three days. This happened in the case of Constantinople, although order was then quickly restored and Sultan Mehmet began rebuilding and improving the capital city in many ways. At various times the sultans also could not control the behavior of their irregular troops, that is, mercenaries or militias. These groups, especially late in the Empire's history, could wreak an appalling amount of havoc on minority groups. In general, though, the sultans preferred to negotiate with rebellious subjects rather than crush them in expensive military campaigns; and at least during the reign of the Empire's first ten "good sultans" (through Suleiman the Magnificent), the rule of law provided relative safety for groups within the realm.

There is no doubt that the economies and societies of southeastern Europe lagged behind Western Europe after the Ottoman invasion. However, stagnation in these lands was certainly not total, and many of the differences between the Balkans and Western Europe had already manifested themselves before Turkish control was secured. That the Balkans missed out on the age of exploration and expansion over the Atlantic Ocean, for instance, is not attributable to deleterious Turkish influence. The Ottomans also spurred some important kinds of economic growth, but indeed not enough to provide for the Balkans' rapid or thorough development.

The Turks favored certain non-Muslim groups as administrators. The Greeks enjoyed the enviable role as head of the Christian *millet* (which at first also included the Romanian, Albanian, and various Slavic Christians of the Empire). Due to their commercial experience, Greeks were also highly valued and rewarded by the Turks for their work as sailors, translators, and merchants. Eventually a group of secular Greeks known as Phanariotes rose to extremely important positions in the Ottoman government, often serving, for instance, as governors of provinces. The Turks distinguished themselves, at least initially, by their enthusiasm for what one might call "meritocracy," recognizing the contributions of talented and loyal subjects regardless of their ethnicity or religion.

A great deal has been written about how different the Balkans are from the rest of Europe. On the one hand, this region was originally Orthodox (as opposed to Catholic or Protestant); on top of that, Islam came to influence it greatly. It is easy to exaggerate the importance of these "cultural divides" and to use unjust stereotypes to label the Balkans "backwards" or "savage." Still, today the cuisine, languages, and folk customs of the Balkans very much bear the stamp of centuries of interaction with the Middle Eastern cultures of the Ottoman Empire. And the centuries of what the Greeks called *turkokratia* ("Turk-ocracy" or "Turkish domination") seem to have left Balkan peoples with a distrustful attitude towards government in general, which they tend to regard as alien and depradatory. This attitude has, in turn, hindered the growth of democratic institutions and a responsible, politically active citizenry.

In sum, the Ottomans, who had trouble enforcing highly centralized rule anywhere in their realm due to geography and cultural characteristics brought with them from Asia, knew in addition that indirect rule of the Christians in the Balkans would be more profitable and less likely to trigger revolts. In addition to the natural friction caused by one religious group ruling over another, however, the indirect Ottoman system also allowed the Christian ethnicities to cultivate a sense of separateness through their religious hierarchies. In the Balkans, this was the seedbed for the growth of nationalism, a force which would eventually help break the Empire apart.

The Ottoman Turks originally came from Central Asia. They arrived in Anatolia in the thirteenth century and settled down on the eastern frontier of the Byzantine Empire as one of the many successor states of an earlier Turkish Empire, that of the Seljuks. The strength and possessions of the Ottomans grew very quickly for a variety of reasons, but this success changed the composition of the population of their lands and also necessitated massive changes in their governmental structure.

The Ottomans proved themselves adept at blending their ideas and institutions with those of peoples they conquered. For example, they adopted many of the successful governmental practices of the Abbasid Empire of Baghdad and of the Seljuks, which helped them along the path of their evolution from nomadic, conquering people to administrators of a long-lived and highly developed empire. There was to be a constant tension in the Ottoman culture between "frontier" and "civilized" values for much of its existence. In military terms, for instance, one might call this the difference between the values of an independent warrior chieftain and those of an officer in a hierarchy below the sultan; in religious terms, it was the conflict between the values of the *ghazi*, or warrior for the faith, and those of rulers whose chief concerns were tax collection and the stability of the realm.

The conquest of Constantinople added another layer to this mixed Ottoman identity. Indeed, this aspiration of the sultans—especially, it seems, of Mehmet the Conqueror, who was steeped in the lore of Alexander the Great—to sit on the throne of the Eastern Roman emperors has come to epitomize not only Ottoman military prowess and their expansion into overwhelmingly Christian territory (the Balkans); but also the completion of the process whereby the sultans were transformed from tribal leader (*bey, beg,* or *emir*) to caesar or khan, titles that they began using as the Empire grew. In other words, with the conquest of Constantinople the Empire had "arrived." Its population was vast and diverse in ethnicity and faith; its capital was in Europe, the direction in which its future conquests lay; and its leader walked the streets of the last capital of the great Roman Empire, cloaked in the authority of classical tradition.

In the early Middle Ages, the Holy Land, North Africa, and then Spain fell under the control of the Arab (Abbasid) Empire. This greatly angered European political and military leaders, who considered the Muslim Arabs (as well as the Turks and Kurds who were part of these new Muslim political configurations in the Middle East) infidels and barbarians. The sad and bloody period of Crusader warfare against these Muslim states, from about 1095 to about 1350, is a well-known and important example of this intercommunal hatred. But the animosity continued after the Crusades, and was directed first at the Seljuk Turks as they began encroaching on Byzantine territory in the eleventh century, and then at the Ottomans, who began doing so in the fourteenth century. When Constantinople fell to Mehmet's army in 1453, attempts were made in the rest of Europe to raise new Crusades against the Turks.

There had already been two major campaigns against the Turks before 1453 as rulers, knights, and soldiers from Central and Western Europe joined with some local Balkan peoples to try to stem the tide of Ottoman advance. In the first, in 1396, Sigismund, the king of Hungary, assembled a rowdy and undisciplined force which also included Frenchmen, Germans, English, and Dutch. With the blessing and encouragement of Pope Boniface IX, they marched down the Danube River and joined with local Romanian forces. At the city of Nicopolis they were annihilated by the powerful Ottoman Sultan Bayezid, who had as his nickname "Yildirim," or "the Thunderbolt." Ironically, Bayezid's army included important numbers of European Christian vassals or mercenaries, including Serbs.

The second major crusade was an even more bizarre and complicated affair. By the 1440s, much more local resistance to the Turks had sprung up, mostly because the Turks were proving more and more successful and extending their holdings rapidly. The most famous of these local

"Turk fighters" was John Hunyadi, a Hungarian, who joined with Prince Vlad ("Dracul," also known as "the Impaler", the historical prototype for the fictitious literary character later known as "Dracula"), George Brankovic of Serbia, and Skanderbeg, the Albanian national hero. Pope Eugenius called together the forces of Hungary, Poland, France, the German states, and Venice, who were also joined by Greek units. In 1444 these forces engaged the Turks and were, once again, quickly and decisively defeated. The Sultan, Murad I, continued fighting successfully against his Balkan enemies after the West European forces departed. By this point, Constantinople itself was surrounded, the Byzantine Empire was extremely weak, and other Europeans had given up trying to help save it. The stage was set for the fall of Constantinople.

The defeat of the Byzantine Empire—utterly complete by the early 1460s—put all of Europe's powers on notice. The Ottomans had accomplished what the Arabs, the Seljuks, Mongols, and the various Balkan empires had failed to do. The Ottomans were now clearly a force to be reckoned with, and their victories continued after the fall of Constantinople. By the mid-sixteenth century, they controlled the Romanian principalities of Moldavia and Wallachia as well as almost all of Hungary, Croatia, northern Africa, Mesopotamia, Arabia, and the Holy Land. The Empire was at its peak under Suleiman the Magnificent (ruled 1520–1566). Among many other feats, he conquered the important city of Belgrade and the highly fortified island of Rhodes (the last of the medieval Crusader states set up by Western knights). Suleiman had an enormous and positive cultural and political impact on the domestic life of the Ottoman Empire, but he is most remembered in Europe for his invasion northward that resulted in the siege of Vienna in the fall of 1529. This invasion underscored the impact of Mehmet's victory of 1453. Circumstances in Europe were now favorable for the entrance of the Turks into the politics of Central Europe and into the military calculations of all of the Great Powers, as the most powerful countries of Europe were known at the time.

Europe in the early sixteenth century was in the throes of the Reformation and was being buffeted by the great rivalry between the Habsburg Empire and France. King Francis I of France invited Suleiman to become his ally. He did this in an effort to limit the growth of the Habsburg Empire under Charles V, who was faced with rebellions among Protestants and peasants in his realm and also with Hungarian separatism. Suleiman, for his part, hoped to rule Hungary indirectly by creating a vassal of the anti-Habsburg nobleman Janos Zapolya, and he also wished to rack up more victories to satisfy his troops' desire for booty (a main source of their upkeep). This combination of events led, then, to the French alliance with the Ottomans, an alliance between a Christian and a Muslim country that would have been unthinkable in the era of the Crusades. For several hundred years, the French and the Ottomans would often make common cause against their mutual enemies; later, it would be the British who would offer the Turks the most assistance, giving way to German influence in the Empire only just before World War I. After a second unsuccessful siege of Vienna and then the Treaty of Karlowitz in the late 1600s, the Ottoman Empire would slowly begin to recede. The disposition of its lands became known as "the Eastern Question," as the other Great Powers (and many small ones emerging among the non-Muslim peoples of the Empire) fought to expand at the Turks' expense. Because it was unable to carry out far-reaching financial and military reforms, the Empire became known in the 1800s as "the Sick Man of Europe." But for now, in a massive departure from tradition, the Muslim Ottoman presence among the Great Powers had been established, thanks in large part to the conquest of Constantinople in 1453.

SELECTED BIBLIOGRAPHY

Babinger, Franz. *Mehmed the Conqueror and His Time*. Princeton, NJ: Princeton University Press, 1978. Discusses the Ottoman role in reviving the old imperial city.

Brown, L. Carl, ed. *Imperial Legacy: The Ottoman Imprint on the Balkans and the Middle East*. New York: Columbia University Press, 1996. This recent collection of essays examines the meaning of the term "Balkan" and the effects of Ottoman rule on the recent wars in Yugoslavia.

Chirot, Daniel, ed. *The Origins of Backwardness in Eastern Europe: Economics and Politics from the Middle Ages until the Early Twentieth Century*. Berkeley: University of California Press, 1989. This intense study of the differences between East and West Europe raises many important issues.

Dvornik, Francis. *The Slavs in European History and Civilization*. New Brunswick, NJ: Rutgers University Press, 1962. Historical development of the Slavic peoples, especially in the Balkans, is set in a European-wide context.

Fine, John V. A. *The Early Medieval Balkans*. Ann Arbor: University of Michigan Press, 1983. This important volume traces the early history of the Byzantine Empire and evaluates Constantinople's role in the Balkans and the Near East.

——. *The Late Medieval Balkans*. Ann Arbor: The University of Michigan Press, 1987. A successful continuation of the author's earlier volume.

Geanakoplos, Deno J. *Greek Scholars in Venice: Studies in the Dissemination of Greek Learning from Byzantium to Western Europe*. Cambridge, MA: Harvard University Press, 1962. In this work the symbiotic relationship between the

Balkans and Western Europe in the era of the Reformation receives its fullest treatment.

Jelavich, Charles and Barbara, eds. *The Balkans in Transition*. Berkeley: University of California Press, 1963. This classic work studies the impact of the Ottomans on Balkan developments after the fall of Byzantium.

———. *The Establishment of the Balkan National States, 1804–1920*. Seattle: University of Washington Press, 1977. The best study of Ottoman influence during the all-important period of national revolutions in Serbia, Greece, Bulgaria, Romania, and Albania.

Kafadar, Cemal. *Between Two Worlds: The Construction of the Ottoman State*. Berkeley: University of California Press, 1995. This specialized study focuses on the initial stages of Ottoman history.

Longworth, Philip. *The Making of Eastern Europe: From Prehistory to Postcommunism*. 2nd ed. New York: St. Martin's, 1997. This general survey offers a provocative, scholarly reassessment of Balkan "backwardness" dating from the Ottoman period.

Mango, Cyril. *Byzantium: The Empire of New Rome*. London: Weidenfeld and Nicolson, 1980. Pre-Ottoman Byzantine culture receives extensive treatment in this lively volume.

Mansel, Philip. *Constantinople: City of the World's Desire*. New York: St. Martin's Press, 1996. This work features a richly illustrated historical and cultural portrait of Constantinople's long life.

Riasanovsky, Nicholas. *History of Russia*. 6th ed. New York: Oxford University Press, 2000. This classic text of Russian history presents a good survey of Russia's relationship with the city of Constantinople and its legacy.

Runciman, Steven. *Byzantine Style and Civilization*. Baltimore, MD: Harmondsworth, 1975. One of the twentieth century's greatest historians of Byzantium brilliantly explores the cultural history of the empire.

———. *The Fall of Constantinople, 1453*. Cambridge, Eng.: Cambridge University Press, 1965. A detailed account of the Ottoman capture of the fabled city.

———. *The Great Church in Captivity. A Study of the Patriarchate of Constantinople from the Eve of the Turkish Conquest to the Greek War of Independence*. Cambridge, Eng.: Cambridge University Press, 1968. Dated but still valuable, this work studies the fate of Orthodox Christianity under the Muslim Ottomans.

Sherrard, Philip. *Byzantium*. (Series: *Great Ages of Man*) New York: Time, Inc., 1966. Part of *Time's* "Great Ages of Man" series, this is a credible, well-illustrated introduction to the complex matter of the Byzantine Empire.

Stavrianos, Leften S. *The Balkans since 1453*. New York: Holt, Rinehart, 1958; reissued 2000. A venerable volume used by thousands of graduate students, this is an eminently reliable, comprehensive, and readable survey which extends well into the twentieth century.

Sugar, Peter F. *Southeastern Europe under Ottoman Rule, 1354–1804*. Seattle: University of Washington Press, 1977. A careful yet comprehensive examination of Ottoman rule in the Balkans, this volume is especially helpful in describing the Ottoman inheritance in the Balkans in light of the resurgence of ethnic nationalism in the region.

Vasiliev, A. A. *History of the Byzantine Empire, 324–1453.* 2nd ed. Madison: University of Wisconsin Press, 1952. Dated, but still one of the best general histories of the Byzantine Empire.

Vucinich, Wayne S. *The Ottoman Empire: Its Record and Legacy.* Princeton, NJ: Princeton University Press, 1965. In addition to being a very good general survey, this volume also contains a valuable selection of primary source documents.

Ware, Timothy. *The Orthodox Church.* 2nd ed. New York: Penguin, 1993. The most recent general survey of the history of the Orthodox Church.

8

The Conquest of the New World, 1492–c. 1550

INTRODUCTION

On August 3, 1492, the Genoese sailor Christopher Columbus set sail in three small ships from the Spanish port of Palos. Columbus, who sailed under the flag of Spain, headed west in the hope of finding a new route to the "Indies," or east Asia, whose spices and other products brought a high price in Europe's markets. He made landfall on October 12; but instead of reaching Asia, Columbus had found a "New World" that included the continents of North and South America. While Columbus never acknowledged this (he maintained until his death in 1506 that he had in fact discovered islands lying just off the east coast of Asia), others reached a different conclusion and soon followed him to the New World in order to gauge its potential, especially the possibility that gold and/or silver could be found in abundance.

Columbus himself made three more voyages during which he discovered additional Caribbean islands, scouted the eastern coast of Central America, and visited the coast of South America not far from the mouth of the Orinoco River. Amerigo Vespucci, a Florentine sailing for Spain, ranged even further afield. Between 1497 and 1505, he traced the coast of Central and South America almost as far south as the mouth of the La Plata River, which lies between present-day Uruguay and Argentina. The newly discovered land was named America in his honor. A few years earlier and farther to the north, John Cabot, another Italian, ex-

Hernán Cortés' forces capture Mexico City, 1521. This important event in the history of Spanish imperial expansion brought a bloody end to the Aztec Empire. (Reproduced from the Collections of the Library of Congress)

plored the coast of Newfoundland as far south as New England for his sponsor, the king of England. In 1513 the Spaniard Vasco Núñez de Balboa sighted the Pacific Ocean from a hill in present-day Panama, a discovery that first revealed that huge body of water to the European explorers. Seven years later, in 1520, at the southern tip of South America, the sailor Ferdinand Magellan crossed from the Atlantic Ocean into the Pacific on a voyage that was to circumnavigate the globe. With Magellan's voyage, any lingering doubt that Columbus had indeed discovered something new and quite far removed from the Indies vanished.

These early explorations encouraged successive waves of Europeans who tended to settle permanently. The Spanish led the way. Motivated in part by a lust for gold, in part by a desire to spread Christianity, and in part by the sheer adventure involved, the Spanish quickly settled many of the Caribbean islands, including Cuba, Hispaniola, Jamaica, and Puerto Rico. They soon moved beyond the Caribbean, establishing settlements in what are now Panama and Colombia.

The Caribbean natives offered little resistance to the encroaching Spaniards, and with little or no gold to be found in the Caribbean the Spanish turned to agriculture. They established an economic system based on the *encomienda*, or manor. The Spanish acted as lords of the land, while the native Indians were required to provide the requisite labor. The Spanish proved to be brutal taskmasters. Unaccustomed to the backbreaking work now required of them and ravaged by European diseases such as smallpox, the Indians died at an alarming rate. It is estimated that the native population of Hispaniola decreased by almost 75 percent in the 15 years immediately after Columbus first set foot on the island. The devastation of the Indians produced a severe labor shortage that ended only with the introduction of black slaves from Africa into the Caribbean. Slavery subsequently spread to South, Central, and North America.

Failure to find gold in the Caribbean did not lessen the Europeans' desire for the precious metal. Rather, their lust for gold intensified when Caribbean Indians told tales of mainland tribes who lived in large and wealthy cities where gold and silver figuratively paved the streets. One of those inflamed by these stories was Hernán Cortés, the son of a minor Spanish nobleman. Born in 1485, Cortés had attended the University of Salamanca before journeying to the New World in 1504 where, in 1519, he found himself in the service of the governor of Cuba. Rumors of a great and opulent Aztec Indian empire centered in Mexico's interior persuaded the governor to send Cortés to investigate. He gathered an expeditionary force of 600 men and several horses, and set sail for Mexico. Along the way he told his followers, "I come, not to cultivate the soil like a laborer, but to find gold." He also determined to make himself governor, independent of his nominal superior in Cuba. Upon landing in Mexico, Cortés established the town of Veracruz, which would eventually become one of Mexico's most important ports. He also burned his vessels; there would be no retreat, his forces could only go forward.

Cortés's objective was the empire of the Aztecs, a warlike people who had come down from the north to establish their capital in 1325 at Tenochtitlán. The Aztecs were conquerors. They subjugated their immediate neighbors and moved farther afield to bring even more tribes under their sway. With this expansion, the Aztecs intended to secure prisoners who would then be used for human sacrifice. The Aztecs worshiped the sun god and they believed that the god would return (the sun would rise) on a daily basis only if it was fed a steady diet of human hearts drawn from still living victims. Hence the need for a virtually unlimited supply of captives. Naturally, the vanquished tribes resented this, but they were too weak to throw off the Aztec yoke.

The Aztecs were also quite advanced in many ways. Their capital was as large and populous as any in Europe at this time. It was clean, supplied with water by a massive aqueduct, and well built with sturdy stone houses and magnificent temples. The Aztecs also had an effective legal code, and they had developed an accurate solar calendar. Their economy was robust, including not only conquered wealth but also mining, trade and commerce, and agriculture. Quite unique in themselves, the Aztec accomplishments are even more stunning when one considers that the Aztecs lacked the wheel, horses or other beasts of burden, and iron and steel.

At first glance, Cortés seemed to stand no chance against this mighty empire; but a combination of luck and superior technology, especially weapons, carried the day for the Spaniard. According to Aztec legend, an ancient god called Quetzalcóatl had left the community many years before. However, Quetzalcóatl, who was white and bearded, had promised to return someday. Although the purpose of his return was not specified, the Aztecs did not look forward to it. When word of Cortés' landing in Mexico reached Monctezuma, the Aztec ruler, he feared for the worst. Monctezuma sent a delegation to Veracruz with gifts for Quetzalcóatl/Cortés and a request that he depart. Gold was among the gifts, and this convinced Cortés to not only stay but also to move inland.

Cortés and his men trekked through the coastal jungles and over high mountain passes as they marched toward Tenochtitlán and the presumed source of the gold. Along the way, the tribes whom the Aztecs had conquered aided the Spaniards, apparently seeing in the white men either gods or, at the least, a realistic threat to the Aztecs who had terrorized them for so long. When Cortés and his men arrived at the Aztec capital, Monctezuma greeted them warmly. The warmth quickly disappeared, however, and the Spaniards imprisoned Monctezuma. In the midst of a subsequent riot, Monctezuma was killed—perhaps accidentally—and Cortés was forced to withdraw from the city.

After receiving reinforcements from Veracruz, Cortés used his horses, advanced weaponry, and support from the Indians who hated the Aztecs to retake Tenochtitlán in 1521. He virtually destroyed the Aztec city, looting it of tons of precious metals as well. As a replacement for Tenochtitlán, Cortés constructed a town nearby that was to become Mexico City. His triumph, but especially the treasure that he shipped back to Spain, earned Cortés the gratitude of the monarchy which then named him governor of New Spain, the name given to the territory that he had conquered. As governor, Cortés effectively organized the economy of New Spain; mines insured a steady flow of gold and silver, and the encomienda system was imposed on the natives.

Cortés was amongst the most famous of the conquistadors, or conquerors, who boldly and sometimes recklessly sought to subdue the New World's natives in the hopes of finding fame and fortune. His renown was equaled by that of Francisco Pizarro, who destroyed the Inca empire of South America a decade or so after Cortés's success in Mexico.

Pizarro, an astonishingly brutal man from an obscure background, was born in 1470. After a long career as an insignificant soldier of fortune, Pizarro, a lifelong illiterate, managed in 1530 to secure the consent of Spanish king Charles I (Charles V of the Holy Roman Empire) to lead an expedition into South America's Andes Mountains in search of the Inca empire that was rumored to be fabulously rich.

With approximately 180 men and a few dozen horses, Pizarro scaled the Andes and confronted the Incas in their Peruvian highland home. Like the Aztecs, the Incas had developed an advanced civilization featuring extensive irrigation and terracing for the benefit of agriculture and an exceptional road system that facilitated communications and trade and commerce. However, like the Aztecs the Incas were technologically backward compared to the Europeans and no match for Pizarro's superior firepower.

Like Cortés, Pizarro was also lucky. When he arrived in Peru, the Incas were in the midst of a power struggle to determine who would rule. Pizarro took advantage of the chaos to seize the Inca leader, Atahualpa, in a bloody skirmish that resulted in many Inca casualties but no Spanish deaths. Holding Atahualpa for ransom, Pizarro demanded that the Incas fill a large room with gold and surrender an even larger amount of silver. Despite Inca compliance with these demands, Pizarro ruthlessly strangled the Indian leader and proceeded to conquer the Inca empire. In 1541 Pizarro was murdered by one of his own men.

Other conquistadors hoped to emulate Cortés and Pizarro, but none were nearly as successful. Nevertheless, their victories gave to the Spanish crown a seemingly limitless storehouse of gold and silver, to say nothing of land and people.

INTERPRETIVE ESSAY
Clifford L. Staten

The conquest of the New World by Hernán Cortés, Francisco Pizarro, and the other conquistadors dramatically changed the development of the Americas, the world economy, and the European nations. It provided a means for centralizing power and authority in the European nations as the monarchies sought to further their control over the nobles and merchants in their own countries. The conquest played a major role in the development of an international economy. It forced the New World to become part of the Old World—forever connected and influenced by both economic and political events in Europe. In the New World the conquest wiped out much of the indigenous peoples and their political, economic, and social institutions. The New World developed its own unique characteristics that were evident in its social class structure, ethnic and racial make-up, religion, land-tenure system, political and economic institutions and processes, and culture. The legacy of the changes wrought by the conquistadors is still evident today in that area of the New World known as Latin America.

The Spanish conquest of the New World was swift, ruthless, and extremely brutal. In 1519 Cortés discovered a plot by the indigenous people of Cholula to kill his men. He retaliated by murdering nearly 3,000. He conquered the Aztecs and leveled the capital city of Tenochtitlán (present day Mexico City) within two years. Cortés's final assault on Tenochtitlán left tens of thousands dead in the city. The number of dead was so great that Cortés commented, "A man could not set his foot down unless on the corpse of an Indian." When the Inca Emperor Atahualpa refused to convert to Christianity, Francisco Pizarro immediately slaughtered 2,000 Indians. The captured emperor tried to pay off his ransom with seven tons of gold and 13 tons of silver. Pizarro took the gold and silver, and then executed the emperor. He conquered the Incas within three years.

Reliable studies indicate that between 1519 and 1523 the indigenous population of central Mexico was reduced by nearly 40 percent and by nearly 95 percent between 1519 and 1605. Data from Peru indicate a decline in the indigenous population of more than 50 percent from 1570 to 1620. Although some of this was due to the superior weaponry (armor, crossbows, metal weapons such as swords and lances, the use of the horse for cavalry, and gunpowder) of the Spanish, most of it was due to the introduction of diseases such as influenza, measles, smallpox, and typhus. In fact, smallpox was ravaging the Aztec capital when Cortés had it under siege. During the conquest, Cortés and Pizarro took advantage of the religious beliefs of the indigenous peoples. They also used divide and rule tactics by winning the support of many of the other indigenous peoples whom the Aztecs and Incas had conquered. By 1535, only 43 years after Christopher Columbus arrived in the New World, the Spanish Crown created its first viceroyalty (a representative of Spain served as the Viceroy or governor of the area) in Mexico, or New Spain as it was then called.

In many ways, the conquistadors recreated Spanish society in the Americas. Reflecting the Spanish desire to live in urban areas, many of Latin America's major cities were founded in the 1500s: Asunción, Bogotá, Buenos Aires, Havana, Lima, Mexico City, Quito, and Santiago. Cities were modeled after the Spanish; Catholicism became the dominant religion; the Church became the primary educator; and Spanish became the official language. The political processes were centralized under the monarchy and local elitist rule; titles of nobility were granted; large landed estates (haciendas) were created; and a strict, social class hierarchy was established. Yet, in other ways the New World took on its own unique characteristics.

There were two important events that occurred in 1492 that set the stage for the conquistadors. The first was Columbus' discovery of America for the Spanish Crown. In summarizing his first voyage in a letter to the Crown, Columbus spoke of the splendid opportunity to bring the heathen to God. The second event was the triumph of Spain's Christians over the Moors (Moslems). After centuries of conflict, Spain finally forced the Moors to leave Granada, their last territorial possession on the Iberian peninsula, and go back to North Africa. These events help to explain the missionary zeal of the conquistadors and their passionate desire either to kill the infidels (non-Christians) or convert them to Christianity. The conquistadors were successful in converting the conquered, indigenous peoples of the New World to Catholicism, but the Catholicism that came to be practiced reflected a strong infusion of indigenous religious traditions.

Many factors facilitated this religious syncretism. The indigenous peoples had a long history of assimilating the major components of the religion and culture of their most recent conquerors. The Catholic churches that were built may have had Spanish architects, but the craftsmen were the indigenous peoples who applied their own cultural tastes and designs to the new structures. Catholic churches were often constructed with the very stones that were used to build the indigenous religious temples. Many times they were built on or near the very sites where the religious temples of the indigenous peoples had existed. Thus, it was natural for indigenous peoples to continue to make religious pilgrimages to these sites. The Aztec religion was full of pomp and ceremony just like Catholicism, and the large number and variety of Catholic saints were consistent with the large number and variety of gods found in the indigenous religions. Similar teachings concerning punishment and reward also facilitated the blending of the religions. It is important to point out that many of the Catholic missionaries tolerated and even accepted this blending of Christianity with the religious traditions of the indigenous peoples. For example, in 1531 close to the sanctuary of the Aztec goddess Tonantzin outside Mexico City, an Indian named Juan Diego claimed to have seen an image of the Virgin of Guadalupe coming to bless and heal her suffering people. The Catholic Church officially adopted this myth in 1648 and the Virgin of Guadalupe became a symbol of salvation for the oppressed. This hybrid version of Catholicism (Christianity) played a crucial role in the societal development of the New World.

The conquest of Latin America by the conquistadors created a social class structure based primarily upon race and ethnic background with white Europeans at the top, indigenous peoples and slaves at the bottom, and mixed races in the middle. Cortés and Pizarro came to the New World not only seeking wealth but also social status. Cortés was of minor nobility, the son of a captain in the infantry. He had failed as a student at the University of Salamanca. Pizarro was the illegitimate son of a Spanish gentleman and as a child was a swineherder, a keeper of pigs. He never learned to read or write. In fact, most of the conquistadors were not from the elite social classes and under the strict social class hierarchy of the Iberian peninsula there was virtually no chance for them to become part of the Spanish elite. But those who became soldiers and conquered the New World could gain immense wealth and achieve elite social status. The conquistadors and their immediate descendants (often called creoles, those born in the New World of Spanish or European parents) would come to occupy the top tier of the social class structure and make up the "better families" of Latin America.

The indigenous peoples occupied the bottom of the social class structure and were viewed primarily as laborers. In areas where the indigenous population was small or non-existent, the Spaniards and the Portuguese imported black slaves from Africa as laborers. Spanish America imported more than 1.5 million Africans as slaves between 1518 and 1870, and Portuguese America imported more than 2.5 million by 1810. Indigenous peoples and blacks became a permanent lower class that continues to be evident in much of present-day Latin America.

During the era of Cortés and Pizarro, there were very few white, or European, women in the New World. As a result, many Spaniards took Indian women as their consorts. Cortés, for example, took a young "outgoing, meddlesome, and beautiful" Indian woman who became his interpreter, teacher, spy, and lover. The Spanish called her Doña Marina, "the navigator," while the indigenous peoples called her La Malinche, "the traitor." It is interesting to note that one of the most pejorative terms in Mexico today is *malinchista*, which refers to a person who collaborates with the enemy. The mixed-blood son of Cortés and La Malinche, Don Martin Cortés, represented the first mestizo, a mixed race of European and indigenous peoples. There is a plaque on a small church that looks out over the remains of the pre-Hispanic pyramids known as the Plaza of the Three Cultures in Mexico City that reads, "On August 13, 1521, heroically defended by Cuauhtemoc, Tlatelolco fell into the hands of Hernán Cortés. It was neither a triumph nor defeat: it was the painful birth of the mestizo nation that is Mexico today." Today, mestizos make up the largest ethnic group throughout much of Latin America.

In some areas Africans were imported as laborers because of the small number of indigenous peoples. The mixed-blood children of Europeans and slaves created the mulatto ethnic group that is the largest in much of the tropical lowlands of Brazil and the Caribbean Basin today. Similar to the mestizo culture, mulattos reflect the blending of European and African traditions. This can be seen in the fusion of Catholicism with African religions, which is most prominent in Cuba, Haiti, and Brazil.

Given that the conquistadors were soldiers who were intent upon spreading the word of God, it is no coincidence that two of the three dominant political institutions in Latin America until the beginning of the twentieth century were the military and the Catholic Church. These two institutions and the so-called oligarchy, or large landowners, were the dominant players in the emerging Latin American political system that was designed primarily for the maintenance of the established social class hierarchy.

The Europeans, creole families, and later the "better" mestizo families who could trace their roots to the Europeans were able to dominate the economy through access to land, land ownership, control of the labor force, and access to finances from Europe. As a reward for their military conquests, the Crown gave many of the conquistadors immense tracts of land. As early as 1513, it also gave instructions to many of them to take "farmers so that they may attempt to plant the soil." It is important to note that private property was a European concept. The indigenous peoples of the Americas viewed land as part of the community as a whole not to be possessed by individuals. The communal land (known as *ejido* in Mexico) of the indigenous peoples gradually became privatized, the European elite and the Catholic Church owning most of it. This represents the beginning of a process whereby land came to be concentrated in the hands of a small, elite group in Latin America. The vast disparity of land ownership and unequal access to land created tremendous economic inequality among the social classes of Latin America. Land and wealth came to be concentrated in the hands of the few, with the vast majority living in poverty. This would become a major factor underlying the political instability found in many Latin American countries. In the twentieth century land ownership, access to land, and land reform would become the rallying cry for revolutionary struggles in countries such as Cuba, Bolivia, El Salvador, Guatemala, Mexico, Nicaragua, and Peru.

Ownership of land enabled the white, European elites to control an economy that came to be dependent upon the export of wealth (gold and silver), cash crops (cacao, indigo, coffee, bananas, sugar, cotton, cattle, and wheat), and raw materials (copper, tin, and rubber) initially to Spain and later to Europe and then the United States. The elites also had access to finances largely because of their connections to the ruling elite in Europe. Finances were needed to fund and develop the export of cash crops and raw materials to Europe.

The export of wealth, cash crops, and raw materials also required access to and control over cheap labor. Through various forms of coercion, indigenous peoples and black slaves provided much of the labor. For example, under the *encomienda* system the large landowners were given trusteeship by the Spanish Crown over the indigenous peoples living on their land who were then required to work on the estate. Under this system the landowner, or *encomendero*, provided religious instruction and education for the indigenous peoples. He also provided for their protection. In return, the indigenous peoples provided labor or tribute for the landowner. Cortés received *encomiendas* throughout Mexico, including 22 villages with a population of about 22,000 and an area of about 25,000 square miles. The landowners were terribly cruel toward the laborers. Based on an account written by Bartolomé de las Casas, a Catholic monk, a rebel Indian named Hateuy stated before being put to death, "If the Christians go to heaven, I do not want to go to heaven. I do not wish ever again to meet such cruel and wicked people as Christians who kill and make slaves of the Indians." The landowners often employed the military to insure a docile and compliant labor force.

The development of patron-client relationships provided another way to control laborers. A patron-client relationship occurs between two people who are not equal in terms of wealth and power. In this relationship each person obtains what he desires or needs to survive from the other. For example, many laborers worked on the large estates. The landowner provided a house, a small plot of land to grow food, religious instruction, medical support, and burial expenses for the laborer's family. In return, the laborer worked the landowner's crop, provided votes in elections (if elections were held), and gave the landowner respect and deference to his position in society. This relationship provided security for both the landowner and the laborer. It was responsible for much of the social and political stability in rural Latin America. Similar patron-client relationships would also be developed in urban areas and become institutionalized throughout the political processes. These relationships help us to understand the stability of the social class hierarchy throughout the history of Latin America.

The Catholic Church also played a major role in preserving the social class hierarchy. In addition to its moral authority and the fact that it was the largest landowner in all of Latin America until the beginning of the twentieth century, the Catholic Church held a virtual monopoly on education. Indigenous peoples were taught to accept their status, that it was the will of God for them to occupy the bottom of the social class system. They were told that poverty would be rewarded in their next life. Any challenge to the will of God was considered blasphemy. Thus, the Church served to socialize the indigenous peoples into accepting the status quo and the established social class hierarchy.

The conquistadors and their descendents who were at the top of the social class system reflected Iberian (Spanish and Portuguese) values, culture, and political philosophies. These values legitimized monarchical, elitist, non-democratic rule. The Catholic Church also reinforced these political and social values. It followed the teachings of Saint Thomas Aquinas, who is generally recognized as the greatest philosopher that Catholicism has ever produced. The Church preached that a few individuals by the grace of God were less fallible than the vast majority of people and, thus, these individuals (white Europeans) should be in positions of authority because they could "interpret and execute God's will in a superior way." In other words, there existed a natural hierarchy among people. These values served to legitimize both the social class structure and authoritarian, elitist rule. This is significant because these values obstructed the growth of democratic values and help us to understand the absence of democracy in Latin America for much of its history. They also help to explain why much of the study of politics in Latin America tends to focus on the relationships among the most powerful groups.

One of the most enduring legacies of the conquistadors is the significance of the military in Latin America's political systems. The military, for better or worse, has always been a source of political leadership (known as the *caudillo*, or strong man) and the military has directly ruled almost every country at least once in its history. Even elected, civilian governments in Latin America cannot escape the military's influence and power in certain policy areas. Yet, the military could never rule without at least minimal cooperation of other powerful groups in Latin America. Politics in Latin America is viewed as a continual negotiating and bargaining process among powerful groups. From Cortés and Pizarro to the beginning of the twentieth century the military, the Catholic Church, and the landowners were the most powerful groups. Each group had its own power base: the military controlled the means of violence and coercion; the Church had both moral authority and economic power through its vast land holdings; and the landowners controlled the economy. Each group had its own particular goals: the military wanted the best weapons, high salaries, and attractive retirement plans; the Church wanted to maintain its monopoly on education and to save souls; and the landowners wanted protection of their property, access to cheap labor, control over labor, and low taxes. All three had the common goals of maintaining the social class structure and political stability. All three groups depended upon each other to achieve both their individual and common goals. To be successful required constant bargaining and compromising among the three groups. The make-up of these powerful groups has changed since the beginning of the twentieth century, but the essential bargaining process among them continues to define politics in Latin America today.

Latin American cultural values today can also be traced to the Spanish conquest. Two of the most important cultural values are *machismo* and its female counterpart *marianismo*. The early conquistadors were lauded for their military conquests, physical strength, and sexual prowess. *Machismo*, or manliness, is an attraction to the power, authority, strength, and sexuality of male leaders. The Spanish writer Salvador de Madariaga states that, "dictatorship is observable not only in the public man . . . at the head of state [government], but in every one of the men at the head of every village, city, region, business firm or even family." *Machismo* manifests itself not only in the political processes of Latin America but also in clear distinctions between accepted male and female behavior. Men are valued as leaders and women are valued as keepers of the household and family. Men are expected to exert authority whereas women are praised for their loyalty. It is expected that men will engage in extramarital affairs while women are supposed to ignore these indiscretions for the good of the family.

Closely related to *machismo* is *marianismo*. *Marianismo* asserts the spiritual superiority of women over men in Latin America. It is linked to the importance that the Catholic Church places on the Blessed Virgin Mary. This spiritual superiority is a source of power for women not only within the family but also occasionally in public life. Eva (Evita) Peron of Argentina used this image of spirituality as a source of political power. The tremendous popularity and adoration showered on her by the people of Argentina was an illustration of *marianismo* in public life.

The conquistadors, as noted previously, came to the New World seeking wealth—in particular, gold and silver. Cortés remarked, "The Spaniards are troubled with a disease of the heart for which gold is a specific remedy." They plundered the vast amount of gold and silver held by the indigenous peoples of the Americas. Pizarro, for example, accumulated more than eight tons of gold artifacts from the Incas during a four-month period in 1532. By 1534 it is estimated that he had accumulated 24 tons of gold. These gold artifacts included jewelry and ornately carved birds, trees, and animals. Pizarro had most of these priceless cultural pieces melted down and shipped back to Spain. Gold and silver (and later, raw materials such as tin and copper and cash crops such as tobacco, rubber, indigo, cacao, sugar, coffee, and cotton) in the New World colonies were exported back to the "mother" country. The primary purpose of this trade, especially that in gold and silver, was to increase the wealth and power of the central governments (monarchies at that time) of Spain and Portugal. It gave the monarchies the means to further their control over the local nobles, barons, merchants, and peasants. This centralization of control and power by the European monarchies during the fifteenth and sixteenth centuries is part of the process known as state building. This process is extremely significant because it helped to lay the foundation for the creation of the modern nation-state that exists today in Europe. Trade with the New World also provided the means to finance industrialization and to support the growing urbanization of Europe.

Potatoes and corn were two of the crops introduced into Europe from the New World. They are two of the four most important food crops in the world. The potato helped to change Europe by providing an abundance of food that facilitated the processes of urbanization and industrialization. Corn changed animal husbandry by supplying the food to promote its dramatic increase. There is no doubt that the introduction of these cheap and abundant food products played a major role in the rise of the modern state and the industrialization in Europe.

Trade between the New World and the Old World expanded rapidly after the New World was conquered. Trade routes were established. The exchange of wealth (gold and silver), cash crops, and raw materials in the colonies of the New World for processed and luxury goods from the home country in the Old World formed the basis for the growth of a division of labor in the expanding world economy. This division of labor is significant because it helps to explain the historic differences in the level of economic development and the amount of overall wealth found in the Old World (Europe) compared to that in the New World (Latin America). The key to understanding the greater wealth found in the Old World was the unequal exchange between it and the New World. The Old World, for example, took raw cotton and turned it into cloth or clothing. In other words, technology and educated laborers added value to the raw cotton when cloth was created. This is important because regions or countries that produce more value-added products are almost always wealthier and more developed than those that produce fewer value-added products. For most of its history, Latin America has been a primary provider of raw materials and has been less developed economically than Europe or the United States.

The conquest of the New World laid the foundation for a world economy that was controlled by the wealthier, European countries and later, the United States. At the top of the social class structure in the New World were those elite families that controlled the local economy through land ownership and access to the land. But the oligarchy in the New World had to sell its cash crops and raw materials to the Old World because there was no local market for them. In other words, the oligarchy or the elites in the New World were dependent upon Europe for markets. They were also dependent upon the Old World for finance and technology. This dependence, or vulnerability, gave the European countries a degree of control over Latin America's economic development. Elites in the New World had to follow certain trade rules established in Spain or the Old World. For example, from the time of the conquest until the last part of the eighteenth century the Spanish followed the trade doctrine of mercantilism. This meant that Spanish America could only trade with certain ports in Spain and were forced to use Spanish ships. Spanish America was limited solely to the export of the raw materials that Spain needed. The Crown protected technology. This economic doctrine served to limit both the economic and political development of Latin America. In the nineteenth century economic liberalism, or the principles of free trade, became the dominant economic doctrine, but the outcome was much the same. The world division of labor continued under a different set of European trade rules and Latin America continued to be dependent upon the markets, the finance, and the technology of the wealthy, European countries. From the time of Cortés and Pizarro through today, economic and political development in Latin America was directly influenced and in some cases controlled by events and decisions made in Europe.

The conquest of the New World by Spain and Portugal represents a pivotal point in the history of the world. A synthesis of indigenous, European, and African cultures, values, and traditions remade the New World, or Latin America. The centralization of power and authority that eventually allowed the creation of the modern nation-state remade the

Old World. The conquest and colonization provided the means for the initiation of the processes of urbanization and industrialization in the Old World. An international economy expanded rapidly as the New World and the Old World became forever linked economically and politically. But this linkage took the form of economic dependence that left the New World vulnerable to political and economic decisions made in the Old World. The outcome is that Latin America has never been completely in control of its own economic and political destiny.

SELECTED BIBLIOGRAPHY

Berler, Beatrice. *The Conquest of Mexico: A Modern Reading of William H. Prescott's History*. San Antonio, TX: Corona Publishing, 1988. This is an abridged and popularized version of Prescott's classic *The History of the Conquest of Mexico*.

Burns, E. Bradford. *Latin America: A Concise Interpretive History*, 6th ed. Englewood Cliffs, NJ: Prentice Hall, 1994. One of the most readable and insightful histories of Latin America; especially strong on the origins of Latin American society.

———, ed. *Latin America Conflict and Creation*. Englewood Cliffs, NJ: Prentice Hall, 1993. This text introduces the reader to some of the classic works on Latin American history. The discussion of the initial encounter between the indigenous peoples and the Spanish is particularly good.

Cabo, Bernabe. *History of the Inca Empire: An Account of the Indian Customs and Their Origin Together with a Treatise on Inca Legends, History and Social Institutions*. Translated by Roland Hamilton. Austin: University of Texas Press, 1983 (reprint edition). This is an excellent account of the history of the Incas.

Clendinnen, Inga. *Ambivalent Conquests: Maya and Spaniard in Yucatan, 1517–1570*. Cambridge, Eng.: Cambridge University Press, 1987. This study shows how the Mayans adjusted to Spanish rule while maintaining a sense of community.

Cortés, Hernán. *Letters from Mexico*. Edited by Anthony Pagden. New Haven, CT: Yale University Press, 1987. This is the classic text containing the letters of Cortés and edited commentary.

de Batanzos, Juan, Roland Hamilton, and Dana Buchanan, eds. *Narrative of the Incas*. Austin: University of Texas Press, 1996. This is an excellent edited account of the history of the Incas.

de Fuentes, Patricia. *The Conquistadors: First Person Accounts of the Conquest of Mexico*. Norman: University of Oklahoma Press, 1993. This collection was originally published in 1963 and contains firsthand accounts of the conquest from the participants.

Diaz del Castillo, Bernal. *The True History of the Conquest of New Spain*. 5 vols. London: The Hakluyt Society, 1908. This classic presents the eyewitness account of the conquest from a soldier's perspective.

Leon-Portilla, Miguel, ed. *The Broken Spears: The Aztec Account of the Conquest of Mexico*. Translated by Lysander Kemp. Boston, MA: Beacon Press, 1961. This presents a view of the conquest from the perspective of the indigenous peoples.

McClintock, William H. *Prescott's The Conquest of Mexico*. New York: Julian Messner, 1948. This is an abridged and popularized version of Prescott's classic *The History of the Conquest of Mexico*.

Prescott, William H. *The History of the Conquest of Mexico*. New York: Modern Library, 1998. This is the classic historical account of the conquest by which all others are compared. Originally published in 1843, it is meticulous in detail and discussion, but its length can be intimidating to the non-historian and casual reader.

———. *The History of the Conquest of Peru*. New York: Modern Library, 1998. This volume sets the standard by which others are measured. Frequently reissued since its original publication in 1847, it can sometimes overwhelm the reader.

Riding, Alan. *Distant Neighbors: A Portrait of the Mexicans*. New York: Vintage Books, 1986. This book provides the general reader with excellent insights into the complicated Mexican society, especially the blending of Spanish and Indian cultures which has created the mestizo personality and culture in Mexico.

Schwartz, Herman. *States versus Markets: History, Geography, and the Development of the International Political Economy*. New York: St. Martin's Press, 1994. This classic text on international political economy provides an excellent explanation of both the internal and external reasons for mercantilism and the conquest of the New World.

Skidmore, Thomas and Peter H. Smith. *Modern Latin America*, 4th ed. New York: Oxford University Press. This is one of the best-written, concise histories of Latin America; the overview of the Spanish conquest is particularly good.

Stern, Steve. *Peru's Indian Peoples and the Challenge of the Spanish Conquest: Huamanga to 1640*, 2nd ed. Madison: University of Wisconsin Press, 1993. This study focuses on the interaction of Peru's native population with their new Spanish rulers.

Thomas, Hugh. *Conquest: Montezuma, Cortes, and the Fall of Old Mexico*. New York: Simon and Schuster, 1993. This presents an excellent synthesis of the literature on the conquest of Mexico.

Martin Luther burning a papal bull, c. 1519. This sixteenth-century painting shows Luther during his protest campaign against various practices of the Roman Catholic Church. (Reproduced from the Collections of the Library of Congress)

9

The Protestant
Reformation, c. 1517–1648

INTRODUCTION

The Protestant Reformation, which is generally considered to have begun in 1517, came about after well over a century of growing problems within the Roman Catholic Church. As early as the fourteenth century, religious and civic leaders were calling for church reform "in head and in members," and humanists of the early Renaissance were quick to criticize corruption in the Church.

At the local level, parish priests, of peasant stock themselves, were all too often immoral, violating their oath of celibacy, and ignorant, unable to understand the Latin words they mumbled at Mass and given to reliance on fables and superstition. Clerical supervision was almost nonexistent; many higher-ranking church officials held several lucrative sinecures but seldom carried out the responsibilities of these positions. Many of the popes of the fifteenth and early sixteenth centuries set bad examples by indulging in intricate political intrigue and living like secular princes in lavish residences, often with mistresses and children.

One of the earliest efforts at reform was a Dutch-based movement called the Brethren of the Common Life, which sprung up in the middle of the fourteenth century. Its members tried to live a simple life while teaching religion in local schools and helping the sick and needy. Its spiritual sentiments were described in *The Imitation of Christ*, a popular work by Thomas à Kempis, that urged readers to model their lives after that of Christ.

Despite the evident problems in the Roman Catholic Church, the vast majority of Europeans in the fifteenth century maintained their strong belief in its teachings, continued to give it their financial support, and made arduous, often lengthy, pilgrimages to Rome. But problems persisted and in 1512, Pope Julius II convened a church-wide council of bishops to discuss possible reforms. Although the council met intermittently until 1517, little concrete action was taken, except to charge the papacy with the responsibility of cleaning up the bureaucratic corruption of church officials.

Most historians credit Martin Luther (1483–1546) with launching the Protestant Reformation. Son of a German copper miner, Luther nevertheless had a university education, studying law and earning a master's degree in 1504. When he was badly frightened by a thunderstorm, Luther gave up the notion of becoming a lawyer and instead entered an Augustinian monastery in 1505. He became a priest in 1507, and further study led to a doctorate of theology and a professorship at the University of Wittenberg.

During his years of study, Luther came to believe that salvation, the goal of every Christian, came not through fealty to the rituals of the established church but rather by means of a simple and direct faith in God. One of the most controversial rituals of Luther's time was the selling of indulgences. An indulgence was essentially a church-authorized exemption from the penalties of a sin. First granted to the Christian crusaders in the twelfth century, the practice had evolved to a point where indulgences could be purchased almost anywhere for the right price. To many, it must have seemed like a win-win situation: the purchaser of the indulgence, the sinner, received forgiveness for his sins, and the seller of the indulgence, the church, had a lucrative additional source of income.

The sale of indulgences troubled Luther, who thought it undermined the need for true faith and was corrupting those who were selling them. In 1517, he wrote a letter to his archbishop, enclosing an essay, "Ninety-Five Theses on the Power of Indulgences." In his essay, he criticized indulgences as crass and counterproductive to the development of faith based on the Gospels. Apparently Luther also posted his "Ninety-Five Theses" on the door of the church at Wittenberg Castle, although some scholars assert that this dramatic event never happened. Regardless, the essay was printed and distributed throughout the Holy Roman Empire and made Luther a well-known and controversial public figure.

After two years of often heated public discussion, Luther and a Catholic defender, John Eck, debated the question of indulgences at Leipzig. Luther went a step further and denied the total authority of the pope and the infallibility of papally-convened councils. Church officials in Rome tried to silence Luther by publicly condemning his views, burning his books, and giving him a month to recant or be excommunicated. By January 1521, when the excommunication order was to be implemented, criticism of the pope and the church in the Holy Roman Empire had risen almost to a fever pitch, and Luther was summoned to appear before Emperor Charles V to recant. He refused, and only the generous offer of protection from Duke Frederick of Saxony prevented him from being captured and probably executed.

Meanwhile, in Switzerland, Huldrych Zwingli, a humanist and follower of Desiderius Erasmus's teachings, broke from the Roman Catholic Church. Zwingli believed that true faith was found in the Bible, and that the rituals associated with the church in Rome were of no use to faithful Christians. Zwingli attacked many of the hallowed institutions of the church, including even the Mass. In 1529, he and Luther publicly debated the meaning of communion, or the Eucharist. He and Luther disagreed sharply over the issue of transubstantiation, or whether the body and blood of Christ were literally present in the bread and wine of communion, or whether they were only symbolically present. Luther and Zwingli hoped to find agreement on this issue but were unable to do so.

Beginning in 1530, German leaders tried to find ways to reconcile the diverging religious views of Catholicism and Lutheranism. The Diet of Augsburg (1530) was a conference that brought both sides together but broke up with a Catholic demand that Lutherans recant and return to the church of Rome. Charles V tried to effect some kind of compromise in the 1540s; his efforts failed and a religious war broke out in 1547. The Peace of Passau (1552) that ended this conflict guaranteed religious freedom to Lutherans. Three years later, the important Peace of Augsburg set into law the principle that the ruler of a particular territory would determine the religion to prevail there. Those dissatisfied with the choice the ruler made would be free to emigrate elsewhere.

In England, the Protestant Reformation took a much different course than it did in Germany. Ever since the late thirteenth century, there had been rivalry between the crown and the church over matters such as taxes, the judicial authority of the Roman Catholic Church, and clerical property rights. In the fourteenth and fifteenth centuries, the rise of humanism further heightened the conflict. The ideas of Luther were being circulated in England by the 1520s, and William Tyndale translated the New Testament unto English, much as Luther had translated it into German, acts that the church hierarchy deplored. Sir Thomas More, also a humanist, and Cardinal Thomas Wolsey defended the church against the rising demands for reform, and King Henry VIII personally praised Catholic sacraments in the face of Luther's criticism.

Then Henry's personal life intervened. Married for 18 years to Catherine of Aragon and still without a male heir, Henry was understandably concerned about his succession. His one daughter, Mary, would find it difficult to win acceptance in the patriarchal society of sixteenth-century England. At this time, Henry was much attracted to Anne Boleyn, a young lady-in-waiting to Catherine. Surely, thought Henry, Anne could and would produce a male heir. But the Roman Catholic Church did not condone divorce, even for kings, and would not consent to the annulment of an 18-year marriage. After Henry fired Cardinal Wolsey in 1529 for failing to secure an annulment, his new, more secular advisers suggested that since the king ruled England in temporal affairs, why should he not also rule England in spiritual affairs? If that were the case, then Henry could annul his own marriage or grant himself a divorce.

Between 1529 and 1536, a compliant Parliament passed the legislation that effectively placed the church under the monarch's control. Henry succeeded in terminating his marriage to Catherine and wed Anne Boleyn. Parliament also cut off payments from English clergy to Rome and granted the king authority to make religious appointments. Anne Boleyn's offspring were declared to be legitimate heirs of Henry, who was formally anointed as the "only supreme head" of the church in England. These last two acts were too much for Thomas More, who paid with his life for his strenuous objection. Despite his radical break with Rome, Henry remained the conservative head of a conservative church, enforcing rules of clerical celibacy and reaffirming the traditional sacraments of the church, such as the Eucharist. Only after Henry's death in 1547 were more radical Protestant reforms implemented in England.

In France, Protestantism had a considerably tougher time surviving. Luther's ideas filtered into France during the 1520s and met fierce resistance from the church establishment in Paris. In 1525, the Holy Roman Emperor, Charles V, a dedicated foe of the Reformation, captured the French king, Francis I, in battle. In order to curry favor with Charles V and win their king's freedom, the French government cracked down on the small but growing Protestant movement. A decade later, Protestant activism brought on another period of stern repression that forced many Protestant leaders into exile.

In 1559, France was thrown into turmoil by the untimely death of King Henry II and the succession of his teenage sons, Francis II, who lived only a short while, and Charles IX. Three families, wealthy and influential, vied to win the favor of the new young kings; of these, the Guise family, which controlled eastern France, prevailed. Very staunchly Catholic, the Guises pushed Francis and his court into supporting repressive, conservative Catholic policies that put the French Protestants, known as Huguenots, on the defensive. In this, they were aided by the two families that had lost out in the struggle for royal influence.

The consequence of this was a series of conflicts known as the French Wars of Religion that began in 1562 and lasted for more than 30 years. These wars featured some horrific brutality, notably the St. Bartholomew's Day massacre on August 24, 1572, when, in coordinated raids across France, Catholic partisans killed some 20,000 Protestants. Finally, the Edict of Nantes ended the prolonged conflict on April 13, 1598. Although France remained officially a Catholic country, the edict guaranteed religious freedom to Huguenots and other religious minorities, including the freedom to worship publicly, to be admitted to universities, and to build and maintain fortified towns. While the Edict of Nantes ended the bloodshed, it did not create religious harmony and toleration. Less than 100 years later, Louis XIV revoked the edict, forcing the emigration of many Huguenots to other parts of Europe, where they eagerly allied themselves with Louis' enemies Those who stayed in France were driven underground and became a formidable resistance force against the king and his church.

The travails of the Reformation in France should not lead us to overlook the work of the great French Protestant, John Calvin (1509–1564), the founder of Calvinism. Well-born and well-educated in France, Calvin became linked with the humanist movement and converted to Protestantism in 1534. Forced to leave France to escape persecution, Calvin went to Geneva, in Switzerland, where he formulated the structure and catechism of his new church, and then to Strasbourg, where he wrote *Institutes of the Christian Religion*, a tract that many cite as the basic statement of Protestant faith. Returning to Geneva in 1540, he became involved in relating his form of Protestantism to society. He believed that a good Protestant practiced his religion in his secular life as well as in church; his church, moreover, had a great deal of authority to punish those who broke the strict moral code Calvinism forced upon its adherents. Under Calvin's leadership, Geneva became a center for Protestant exiles and refugees.

One of the responses Catholic leadership made to the growing popularity of Protestantism was to undertake reforms within the church. Some of this reform was seen in the formation of new religious orders, such as the Society of Jesus, created in the 1530s by a remarkable cleric, Ignatius of Loyola. The Jesuits, as the followers were called, lived highly disciplined lives but were not afraid to flout church authority and experiment with religious innovations. Ignatius wrote *Spiritual Exercises*, a devotional book designed to help Catholics maintain (or regain) their self-discipline and spirituality.

The central Catholic hierarchy, also concerned with the rise of Protestantism, organized the Council of Trent to bring about internal reform. The Council, which met in three sessions between 1542 and 1563, did institute some reforms in church management and discipline but did not make any changes in doctrinal authority. Local bishops were told to live in their own diocese and were authorized to exert more control over the performance, appearance, and behavior of local priests. To further these ends, the Council directed that seminaries be built in every diocese.

INTERPRETIVE ESSAY
Ineke Justitz

In the second half of the sixteenth century, a woodcut appeared in Germany that depicted Luther being butchered by Zwingli, Calvin, and other Protestant reformers. In the background, a table is set, and big kettles over a fire suggest a plentiful meal. The print warned: "See how this wretched Lutherdom is martyred, quartered, butchered, ground-up, cut up, boiled, fried, and finally completely devoured by its own champions." The woodcut was part of a Catholic propaganda effort to counter the Reformation that had split western Christianity into Roman Catholic and Protestant churches. From the Catholic perspective, the image accurately represented the divisive nature of the Reformation that, in the end, pitted not only Protestants against Catholics but also Protestants against Protestants. Yet, this shocking image inadvertently conveyed an important truth about the Reformation: When reformers such as Luther,

Zwingli, Calvin, and others successfully questioned the authority of the pope and the legitimacy of the Catholic Church—the most powerful man and the most powerful institution in the western world—then any and all authority could be questioned. Martin Luther (1483–1546) discovered this truth in his lifetime along with other reformers who offered different interpretations of Scriptures and found followers. The rulers of early modern Europe (1450–1650) discovered this truth from their rebellious subjects who no longer accepted the idea that the rule of monarchs was God-given and therefore unassailable. By the end of the sixteenth century, both church and state tried to control these independent tendencies by assuming a greater role in the lives of their subjects.

The woodcut illustrates the great significance of the Reformation for the history of Christianity and for everyone touched by the Christian faith in one way or another. The sixteenth-century Reformation gave those who were dissatisfied with the spiritual experience offered by the Catholic Church a new and profoundly satisfying understanding of the Christian faith. At the same time, the Reformation caused the Catholic Church to bring about meaningful reforms in clerical education and administration and to reaffirm its core teachings. However, the impact of the Reformation goes beyond the history of the Christian Church. The Reformation raised complex issues—theological, political, economic, social, and cultural in nature—that touched all sixteenth-century Europeans in important ways. This essay will examine these issues mainly from a German perspective.

At this point it is important to note that early modern Christians were concerned about the salvation of their souls, about eternal life once their existence on earth had ended. However, the Catholic Church, in its pursuit of power and wealth, paid too little attention to their spiritual needs. Corruption was rampant. Important church offices could be bought at a price. The parish clergy were frequently uneducated. While the Church had a long tradition of reforming its institutional behavior, time and again vested interests prevented a thorough clean up. The Church also had a long tradition of opposing challenges to its core teachings or doctrine. For example, in fourteenth-century England, John Wycliffe (ca. 1330–1384) called for doctrinal and ritual reforms quite similar to those demanded by Luther nearly 200 years later. The Church condemned many of his doctrines, and Wycliffe was forced to retire from his position at Oxford University. In the early fifteenth century, Wycliffe's writings influenced the work of the Czech John Huss (1372–1415) whose doctrinal, ceremonial, and economic reforms threatened to undermine the power of the traditional church hierarchy. In 1415, Huss was executed for his heretical beliefs.

A century after Huss's death, reform could not be stopped because, as the historian Euan Cameron has pointed out, two challenges came together striking at the core teachings of the Church and undermining its very foundation. The Catholic Church taught that it possessed a huge repository of grace that it controlled through the sacraments, important rituals believed to have been instituted by Jesus Christ. They were Baptism, Confirmation, Communion, Marriage, Penance, Extreme Unction (last rites), and Holy Orders (ordination). Through the sacraments, administered by the priesthood, the repentant sinner received God's grace and was ultimately saved from eternal death. Martin Luther and other reformers challenged these teachings and insisted, instead, that grace flowed freely from God to the believer. He urged Christians to have faith as they accepted His gift of grace. This message denied the Church its most important role because salvation no longer depended on the institutional Church. If that were true, then Christians did not have to tolerate the Church's institutional shortcomings either.

Within the Reformation message were the seeds of dissent and rebellion. At the core of Luther's theological insights were three convictions: First, God's grace came as a free, unconditional gift. In accepting this gift, Christians were justified (made righteous) by faith alone. They were free—no longer enslaved to sin. Second, the Bible informed the Christian life; as the Word of God, Scriptures were the sole foundation of the Church. Everyone could discuss and understand Scriptures; their explication was no longer the exclusive domain of theologians. The role of the church was to lead the believers to God through His Word. Finally, every Christian had a direct relationship with God, and every Christian was like a priest—an idea commonly called "the priesthood of all believers." The clergy did not stand in a special relationship to God. Together, these beliefs suggested that Christians were free to explore the Bible, to disagree over different interpretations, and to congregate with like-minded believers.

From the 1520s on, lively debates over the meaning of Scriptures fueled an atmosphere of tension and excitement in which many clerics and laypersons rejected the "old" faith for what they called the "true teachings." In Switzerland, the priest and reformer Huldrych Zwingli (1484–1531), who disagreed with Luther on the meaning of the sacraments, died in a war against Catholic districts over the spread of the Reformation. In Germany in the 1530s, the Anabaptists—rejecting infant baptism—interpreted the Scriptures to mean that only adult baptism brought people into a true covenant with Christ. They lived in communities separate from the secular world and found themselves persecuted by Catholics and Lutherans alike. In the 1540s, the French lawyer, theologian, and reformer John Calvin (1509–1564) organized in Geneva, Switzerland, a theocratic municipal government to supervise God's chosen people. His concept of predestination—an all-powerful, all-knowing God elected some to eternal life and others to eternal death—became a central tenet of the Reformed Faith. From the 1560s until the end of the sixteenth century, Calvin's followers in France, called Huguenots, clashed with the country's Catholic monarchy in a series of bitter civil wars driven on both sides by religious fervor and political ambitions. Between 1566 and 1588, the Calvinist Dutch revolted against their Catholic Spanish overlords and established a republic in the Netherlands. In their particular political contexts, these Protestants found in the ideas and the language of the Reformation the will to rebel against monarchs who refused to tolerate their religious convictions and who rejected their political aspirations.

By the end of the sixteenth century, the Reformation had not only shattered the unity of western Christianity, but it also threatened the political power of many rulers for whom the idea of Christian freedom meant anarchy. This became clear as early as 1525–1526 when German peasants, together with urban artisans, revolted against their noble lords. Under the banner of Christian liberty, the peasants rejected their servile status and demanded the return of their traditional rights that their lords had stripped away. By 1526, the German nobility had restored order in their lands. In the process, they killed between 60,000 and 100,000 peasants. Luther and many other reformers sided with the nobility. For the ruling elites, the reform movement had turned into a double-edged sword. They might use the Reformation to curtail the power of the Catholic Church in their own lands, but they were loath to accept the Gospels' message of social justice which empowered their rebellious subjects. Therefore, they began to supervise and direct the reform movement into channels that did not threaten their position and power. In large part, the Reformation owed its survival to the close cooperation that developed between the reformers and the rulers who had rejected the "old" faith.

European rulers had long resented the power of the Catholic Church over their subjects. French, German, and English kings alike rejected the pope's claim of being God's vicar on earth who commanded prince and pauper alike. They demanded that the church not intervene in their national affairs, but time and again the popes in Rome—using threats of excommunication—insisted that they exercised a sacred power greater than any king could possibly wield. With the Reformation came the opportunity for monarchs to ignore a weakened papacy and to assert their undisputed sovereignty. From the sixteenth century on, they would control the church in their own lands. The case of the English King Henry VIII is perhaps best known. In 1527 he asked the pope to annul his marriage to the Spanish princess Catherine of Aragon. In terms of international diplomacy, she was no longer relevant. Moreover, Henry wanted to marry Anne Boleyn who might bear him the son Catherine never produced. As a devout Catholic, Catherine opposed Henry's wishes, and so did the pope. In response, Henry more or less granted himself a divorce by proclaiming a reformation of the church with himself as its head.

While Henry directly asserted his control over the Church of England early on, German princes first had to gain political autonomy before they could command a territorial church. Medieval Germany was fragmented into a multitude of small territories (principalities, duchies, counties, as well as imperial cities) which all belonged to the Holy Roman Empire. The rulers of these territories (the German princes) were often devout Christians, and many welcomed the Reformation; however, they also seized every opportunity to assert their independence from the Holy Roman Emperor to whom they owed their land and their allegiance. In the first half of the sixteenth century, these princes succeeded in their drive toward independence when external enemies weakened the empire at the same time that the turmoil of the Reformation rocked it internally. The combination of these forces played into the hands of these pious, yet pragmatic princes because Emperor Charles V (r. 1519–1556) could not effectively fight and control these diverse forces that worked to defeat him and his ideas.

Charles V ruled much of continental Europe as well as Spain's vast colonial empire in the western hemisphere. The most powerful man on earth next to the pope, Charles was also an unwavering Catholic who believed that the unity of universal rule preserved both his Holy Roman Empire and the Catholic Church. "One God, one Faith, one King" had long been the guiding principle of imperial rule. This principle broke down in the sixteenth century under the weight of an alliance of Protestant German princes in a hostile international political environment. In the 1520s and 1530s, the Emperor fought his external enemies first: the

Ottoman Turks who threatened Vienna on the eastern end of his empire, and the French who not only engaged his troops in northern Italy but also supported the Protestant German princes in their struggle against the Emperor. Only in the 1540s did Charles forcefully respond to the challenges posed by these princes who enjoyed broad popular support by a public who equated the Emperor with the hated Church of Rome. After an initial imperial victory, a reconfigured alliance of German princes in 1552 drove a humiliated Charles out of Germany. With the religious Peace of Augsburg in 1555, the German princes were now sovereign rulers who determined whether their subjects would be Lutheran or Catholic. They had secured the survival of the Reformation in Germany.

Charles V divided the Holy Roman Empire between his brother and his son and resigned in 1556, profoundly saddened by the fact that he had not been able to keep church, faith, and empire together. The confluence of political ambitions and religious convictions in the sixteenth century helped bring about the demise of the most powerful empire in the world, although it continued to exist in a diminished form until Napoleon put an end to it in 1806. It also guaranteed Germany's fragmentation, because the princes zealously guarded their independence until the second half of the nineteenth century when Prussia unified Germany under its leadership.

After the religious settlement of 1555, the reform movement continued, but its focus changed. While the rulers consolidated their power and established their early modern states, territorial churches emerged which allied themselves with these states. A territorial church identified itself with the country (the territory) in which it was founded and organized. It looked to its own territorial ruler for guidance and support. In this context, it is important to mention that sixteenth-century Europeans were unfamiliar with such principles as the separation of church and state, freedom of religion, and popular sovereignty. To them the political community (be it a village or a city, a county, duchy or a principality) was at the same time the religious community. The two were inseparable. Salvation was still a communal affair. This meant, for instance, that the salvation of an entire community was threatened if some of its members did not behave as good Christians should—hence, accusations of adultery or witchcraft were taken very seriously. Thus, it should come as no surprise that many rulers felt responsible for the spiritual well-being of their communities and actively intervened in matters of faith whenever they believed it necessary. Precisely because of their piety and devotion, they used their territorial churches as an instrument of social control. Of course, it is difficult to determine where their religious convictions ended and their political ambitions began.

Between 1560 and 1650, the territorial churches formulated their doctrinal positions and established their church organizations. In this process called "confessionalization," the churches acquired their own particular identity through a distinct confession of faith, worship, and church discipline. Moreover, as Renaissance church historian Heinz Schilling has noted, each of the three great church communities, Lutheran, Reformed, and Catholic, made separate alliances with the political entities of the day, increasing their ability to exert ecclesiastical control. The members of these churches had distinct expectations about the meaning of their confession, and they experienced this confession as exclusively theirs— quite apart from the others. Successful confessionalization meant that people identified themselves as Lutheran, Reformed, or Catholic, and that they believed, thought, and behaved according to the norms of their particular confession.

An example from a 1565 church visitation of several rural parishes in Lutheran Saxony (Germany) shows how difficult it was to instill the beliefs and values of the Reformation into the average peasant. A church visitation was an inspection of the parish and its pastor. In this case, five to ten officials traveled to the parishes. Church overseers (superintendents) were accompanied by scribes who compiled extensive reports that were delivered to the prince or ruler for further action. Traveling with them were the state's law enforcement officials. The inspectors examined the pastor's knowledge of Scriptures and church teachings; they questioned the parishioners on their understanding of the correct teachings; and they reviewed the parish's financial records.

The inspectors were quite dissatisfied with the perceived lack of commitment to the Lutheran teachings. Visiting over 40 parishes, they found that 45 percent of the pastors failed to provide good pastoral care. They fired six pastors who refused to renounce their allegiance to the pope. (Thirty years later, the inspectors would have the pastors swear an oath of loyalty on their confession of faith.) They retired eight pastors. They were dissatisfied with an additional five pastors but kept them on because of a severe shortage of pastors. The pastors, on the other hand, complained about their parishioners for refusing to tithe, to pay fees and the inheritance tax, to maintain the church and the parsonage. Several men in one parish refused to celebrate the Eucharist. Apart from the deplorable pastoral care, the financial status of the parishes proved utterly inadequate to support the pastor and his family. The inspectors sensed the urgent need to organize, to teach, to discipline. Confessionalization became all the more urgent.

However, the inspection of the rural parishes of Saxony suggested that confessionalization would be a slow and arduous process requiring the close cooperation of church and state. These villagers could not be turned overnight into good Christians and good subjects. After all, life returned to normal once the inspectors left, and no one could compel a person to participate in the Eucharist or to learn by heart the Lord's Prayer, the Ten Commandments or Luther's Small Catechism. The ruler might not order a subsequent visitation for another five years. However, when these educated elites arrived in the parish communities, it was abundantly clear to the 250 or so inhabitants that the church could rely on the "coercive power" of the state to enforce its teachings and its discipline. The clergy also knew that they had to meet the expectations of both the church officials and the secular authorities. At the same time, the community was well aware of the fact that the state, in the person of the prince and his representatives, controlled desirable resources, appointments, and, last but not least, the limited use of force. And so people's pragmatism often dictated their cooperation.

The Reformation brought about important social changes, such as a new understanding of marriage and the family, education, and welfare programs. Through these institutions, the state and the church assumed a greater role in people's lives in an effort to shape them into good Christians and good subjects.

For the Catholic Church, marriage was a sacred union that could not be dissolved. However, when Luther and other reformers insisted that the sacrament of marriage did not confer grace, marriage became a civic affair opening the door to the possibility of divorce. However, few marriages were dissolved. For one, marriage courts urged reconciliation and only granted divorce under special circumstances such as long-term abandonment or adultery. For another, the family became the cornerstone of Protestant society that meant that social pressures against divorce remained high. The church and civil authorities began to supervise and legislate morality; they closed brothels, instituted dress codes, and regulated wedding celebrations. They punished men and women for adultery and abortions. It has been argued that the Reformation's focus on the family raised the status of women by celebrating their roles as Christian wives and mothers. While many pamphlets prominently illustrated women in these roles, their actual lives changed little in this harsh sixteenth-century world. Women lived in an increasingly patriarchal society and were expected to fully submit to their husbands.

The Reformation's celebration of marriage contrasted sharply with the Roman Catholic Church's insistence that the celibate life was the superior life. Reflecting on his own sinful nature, Luther concluded that very few men and women were called to lead such chaste and pure lives. Marriage, not celibacy, was the ideal Christian state. He urged nuns and priests to leave their monasteries and to marry. In Protestant lands, marriage became the only respectable option for women who lost the alternative of a religious vocation. While many nuns followed the example of Katharine von Bora, Luther's wife and a former nun, a large number of nuns staunchly defended the monastic ideal and refused to leave their convents. Monastic life disappeared by the late sixteenth century when Protestant authorities did not allow new entrants and the old monks and nuns died off.

Having rejected the special status of the clergy, the Reformation insisted that the Protestant pastors were members of the community who married, paid taxes, and were judged in the same courts as everyone else. In reality, by the end of the sixteenth century, they developed into a distinct clerical class who served both the confessional church and the territorial state. After the peasant revolts of the 1520s, the Reformation began to back away from the idea that everyone could understand God's Word as revealed in Scriptures. The revolts demonstrated the need for properly trained pastors whose sermons would deliver a uniform message and facilitate the right understanding of the Word. However, a severe shortage of pastors meant that laypersons continued to provide pastoral care. In response, the universities expanded their curricula and attracted more young men who felt called to the pastorate. By the end of the sixteenth century, the confessional church could insist on a university degree, which by then some 80 to 90 percent of the Lutheran pastors possessed. As a group, they were set apart from the rest of the community by their education, their calling, and their preference for marriages within the faith. These pastors married within their own group; their wives were the daughters of other clergymen. Their sons became clergymen who again married other pastors' daughters. The result was a distinct clerical class that would serve the confessionalizing church and the state. These pastors formed a web of communication between the state's bureaucratic center and the periphery, where they announced the state's decrees to village communities and urban neighborhoods. The web functioned in both directions, for the clergy also relayed from "below" to "above" information that proved indispensable to accurate and effective management by early modern civil administrations.

In Protestant states, the Word of God—properly taught—remained the foundation of a society in which education became increasingly important. People needed to be able to read the Bible, translated by Luther into a very accessible German, but few people were literate. With the Reformation began a push to establish schools in every town and village where boys and girls learned to read and to do basic arithmetic. They also memorized Psalms, prayers, hymns, and Luther's Small Catechism. Bright boys in the cities might learn the intricacies of Latin, Greek, and mathematics and attend the new universities for the higher education needed to enter church or government service. Literacy rates, estimated at only 5 percent, slowly increased in the sixteenth century; however, the goal of producing good Christians through education remained elusive. In particular in rural areas, where the best pastors refused to go and where education remained irregular at best, people resisted the "new teachings" and instead preferred the familiar comfort of their traditional beliefs and practices.

Welfare reform became necessary when the Reformation rejected the sacrament of penance as a means to salvation. Civic institutions emerged to aid the poor, the disabled, and the orphans. The Catholic Church had traditionally provided poor relief. It tied charitable giving to the sacrament of penance by requiring that the repentant sinner perform acts of charity to complete the sacrament. In this belief system, the poor provided the wealthy with the opportunity to do good works. They shared in a cycle of charity benefiting both in their quest for salvation. After all, God blessed the poor for their poverty and the wealthy for their charity. Over the course of the sixteenth century, charitable giving tended to decline where the Reformation took hold, since people no longer needed to support the perceived extravagance of the Catholic Church. In addition, when the Reformation rejected the sacrament of penance as a vehicle of grace, people understood that works of charity did not merit God's grace. Given the sixteenth-century economic crises, they responded to the new message with their wallets closed. Beginning in the 1520s, the community took care of its poor with municipal welfare programs replacing the charity of the Catholic Church. Local authorities supervised and distributed alms from so called "community chests" which depended on regular contributions from the city's inhabitants and on occasional donations from the rulers. However, when poor relief became a legitimate function of government, the opportunity for social control increased accordingly.

The discussion of poor relief indicates that the Reformation had economic implications. However, they are difficult to measure because the responses to the Reformation and to economic conditions differed over time and from place to place. In addition, the relationships between religious ideas and economic data are not obvious. Many Protestants—reformers, rulers, ordinary citizens, peasants—anticipated that society would benefit financially from the breakdown of the Catholic Church. They believed that confiscated church lands would generate wealth and prosperity for all. However, they discovered that the maintenance of religion in a society that assumed additional responsibilities (such as education and poor relief) required great financial outlays. The income from real estate once owned by the Catholic Church rarely proved enough to satisfy these needs. Yet, the churches and the states met these growing needs, in the process strengthening the bonds between them.

In Germany the Reformation appealed to many people because they earnestly believed in the spiritual superiority of Luther's teachings. At the same time, they greatly resented the financial burdens imposed by the Catholic Church that appeared to tax nearly every aspect of their lives. It also angered the Germans that a share of their money was sent to far away Rome, where it was often squandered on frivolous pursuits by a corrupt papal bureaucracy. In principle, people did not mind paying the clergy for their services as long as these merited salvation and were properly performed. However, the clergy frequently failed to do so—as noted earlier, the parish priest was frequently uneducated and corruption was rampant. Attempts at reform seemed to go nowhere. In addition, these were hard times. Poverty increased as prices rose and wages remained stagnant for much of the sixteenth century.

How did the Catholic Church secure the resources to do God's work, i.e., to maintain the Church and the clergy, educate the youth, minister to the faithful, feed the hungry, and aid the sick? The Catholic Church generated income from its ownership of large tracts of land. Kings made grants of land and pious Christians bequeathed their estates to the Church. In exchange for rent, peasants farmed this land. In addition, they tithed a percentage of their crops to the church. Everyone paid fees to the clergy for officiating at weddings, baptisms, and last rites. Additional fees were due on major holidays, such as Christmas and Easter, usually in the form of bread, eggs, chickens, a rooster, or a few pennies. At least once a year, every Christian confessed his or her sins and made a payment of money to complete the sacrament of penance. Another source of income came from foundations established by wealthy parishioners who wanted the clergy to say prayers or mass—often in perpetuity—for themselves or for deceased ancestors.

Financial relief appeared in sight when the Reformation sanctioned the confiscation (or secularization) of church lands by Protestant princes. Secularization refers to the process of placing church and monastic property under the control of secular authorities and institutions. For instance, the new community chest might receive the income of plots of arable land. Given the impression that the Church possessed fabulous wealth, most rulers expected a financial windfall but found that the income barely sufficed to pay the pastors, fund education, and provide poor relief—tasks previously assumed by the Catholic Church. The new churches faced an additional problem when some people stopped tithing altogether and asserted that their salvation no longer depended on their financial contributions. One seventeenth-century Lutheran pastor sadly observed that "people expect God to feed us, but we are no angels."

While the economic impact of the Reformation cannot be fully assessed, an interesting debate emerged early in the twentieth century on the relationship between Protestantism and the transition to capitalism in early modern Europe (1450–1650). One of the most influential and controversial theories was posited by the German sociologist Max Weber, whose *Protestant Ethic and the Spirit of Capitalism* appeared in 1930 in its first English translation. Weber argued that Protestantism—in particular the Calvinism of the Puritans—had led to the emergence of modern capitalism. He claimed that the Puritan value system had produced a new mind-set which favored experimentation, innovation, and confidence. This new mind-set allowed modern capitalism to emerge, a new economic system which commanded great resources, employed wage labor, and produced profits which it reinvested to generate more wealth, all in a rational, systematic manner.

Weber did not deny the capitalistic organization of early modern business and industry, but he claimed that traditional entrepreneurs lacked the true spirit, the drive, to develop modern capitalism. Traditional business produced in a leisurely manner; it was rational only in so far as it supported the traditional manner of life, the traditional rate of profit, the traditional amount of work, the traditional manner of regulating the relationships with labor, and the essentially traditional circle of customers and the manner of attracting new ones. According to Weber, this traditional "idyllic" society did not rationally produce wealth. In this traditional world, Weber suggested, many social, cultural, and economic barriers prevented the traditional mind-set from conceiving a new approach to the rational organization of capital, labor, and resources. What then brought about the change?

Weber linked the capitalist spirit to the reformed faith of John Calvin, the French reformer whose ideas spread from Geneva, Switzerland, to the Netherlands, Scotland, and England, and to North America with the Puritans. As noted earlier, Calvin taught that God had predestined some men and women to everlasting life and others to everlasting death. Over time the concept of predestination became central to Calvinist doctrine. Calvin also believed that human beings—sinful in their very nature— could do nothing to deserve God's grace, nothing to merit salvation. All that mattered was to place one's trust in God's Word and to have faith and confidence in God's grace. For Calvin, this trust brought peace and serenity.

In his examination of seventeenth- and eighteenth-century Puritans, Weber argued that the concept of predestination brought not peace but anxiety and fear. The believer had a profound psychological need to know that she or he was not among the damned. But how could one know? Here the concept of a calling, or vocation, came into play. All human beings had a calling in life, be they homemakers, ministers, carpenters, or magistrates. Calvin believed that every calling was equally pleasing to God as long as it was performed with excellence. Weber argued that many Calvinists came to believe that success in one's calling might demonstrate one's faith and signal God's grace. Demonstrated success might mean that one was among God's chosen. Hard work and a frugal lifestyle made this success possible. Weber claimed that this drive to succeed generated the wealth to be reinvested. This Puritan ethic was the spirit of capitalism that made modern capitalism a reality.

Weber's theory is problematic because its causal connections cannot be proven and compelling counter-arguments can be made. In addition, historians tend to reject single theories to explain complex social developments, in this case Weber's argument that a religious explanation is central to the development of modern capitalism. Multiple currents and many ideas at different times and places tend to come together in new ways of thinking and new ways of doing business. In sixteenth-century England, the entrepreneurial spirit was evident not only among the Puritans but also among the members of the Church of England. In Scotland, profoundly influenced by Calvin's reformed faith, there were few capitalists. Many capitalists in Calvinist Holland did not believe in predestination. Catholic capitalists made Antwerp in present-day Belgium a highly successful commercial city. Thus, the causal link between the development of capitalism and the religious beliefs and values of seventeenth- and eighteenth-century Puritans is hard to establish. Furthermore, Weber rejects the relevance of late medieval and Renaissance capitalist developments in Italy, Germany, and the Netherlands to the development of modern capitalism. In fact, Karl Marx (1818–1883), a German political philosopher, had earlier argued that hard work, frugality, self-reliance, and rationalism were precisely the qualities of an emerging bourgeois class who expressed their value system in sixteenth-century Protestant terms. For Marx, these bourgeois values explained not capitalism but the success of Protestantism.

In fact, nothing was inevitable about the sixteenth-century Reformation except perhaps the emergence of a movement—sooner or later—which would have corrected the abuses in the Catholic Church. In Germany in particular, complex political arrangements, a tradition of religious devotion, and changing social and economic relationships raised questions that required complex responses on many levels, none of which was inevitable either. The Reformation was born in this context, but its fourteenth- and fifteenth-century ancestry was rich. By rejecting the political and spiritual power of the Roman Catholic Church, the Reformation implied that the legitimacy of authority could be questioned. Many people responded with enthusiasm demanding that their magistrates and rulers support the movement. European rulers responded to the turmoil by defending the Reformation, by expanding the power of their states, and by bringing the territorial churches under their control. With the Reformation began a century and a half of religious and political upheaval, crises, and wars—the clash of strongly held convictions and ambitions. Only after the Thirty-Years' War (1618–1648) did countries stop going to war with one another over religion.

SELECTED BIBLIOGRAPHY

Arthur, Anthony. *The Tailor-King: The Rise and Fall of the Anabaptist Kingdom of Munster*. New York: St. Martin's Press, 1999. Intended for a wide audience, this is the story of Jan van Leyden and his followers who turned the German city of Muenster into a militant theocracy between 1534–1535.

Bireley, Robert. *The Refashioning of Catholicism, 1450–1700*. Washington, DC: The Catholic University of America Press, 1999. Catholicism as it reshaped itself in response to the challenges of a profoundly changing world. Helpful annotated bibliography.

Bouwsma, William J. *John Calvin: A Sixteenth-Century Portrait*. New York: Oxford University Press, 1988. Sensitive discussion of a complex personality whose life is a window into a turbulent, contentious century.

Brady, Thomas A., Jr., Heiko Oberman, and James D. Tracy, eds. *Handbook of European History, 1400–1600. Late Middle Ages, Renaissance and Reformation*. 2 vols. Leiden: E. J. Brill, 1995. Essays on important themes, debates, and directions of research by the leading scholars.

Cameron, Euan. *The European Reformation*. New York: Oxford University Press, 1991. A thorough treatment of the Reformation in all its complexities. Helpful for readers who have some understanding of the topic.

Clasen, Claus-Peter. *Anabaptism: A Social History*. Ithaca, NY: Cornell University Press, 1972. A study of the sixteenth-century Anabaptist movement, includes Hutterites, excludes the Munster and Mennonite experiences.

Dickens, A. G. *The German Nation and Martin Luther*. London: Fontana, 1976. A good introduction to Luther, his times, and the issues.

Dixon, C. Scott, ed. *The German Reformation*. Oxford, Eng.: Blackwell, 1999. A collection of essays illustrating the direction of historical research in the last 20 years. Includes helpful introductions by the editor.

Duplessis, Robert S. *Transitions to Capitalism in Early Modern Europe*. Cambridge, Eng.: Cambridge University Press, 1997. Survey focusing on constraints and changes in agriculture and industry from 1450–1800. Brings out the human experience and the theoretical debates.

Fernandez Alvarez, Manuel. *Charles V*. Translated by J. A. Lalaguna. London: Thames & Hudson, 1975. Sympathetic political biography of Charles V, Holy Roman Emperor.

Hsia, R. Po-chia. *Social Discipline in the Reformation: Central Europe, 1550–1750*. London: Routledge, 1989. Discussion of confessionalization, state-building, and impact on society.

Karant-Nunn, Susan C. *Luther's Pastors: The Reformation in the Ernestine Countryside*. Philadelphia, PA: The American Philosophical Society, 1979. The Lutheran clergy and the village folk they served. Good on the many obstacles confronting the clergy in the first half of the sixteenth century.

Marshall, Sherrin, ed. *Women in Reformation and Counter-Reformation Europe*. Bloomington: Indiana University Press, 1989. This collection of essays explores the experiences and responses of women across Europe to the changes caused by the Reformations.

Oberman, Heiko A. *Luther: Man between God and the Devil*. New Haven, CT: Yale University Press, 1989. Luther driven by his belief that humanity was witnessing the apocalyptic struggle between God and the Devil at the end of time.

Ozment, Steven E. *The Reformation in the Cities: The Appeal of Protestantism to Sixteenth-Century Germany and Switzerland*. New Haven, CT: Yale University Press, 1975. Classic work on the early appeal of the Reformation in the cities.

Potter, George R. *Zwingli*. Cambridge, Eng.: Cambridge University Press, 1976. A lengthy and comprehensive biography that focuses on Zwingli's later years.

Roper, Lyndal. *Oedipus and the Devil: Witchcraft, Sexuality and Religion in Early Modern Europe.* London: Routledge, 1994. Essays taking a psychological approach to issues of gender, magic, and the body in the context of the Reformation and the Counter-Reformation.

Scribner, Robert W. *For the Sake of Simple Folk: Popular Propaganda for the German Reformation.* Cambridge, Eng.: Cambridge University Press, 1981. Analysis of pamphlets to understand the appeal of the Reformation to the common folk.

Scribner, Robert W., Roy Porter, and Mikulas Teich. *The Reformation in National Context.* Cambridge, Eng.: Cambridge University Press, 1994. Collection of scholarly, interpretive essays on the Reformation in Scotland, Scandinavia, Bohemia, Hungary, Poland, and other European countries.

Tracy, James D. *Europe's Reformations, 1450–1650.* Lanham, MD: Rowman & Littlefield, 1999. A discussion of doctrinal, political, and social concerns and changes, this book integrates the many reformations of early modern Europe. Helpful informative notes and a good bibliography.

The Spanish Armada, 1588. This idealized picture gives no clue as to why the Spanish Armada was so badly defeated by an English naval force. (Reproduced from the Collections of the Library of Congress)

The Spanish Armada, 1588

INTRODUCTION

The story of the ill-fated Spanish Armada is rooted in sixteenth-century Europe's exceptionally complex and violent religious and political turmoil. In 1517 the uncertain unity of western Christianity finally dissolved when Martin Luther nailed his famous Ninety-Five Theses to the door of the castle church at Wittenberg. His action unintentionally unleashed the Reformation, a torrent of protest that shattered western Christianity's unity. Those who left the established church were collectively called Protestants. The established church, or more properly the Roman Catholic Church, responded slowly to Protestantism's challenge. However, by the middle of the century an aroused Catholic Church had begun to combat Protestantism vigorously in a movement known as the Catholic Reformation, or Counter Reformation. In many regions the struggle between Protestantism and Catholicism became entwined with other, nonreligious issues, and frequently it degenerated into savage conflict. These Wars of Religion ravaged Europe.

The rich and powerful Habsburg dynasty provided the most important secular support for Roman Catholicism. Charles V, the head of the Habsburg family, not only served as Holy Roman Emperor from 1519, but also ruled over Spain (and its New World possessions), Austria, the free county of Burgundy, the Low Countries (present day Belgium, Luxembourg, and Holland), and much of southern Italy. For both religious and political reasons, the devoutly Roman Catholic Charles strongly backed the Catholic Church during these troublesome times. In 1556 Charles abdicated, dividing his empire between his brother, who received the central European holdings, and his son Philip, who received the rest.

Philip, who ruled in Spain as Philip II, proved a stronger supporter of Catholicism than even his father. This commitment to Catholicism explains in part Philip's difficulties in the Low Countries that ultimately led to the Spanish Armada. The Low Countries, or Netherlands, that Philip inherited were among the richest territories in Europe. Strategically located at the mouth of the Rhine River and bordering the North Sea close by the Straits of Dover and the English Channel, the Low Countries boasted a nice mix of agriculture, fishing, industrial production, and trade and commerce. The southern, or Flemish, regions had been one of Europe's great weaving centers for centuries. Antwerp was Europe's largest port and Amsterdam, in the north, was gaining ground as a banking and commercial center.

Seventeen different provinces comprised the Netherlands. Each province had its own traditions and its own set of laws. Each was fairly autonomous and there was little that held them together save for an inconsequential general assembly and a common ruler who in this case was Charles V, who had been born in the Low Countries and shared its culture. Under these circumstances, both the local nobility and the rising middle classes exercised a great deal of authority under the tolerant gaze of a benign ruler.

Because the Netherlands were at the crossroads of Europe, ideas drawn from all over the Continent tended to surface there. Not surprisingly, soon after 1517 Protestant concepts appeared, receiving a warm welcome despite the Catholicism of Charles V.

The revolt of the Netherlands, which precipitated the Spanish Armada, grew slowly. When Charles V abdicated in 1556, the Low Countries found themselves ruled by Philip II who, unlike his father, had only tenuous connections to the Netherlands and certainly never identified with them. When Philip left the Netherlands in 1559 to reside permanently in Spain, he appointed his illegitimate half-sister, Margaret of Parma, as regent. With Margaret came a flood of Spanish administrators who supplanted an increasingly unhappy local nobility and ignored the traditional rights and privileges of the towns.

Philip's insistence on raising already high taxes also disturbed the Netherlanders. Under Charles, taxes were high but the Low Countries's prosperity cushioned the blow. Nevertheless, voices of protest were raised and in 1540 Charles had to crush what was essentially a tax revolt in the important city of Ghent. Philip, lacking Charles's popularity, faced growing discontent over his tax policy.

Religious differences also played a major role in the revolt of the Netherlands. By mid-century, Protestantism in its Calvinistic form had established deep roots, especially among the merchant and laboring classes. Calvinism was a fairly militant strand of Protestantism and it urged resistance to secular authority, such as monarchs, that did not follow a "godly" path. Protestant fanaticism was equaled if not surpassed by Philip's devotion to the Roman Catholic cause. Even more determined than his father to extirpate Protestantism in the Low Countries, Philip unleashed the Inquisition. He also initiated administrative reforms in order to concentrate more power in his hands and to make it easier to crush Protestantism in a land heretofore distinguished by a degree of toleration.

Philip's heedless policies thus served to unite a disparate population against his religious, administrative, and fiscal initiatives. As the crisis gradually deepened, the first outbreak of what would be 40 years of rebellion occurred in 1566. In that year the Spanish authorities in the Netherlands rejected a petition signed by several hundred noblemen— both Protestant and Catholic—demanding that the Spanish Inquisition be removed from the Low Countries. Following shortly after this insulting rebuff (Margaret's advisors referred to the petitioning aristocrats as "beggars"), but not necessarily because of it, Calvinist fanatics went on a rampage. They invaded any number of churches, demolishing stained-glass windows, images of the saints, holy relics, and anything else smacking of "idolatry." These acts of wanton destruction fractured the fragile unity among the Netherlanders. Devout Roman Catholics were appalled and noblemen, both Catholic and Protestant, had second thoughts about allying themselves with such a mob.

However, instead of capitalizing on this sense of outrage to regain his popularity, Philip opted to send the Duke of Alva, one of his most feared soldiers, and a contingent of Spanish troops to the troubled provinces with orders to deal harshly with the miscreants. Succeeding Margaret as regent, Alva instituted a virtual reign of terror. His Council of Troubles, known popularly as the Council of Blood, executed thousands, and the 10 percent sales tax that he levied on all commercial exchanges crippled the economy. Instead of restoring order, Alva's heavy-handed policies united the Netherlanders in opposition under the leadership of William of Orange, known as William the Silent because of his taciturn nature.

As Alva continued to press his attack, bloody civil war broke out. Hatred of the Spanish became so strong that in 1576 William was able to forge a loose union of the 17 provinces that made up the Low Countries with the avowed objective of ousting the Spanish.

However, the union was not a secure one and with Alva's departure and the arrival in 1578 of Alexander Farnese, the duke of Parma and Margaret's son, Philip's fortunes improved. Through a combination of military might, persuasion, and appeals to religious sensibilities, Parma broke the union and slowly but surely retrieved the southern provinces for Spain. In 1579 the seven northern provinces formed the Union of Utrecht and two years later declared their independence as the United Provinces of the Netherlands. However, Parma continued to make significant progress and the United Provinces's chances for success suffered a major blow when William the Silent was assassinated in 1584.

Nevertheless, even at the very time of William's murder the fate of the Low Countries, or at least the United Provinces, was shifting to a different locale. Suspicious of Spanish designs, England had gradually involved itself in the civil war on the side of the rebels. Protestant, fiercely independent, and fearful of a possible Spanish invasion, England had emerged by the mid-1580s as the great protector of the Dutch rebellion.

England's involvement in the affairs of the Netherlands and Spain's ultimately violent reaction is a tangled story whose origins can be traced to earlier in the sixteenth century. As is well known, in 1533 the English king Henry VIII, who desperately sought a male heir to the throne, divorced his wife Catherine, who was aunt to Charles V. Although it was not his intention, Henry's actions moved England away from Catholicism. Eventually Henry created Anglicanism, a form of Protestantism.

When Henry died in 1547, the English throne passed to his nine-year-old son Edward VI, whose advisors were staunch Protestants. When Edward died in 1553, his half-sister Mary, an ardent Roman Catholic, became monarch. Her persecution of English Protestants earned her the nickname Bloody Mary. She was married to Philip II, but the union had produced no children at the time of her death in 1558 and the English crown then passed to Elizabeth, Henry VIII's last surviving child, who reigned until 1603.

At first Elizabeth's grasp on power was tenuous, but she proved to be an exceptional ruler. She worked diligently to bring religious peace to England and to keep England at peace with the rest of Europe. To that end she devised a religious compromise that satisfied most Englishmen while isolating both Protestant and Roman Catholic extremists. She also conducted an effective diplomacy that kept others, but especially Philip II and Spain, at arm's length.

Despite her considerable skills, Elizabeth faced serious problems that defied easy solutions. When it became apparent that Elizabeth would neither lead England back into the Roman Catholic fold nor turn England into a Spanish vassal, she made enemies of both the Roman Church and Philip II. Fortunately for Elizabeth's adversaries, a vehicle was at hand that might enable them to achieve their goals—Mary Stuart, better known as Mary, Queen of Scots.

This attractive but politically witless woman was the granddaughter of Henry VIII's sister Margaret and the great-granddaughter of Henry VII, the founder of the Tudor dynasty. To some it seemed that Mary's lineage gave her a better claim to the English throne than Elizabeth, who had once been declared illegitimate. The high-spirited Mary, who in 1561 returned to rule Scotland from France, a royal widow at the age of 18, soon ran afoul of the dour Scotch Protestants led by John Knox. Her own muddle-headed indiscretions condemned her, and fearing for her life Mary fled to England in 1568 where she sought refuge with her cousin.

Mary, however, presented a major problem for Elizabeth. Not only was she a Roman Catholic around whom England's disaffected Catholics could rally, but her presence also gave hope to Philip II and the Roman hierarchy, both of whom wanted to substitute Mary for Elizabeth on the throne of England and thereby further their respective interests. Mary did not help her cause when she allowed herself to be dragged into harebrained but nonetheless dangerous plots to topple Elizabeth. Eventually, Mary's involvement in one plot too many forced Elizabeth's hand, and the queen ordered Mary's execution in 1587.

Prior to the execution, Elizabeth's relations with both the Roman Catholic Church and Philip had deteriorated. She had been excommunicated in 1570 and the pope had virtually called for her overthrow. Philip, the Roman Catholic champion of Europe, wished to depose Elizabeth for political and economic reasons as well as religious ones. He still harbored ambitions for a Spanish hegemony over England and he greatly resented that English privateers, the "sea dogs," with the obvious connivance of the crown, were preying on Spain's shipping, especially its transport of silver and gold from the New World. Faced with these threats, Elizabeth had begun to support the revolutionaries in the Low Countries as a way to keep Philip occupied and, consequently, less likely to attack England. With the decline in William the Silent's fortunes and increasing evidence that Philip might use the Low Countries as a jumping off point for an invasion of England itself, Elizabeth's support of the Dutch rebellion deepened.

The execution of Mary, Queen of Scots, ended any hope that she would succeed the childless Elizabeth as ruler of England. It also ended any hesitations that Philip might have had about invading England. Beginning in 1587 he began to marshal his resources for the coming attack. A daring raid on Cadiz by Sir Francis Drake slowed preparations, but by the summer of 1588 the ill-named "la felicissima armada" (the most fortunate fleet) was rounding into shape.

The Spanish plan called for the Armada to sail up the English Channel to the Low Countries. There it would pick up Parma's troops and escort them across the Channel for an invasion of England. It was understood that the Armada would sink the English navy if attacked during the Channel passage.

On May 9, 1588, the Spanish fleet sailed. It consisted of 130 ships with 30,000 men and more than 2,000 pieces of artillery. The duke of Medina-Sidonia, a man with no naval experience, commanded the Armada which entered the Channel late in July. There it encountered the English fleet under Lord Howard and Vice-Admiral Francis Drake. The English force numbered about 150 English vessels, and on the whole they were faster, more maneuverable, and better armed than their opponents. This superior force was also aided by unexpected gale winds, the so-called "Protestant wind," that bedeviled the Armada. Over the course of several days of fighting, the English badly mauled the Spanish flotilla. The remnant that escaped faced a long and deadly return voyage through the North Sea that took a ferocious toll on the survivors. What had begun as a bold stroke by Philip II ended in unmitigated disaster.

INTERPRETIVE ESSAY
Connie S. Evans

As the smoke cleared from the confrontation between England and Spain at Gravelines in the English Channel on July 29, 1588, both sides—and, indeed, the whole of continental Europe—began to assess the meaning of the "defeat" of the Spanish Armada. It is a debate that has continued to the present day. While some historians point to it as one of the most decisive battles in the history of Western civilization, others believe much of its importance rests more on legend rather than on reality.

The immediate consequences were reflected most clearly in the two chief protagonists of the conflict: Elizabeth I of England and Philip II of Spain. Elizabeth, whose brave speech at Tilbury had lent so much encouragement to her uncertain troops, took the victory as a sign from God, and even commissioned a special medal to mark the occasion which alluded to the "Protestant wind" that had swept the Armada from England's shores. The triumph sealed the reputation of "Gloriana" for all time, and Elizabeth reveled in the love and devotion of her people in the aftermath of the Armada. After 1588, for the most part, Elizabeth could do no wrong in the eyes of her people; she who had been willing to "lay down for my God and for my kingdom and for my people, my honour and my blood, even in the dust" deserved no less than unswerving loyalty. It was a loyalty she commanded until her death in 1603.

Though Elizabeth basked in approbation in the aftermath of the Armada, her government did not enjoy the same popularity. The mighty Spanish enterprise had been repulsed, but the war with Spain did not come to an end; indeed, it would rage on for another 15 years. Only in 1604 did it find resolution under Elizabeth's successor, James I. The fortunes of England were now inextricably linked with those of the Dutch, and the English found themselves committed to maintaining a strong navy and a military presence on the Continent. The initial enthusiasm for war faded as the costs mounted; the expenditure from the Exchequer for 1588 was over £400,000, a sum that was regularly exceeded as hostilities deepened. The specter of bankruptcy became a permanent fixture in the English government as a huge debt accumulated that would be passed on to Elizabeth's successor.

While the granting of extraordinary taxes by Parliament met some of the financial burden, it made sense to the queen and her councillors to continue the privateering that had become so much a part of English naval strategy since the outbreak of the war. The rich treasure ships that traveled to Spain from the New World were targets that were too hard to resist. The successes of the Elizabethan "sea dogs," Francis Drake and John Hawkins among them, in capturing these vessels proved alluring for merchants, gentlemen, and the Crown alike. As a result, investments that might have been made in colonization of the New World, in trade with the East, and in loosening the Spanish grip in the West Indies, were all diverted into privateering for almost the entire length of the war.

Philip II, who had micromanaged the entire venture, felt the loss keenly and personally, although he ascribed the loss less to his own mistakes and more to the God he felt had abandoned him and his great cause. Philip recovered relatively quickly, however, and began to set in motion plans for a new Armada which would avenge the loss of its predecessor and restore Spanish pride. To do so required a considerable financial investment that necessitated the imposition of new taxes to cover both the costs of the lost Armada and the assembling of a new fleet. The king's request for these new revenues led to a great deal of criticism throughout the country, occasioned by riots in Castile and outright indictments of what were deemed Philip's financial and personal excesses. In addition, the tremendous loss of life in the Armada brought much grief to the Spanish people and, on a practical level, to Philip as well: he lost most of his experienced naval commanders to death or imprisonment and thus had to recoup not only his material losses but also those of personnel.

While the Inquisition moved to silence his internal critics, Philip found himself faced with a new threat from the Continent. The assassination of Henry III of France in 1589 brought to the throne his nearest male relative, the Huguenot Henry of Navarre. Appalled at the prospect of a Protestant king on the throne of France, Philip's focus on the English and the Dutch lessened. Catholic France, always the traditional enemy of Spain, was now twice as dangerous. Philip's shift in emphasis did not assuage the concerns of the English, who had always feared the Spanish Duke of Parma's 30,000 troops poised for attack from Flanders much more than they had feared the Armada itself; indeed, the Armada, for all intents and purposes, had only been the escort for Parma's army. Many of Elizabeth's councillors believed that Spain's control of the Catholic League, which exerted primacy in northern France, would provide a base from which Parma could launch his troops against England. The renewed hostilities between Spain and France made such a scenario likely, at least to English eyes, and by mid-1591 that possibility led England to place more than 14,000 troops on the Continent. While the French and the Dutch unquestionably benefited from the English presence abroad, the English themselves gained little or no advantage and suffered a serious financial strain.

When Henry of Navarre barricaded Paris in early 1590, Philip concluded that Spanish intervention in France was necessary if French Catholicism was to be saved. Plans for a new Spanish fleet to invade England were abandoned temporarily, and Philip began to open peace negotiations with the Dutch in order to avoid additional conflict that would drain resources from his French venture. He commanded Parma to invade France in mid-1590, and the duke reached Paris with his troops by September. Reinforcements were also sent to Brittany in order to establish a base from which to send expeditions against England.

Philip found himself overcommitted, and with no alternative made overtures to the Dutch, who took advantage of the situation to regain territory previously lost to the Spanish. Philip had to divide his resources in order to face the challenges posed by the French, the English, and the Dutch, and faced an additional problem in 1591 in Spain, when Aragon revolted. Though the revolt was put down, its cost depleted the monies available for Philip's foreign ventures. Philip remained devoted to the idea that the Catholic religion had to be saved, no matter what the cost, and it was his stubbornness on this point that created a stalemate in continental affairs. Without Philip's intervention, the French Catholics would have had little chance of survival, but he was not able to provide enough support to give them a decisive advantage against Henry of Navarre. Consequently, the French civil war could reach no conclusion since both sides were fairly equal due to Philip's support of the Catholics.

When Henry IV had been crowned king in 1589, he had promised to take instruction in the Catholic faith; by 1593 he realized that if he did not make good on his promise there would be no hope of peace. With all parties exhausted by the civil war and with other claimants to the throne from the houses of Bourbon and Lorraine, Henry now knew it was imperative to convert to Catholicism. Bowing to the inevitable, he did so in July 1593. Since Henry had previously made it clear to Elizabeth that he could not hold out against the various pressures ranged against him, there was no possibility that the English found his conversion a surprise. Nonetheless, Elizabeth protested Henry's change of religion vociferously and threatened to remove her troops from Normandy and Brittany. Indeed, by the end of 1593 English troops were gone from Normandy and it looked very much like the rest would be withdrawn shortly afterwards. However, the possibility of Spain using Brittany as a base from which to attack England persuaded Elizabeth not only to keep her troops in Brittany but to reinforce them in 1594. It was clear, however, that the English were remaining in France only in terms of a defensive posture and would no longer be aiding the French king. The capture of Fort Crozon in late 1594 from the Spanish put an end to the necessity for an English presence in France, and Elizabeth withdrew the last of her troops from Brittany by February 1595.

A similar policy was put in place in the Netherlands, when the English declined to send a further 3,000 troops to supplement the Normandy troops which had returned there in 1593. Elizabeth believed that she had spent enough money on the Dutch cause; in any case, none of the monies expended by the English had been repaid and Elizabeth saw no point in further expenditure. Indeed, she made it clear to the Dutch that repayment would be expected at a not-too-distant point in the future.

It made a great deal of sense to Elizabeth to institute this defensive policy in France and the Low Countries as she was being faced with problems closer to home. A plot by Scottish Catholics in league with the Spanish to invade England from a Scottish base showed that there were cracks in the relationship between Elizabeth and her putative heir, James VI of Scotland. Elizabeth's failure to name James as her official heir continued to irritate him, leading Elizabeth to believe, perhaps correctly, that he had some complicity in the plot. Though the invasion never materialized, it damaged relations between the two monarchs; Elizabeth was never to make James her heir officially and only his innate suitability to succeed her insured that he did so in 1603.

Elizabeth sought assurances from Henry IV that he would not make peace with Spain, but she also made it clear that the defense of France was in the king's hands alone. In Elizabeth's eyes, a united France posed as many dangers as did Spain, especially in regard to the Netherlands. She wanted to be certain that France and Spain remained at odds with each other to insure a balance of power in western Europe; she also feared the loss of years of financial investment in the Netherlands, which might become a joint target for both France and Spain. If the Dutch fell to such an attack, England could not be far behind. Therefore, it was imperative to Elizabeth that France and Spain remain at odds. To that end, in 1596 Elizabeth entered into an alliance with Henry IV that was both offensive and defensive; the Dutch made it a Triple Alliance before the end of the year. Though Elizabeth supplied 2,000 troops to Picardy in compliance with the terms of the alliance, she withdrew them when France concluded a peace with Spain.

By 1595 it was clear that civil war had come to an end in France; the Catholic League was disbanded and Philip no longer had a base of support in the heart of the country. The war was now a national one between France and Spain, fought along the French borders. Philip, by this time in a declining state of health, had to deal with mutinies among his armies in France and in the Netherlands (leading in one instance to a temporary truce with Henry IV in 1593); he grew unable to provide support to his troops in Brittany and to French Catholic bases, and by late 1596 realized that he would have to come to terms with at least some of his enemies. The situation in the Netherlands had been steadily declining since the loss of the strategic city of Groningen in 1594, which severely weakened Spain's holdings in the Netherlands. The Dutch, with both riverbanks in their possession, were able, on water, to outmaneuver the Spanish land forces. This conflict as well had become a national one between the Spanish-held portions of the Netherlands and the fledgling Dutch republic.

Papal offers to mediate between France and Spain in 1597 led to the signing of a peace agreement in May 1598, which, while it lost Philip no territory, came at great cost nonetheless. His treasury had been depleted in the cause of the French Catholics, and his attention to the conflict in France had meant the loss of many of his holdings in the Spanish Netherlands. There too, Philip was forced to a concession. In 1598 he decided to bestow the Spanish Netherlands upon his daughter, Isabella, who was to be married to Albert, son of Philip's sister, Maria. As rulers, they would be independent of Spain in all matters save those of foreign policy and defense; Philip was determined to secure the Spanish holdings against the Dutch, and also wanted to assure himself of the use of a strategic position for the on-going war with England. Philip hoped that this move would send a signal to the rest of western Europe that a balance of power could be restored, and Spain could relieve some of the pressure under which it labored.

The peace with France and the concessions to the Dutch aside, Philip continued to work for an invasion of England. Elizabeth realized the Dutch could not be left on their own, but she made sure that they were responsible for all payments to the forces with which she supplied them, and further, insisted that repayment begin on the monies advanced to the Dutch over the preceding years. Elizabeth now was in the position of being able to concentrate nearly all of her treasury's resources on the continuing conflict with Spain, which revived in intensity in 1596.

The new Armada which had been delayed by Philip's French venture was finally launched against England in 1596, but massive storms turned it back almost immediately; undaunted, Philip sent it out again in 1597. This second attempt was nearly successful, but it also missed its objective due to storms. The third, in 1599, was diverted by a pressing concern over a combined English/Dutch threat to the Canaries and the Azores. England's response to these repeated attempts by Spain to invade its shores was swift: under the command of Robert Devereux, earl of Essex, and Lord Howard of Effingham, a fleet sailed into Cadiz, a Spanish port on the Atlantic, and sacked the city. A great deal of treasure was taken, to be returned in triumph to Elizabeth. Though a spectacular victory, it had little substantive effect. However, the naval reputation of Devereux had been made, and Elizabeth's fondness for him, coupled with his own ego, led him to mount a subsequent expedition in 1597 against the Armada in Ferrol. This venture, known as the Islands Voyage, was as complete a disaster as the Cadiz expedition had been a success. Essex blamed its failure on everyone and everything but himself, but Elizabeth held him responsible for it and Essex was driven to find a way in which to restore his pride and honor.

Though Scotland had not proven to be a good venue from which to launch a Spanish invasion of England, such was not the case with Ireland. English rule in Ireland, completed by 1300, had slowly been eroded as the English sent to rule the island gradually became Irish themselves. By the time of the Spanish Armada in 1588, discontent with the Protestant rule of Catholic Ireland had reached a peak. Initially, the Spanish flirted with the idea of giving aid to the Ulster chieftain, Hugh O'Donnell, while Hugh O'Neill, earl of Tyrone, toyed with the idea of all-out rebellion. By 1596 it seemed that the moment had come to overthrow English rule in Ireland. The Anglo-Irish co-opted the frustrations of the native Irish and joined in the revolt under the direction of Tyrone, who enjoyed early success with the help of the Spanish.

Essex, seeing a way to restore his battered reputation, petitioned Elizabeth in 1599 to lead an assault upon Ulster, then a central base of the Irish revolt. Instead of becoming the vindication of his hopes for military glory, Essex mismanaged the entire operation and to cover his failures signed a treaty with Tyrone without Elizabeth's permission, an action that was inherently treasonous. When Essex returned to London to explain his actions, Elizabeth received him coldly and banned him from the court. The attempts by Essex to restore himself to the queen's favor eventually resulted in his being charged with treason and executed in 1601.

With the death of Philip II in 1598, his son, Philip III, who succeeded him, continued his policies and was finally able to land 10,000 Spanish troops accompanied by 100 ships at Kinsale in southern Ireland in 1601. Kinsale's distance from the rebel strongholds meant that Tyrone had to make his way there during a harsh winter, and Lord Mountjoy, Essex's successor in Ireland, was able to spring an attack at Kinsale upon Tyrone's weary troops on Christmas Eve. A decisive English victory over the Irish and the Spaniards resulted in a Spanish retreat, which left the Irish rebels with no choice but to surrender. Elizabeth had won, but at great cost: upwards of £2.5 million and 17,000 troops had been required to restore English rule in Ireland.

The Spaniards, foiled in their attempt to use Ireland as a springboard from which to attack England, renewed their efforts against the Dutch; like his father, Philip III wanted the Netherlands to be completely Catholic. The Spanish laid siege to Ostend, and Elizabeth was once again forced to supply some aid to the Dutch; renewed concerns about an attack from the Netherlands had been exacerbated when it was discovered that six Spanish galleys had made it through to Sluys in the Netherlands in 1599. These concerns were somewhat allayed by the ability of the English to destroy another six galleys in a similar attempt by the Spanish in 1602. By January 1603 Spain's council of state acknowledged that it would be impossible to carry through an invasion of England, regardless of where it began; this acknowledgement opened up the real possibility that England and Spain might be able to come to terms, though negotiations to that point had stalled over a variety of issues.

James VI and I, Elizabeth's successor (the queen having died in March 1603), did not wish to continue the conflict and a ceasefire went into effect with his accession. The Spaniards conceded the important points in the peace negotiations which were formalized in London in August 1604. The English would continue to trade with the Dutch, and would not have to withdraw English troops who were in Dutch service; indeed, the English insisted that the Dutch be permitted—although they did not choose to do so—to take part in the negotiations. Though the question of English trade with the Indies remained unresolved, the war with Spain was over. When the conflict between the two nations boiled to the surface again, it would be under the vastly different circumstances occasioned by the Thirty Years' War in 1625.

In practical terms, the Armada and the war that followed proved a costly venture for both countries, both in money and in manpower. In both England and Spain there were active protests at the expense of the war, and these protests showed a widening gulf between the court and the people. The central government, which had to respond to the monarch's demands for funds, was often blamed for the resulting hardships imposed on the people whose purses were tapped time and time again, and who were called upon to serve in the monarch's military. As the war dragged on, there was less willingness to shoulder the burden, and this reluctance was being expressed more boldly over the course of time. England's Parliament, though it managed to meet the crown's demands for war subsidies on each occasion funds were requested, became increasingly concerned that it was not representing the interests of its constituents by continuing to approve every subsidy. Spain faced tax riots, and the government resorted to using the Inquisition to quell the criticism aimed at the king and his policies. While Elizabeth and Philip II lived, there was no question that calls for accountability on the part of monarchs would not gain any purchase, but the seventeenth century saw a distinct change: parliaments began to question subsidy requests and to demand considerations in return for granting them. Over time, the Stuart kings would find themselves dismissing Parliament for years at a time in order to avoid protracted debates about revenues and subsidies. Thus, one of the legacies of the Armada and the war that followed it was that the taxpayers and their legislative representatives began to demand accountability and a greater role in deciding how tax monies were spent. The failure of the first two Stuart kings to accede to such demands eventually led to civil war.

England, as noted earlier, continued its privateering throughout the years of the war, and the investment in privateering drained off monies that might have gone to develop colonies or expand trade to the east. While some historians have argued that the Armada war sent the Spanish colonial empire into decline, such was not the case. By the end of the war, Spain had lost not one colony to England and it would still be some years before English colonization would take hold in the New World. The destruction of the great Armada in 1588 was not the end of the Spanish navy; in many ways, it spurred the Spanish to refine and improve their fleets. The English, by virtue of their island status, were better sailors than the Spanish and continued to be, but they were not able to dominate the seas. English piracy was still effective against Spanish treasure ships, but as the Spanish improved their ships and developed protective convoys, the amount of precious metals and other valuables that arrived in Spain during the course of the war grew exponentially.

Despite the long years of war, Spain failed to establish domination in western Europe and was never able to invade England; its attempt to use Ireland as a base from which to attack England was decisively repulsed. The aura of invincibility that had surrounded Spain for so long was gone; Protestants saw the defeat as God's vindication, while Catholics outside of Spain quietly cheered the breakdown of Spanish hegemony in the Catholic world. After Henry IV's conversion, France was able to reach equilibrium and bring an end to its civil wars; it was also to emerge as a strong counterbalance to Spain and England, thus assuring that the balance of power in western Europe remained stable. The young Dutch republic was rescued from Spanish hegemony, and the Treaty of Westphalia in 1648 made its independence official.

Philip II's dream of reimposing Catholicism on the whole of western Europe was crushed, although Europeans were not quite finished fighting about religion. The Habsburg attempt to force Catholicism on the Calvinists in Bohemia would spark the Thirty Years' War in 1618, while the growth of Puritanism in England became a causal factor in its mid-seventeenth-century civil war. However, if Philip's Armada had been successful and Parma's army had succeeded, the cause of English Protestantism might have failed; certainly the subsequent history of England and Europe as a whole would have been significantly changed. However, the lack of cohesiveness among co-religionists would have made it difficult if not impossible to curb the growth of Protestantism; neither side had the resources to eradicate the other and it was simply a matter of time before each side recognized it was possible to cohabit not only the same continent but the same country and city. Thus, the Spanish Armada and the war that followed it in many ways simply presaged the realities and principles that would be readily acknowledged by the middle of the seventeenth century.

SELECTED BIBLIOGRAPHY

Andrews, Kenneth R. *Elizabethan Privateering during the Spanish War, 1585–1603.* Cambridge, Eng.: Cambridge University Press, 1964. One of the best books on the subject of English privateering; details its role in creating the circumstances that brought about the Armada and the war after.

Doran, Susan. *England and Europe in the Sixteenth Century.* New York: St. Martin's Press, 1999. Argues that English emphasis on privateering during the Spanish war stunted the country's interest in overseas exploration, trade, and investment until the Jacobean period.

Fallon, Niall. *The Armada in Ireland.* Middletown, CT: Wesleyan University Press, 1978. Written before the latest archaeological discoveries, Fallon believes that Ireland's role in the Armada has been overlooked and offers a wide-ranging examination of the wrecks off the coast of Ireland and the experience of the Spaniards who found their way onto the shores of the island.

Fernandez-Armesto, Felipe. *The Spanish Armada: The Experience of War in 1588.* New York: Oxford University Press, 1988. Believes that the myths surrounding the Armada conceal the essential truth of the enterprise, and argues that it had no long-term effects on either the English or Spanish empires; emphasizes the "common experience" of both sides in the conflict.

Howarth, David. *The Voyage of the Armada.* New York: Penguin Group, 1982.

Enthralling account of whys and wherefores behind the Armada; provides an intimate look at Philip II.

Martin, Colin, and Geoffrey Parker. *The Spanish Armada*. London: Hamish Hamilton, 1988. Complements existing archival evidence with underwater archaeological findings to make new conclusions about the extent of the Armada's ineffectualness and the importance of the fireship raid in preventing its triumph.

Mattingly, Garrett. *The Armada*. Boston, MA: Houghton Mifflin, 1959. The classic, standard account of the confrontation; Mattingly convincingly argues for a diminution in the Spanish losses in advance of confirming archaeological evidence and is strong on diplomacy. Ascribes importance of the Armada as much to myth and legend as to its actual significance.

Milne-Tyte, Robert. *Armada! The Planning, the Battle, and After*. London: Robert Hale, 1988. Straightforward, easily accessible account of the plan for, execution of, and immediate aftermath of the Armada, the "flawed enterprise."

Padfield, Peter. *Armada: A Celebration of the Four Hundredth Anniversary of the Defeat of the Spanish Armada, 1588–1988*. London: Gollancz, 1988. Well-illustrated, large-scale volume that concentrates on the campaign of 1587–1588 to ascertain the reasons behind the launching of the Armada. Paints Philip II as the "architect of defeat" and argues that he was forced to the confrontation in order to defend his treasure shipments from the New World as well as his industrial interests in the Netherlands.

Parker, Geoffrey. *The Army of Flanders and the Spanish Road, 1567–1659*. Cambridge, Eng.: Cambridge University Press, 1990. Taking the Spanish perspective, explores the ultimate inability of Spain to put down the revolt of the Dutch. Speculates that, like other powerful countries, Spain was too committed elsewhere in its dominions in order to wage an effective campaign.

———. *The Grand Strategy of Philip II*. New Haven, CT: Yale University Press, 1998. Analysis of the construction of Philip II's global empire; argues that Philip's "flawed 'management style' " was at the heart of the loss of the Armada.

Rasor, Eugene. *The Spanish Armada of 1588: Historiography and Annotated Bibliography*. Westport, CT: Greenwood Press, 1993. Excellent historiographical synthesis of Armada works to 1993, with accompanying annotated bibliography.

Rodriguez-Salgado, Mia J., and Simon Adams, eds. *England, Spain, and the Gran Armada, 1585–1604: Essays from the Anglo-Spanish Conferences, London and Madrid, 1988*. Edinburgh: John Donald Publishers, 1991. Acknowledges the important work being done in Spain on issues associated with the Armada based on new evidence; focusing on Philip II's motives, concludes that the king's decision to go to war led to a reorientation of monarchical power and pins the Armada failure on basic navigational problems.

Thompson, I. A. A. *War and Government in Hapsburg Spain, 1560–1620*. London: Athlone Press, 1976. Offers an analysis of the Spanish government in terms of its ability to administer the war; posits that there were conflicting sys-

tems of administrative control within the Spanish government that con-
travened a continuance of royal absolutism and devolved government
function gradually upon local authorities and private contractors.

———. *War and Society in Hapsburg Spain: Selected Essays*. Brookfield, VT: Ashgate
Publishing Company, 1992. A collection of essays that addresses the issue
of the social and economic impact of war on Spain; building on his earlier
work, Thompson takes an "annalist" approach that reveals the surprising
efficacy of the Spanish government in the sixteenth century.

Wernham, R. B. *After the Armada: Elizabethan England and the Struggle for Western
Europe, 1588–1595*. Oxford, Eng.: Clarendon Press, 1984. How Elizabeth I
and her advisors might have viewed the struggle for western Europe in
the first years after the Armada; argues that policy was determined day-
by-day in response to changing circumstances and events. Suggests that
this period marks the beginning of the division of England into the two
factions of "court" and "country."

———. *The Return of the Armadas: The Last Years of the Elizabethan War Against
Spain, 1595–1603*. Oxford, Eng.: Clarendon Press, 1994. A continuation of
his previous monograph, Wernham argues that Elizabethan policy towards western Europe shifted after 1595 from a day-by-day response to
a more reasoned and thoughtful approach; strictly defensive policies in
France and the Low Countries allowed for a concentration on the dangers
from Ireland, posited as a stepping stone for a Spanish invasion.

Whiting, John Roger Scott. *The Enterprise of England: The Spanish Armada*. New
York: St. Martin's Press, 1988. Seeks to offer an objective reassessment of
the Armada in light of new evidence uncovered in archives and archaeological expeditions; eschewing nationalistic bias, argues that Philip did
not launch the Armada to achieve a conquest of England but rather to
weaken the English to prevent further encroachments on his treasure ships
and challenges to his authority in the Netherlands.

Appendix A

Glossary

Alberti, Leon Battista (1404–1474). Italian architect, painter, musician, and writer; the first to deal scientifically with the idea of perspective.

Angevin. A variant of the word *Anjou*, an old French noble family, some of whose descendants ruled England as Plantagenet kings. Other Angevins ruled the duchy of Anjou in France, and in Naples and Sicily.

Cabot, John (1450–1498). An Italian, whose real name was Giovanni Caboto, Cabot was contracted by King Henry VII of England to lead two expeditions (1497, 1498) across the North Atlantic, during which he explored the Greenland coast, made landfall in Newfoundland and Cape Breton Island, and followed the North American coast down to the 38th parallel.

Carolingian. The name given to a dynasty of kings of France between 751 and 987 and of the Holy Roman Empire between 800 and 918. The name is derived from the French ruler Charlemagne (r. 768–814), who was also Emperor of the West (Holy Roman Empire) from 800 to 814.

Celestial Dynasty. The name given to Chinese ruling dynasties, who believed that their authority to govern came from a heavenly source.

Coronado, Francisco Vazquez de (1510–1554). Spanish explorer who led an expedition (1540–1542) across the southwestern part of what is now the United States in search of the fabled wealth of Quivira. While he never found gold or silver, he was the first European to travel up the Colorado River and see the Grand Canyon.

de Soto, Hernando (1500?–1542). Spanish explorer who led an expedition (1539–1542) from Florida through the southeastern part of what is now the United States seeking gold and silver. He died before the expedition returned home.

Drake, Francis (1540?–1596). English adventurer and navigator who led several expeditions to the Americas and Asia; he was the first Englishman to go around the world. He is perhaps best known as the English vice-admiral whose fleet defeated the Spanish Armada in 1588.

Erasmus, Desiderius (1466?–1536). Dutch Renaissance-era scholar and religious commentator who came to oppose the Protestant Reformation after initially supporting it.

Exchequer. Derived from a word meaning "counting table," the exchequer was (and still is) the department in English government responsible for public finance.

Giotto de Bondone (1266?–1337). Painter, sculptor, and architect who lived in Florence and who some consider to be the first Renaissance artist.

Grand Vizier. The name given to successive prime ministers of the Ottoman Empire. They held their post at the pleasure of the Sultan.

Guild. In medieval and early modern times, a guild was an association of merchants or craftsmen that frequently exercised considerable influence in local governmental affairs.

Huguenot. The name given to French Protestants in the sixteenth and seventeenth centuries. Louis XIV persecuted the Huguenots, and many fled to Prussia, England, Holland, and North America. Scholars disagree over the origin of the name; some think it derives from the German word *Eidgenossen*, or "confederates," while others link it to Besançon Hugues, an early leader in the French Protestant movement.

Inquisition. A Roman Catholic tribunal utilized in Europe and Spanish America in the early modern period to uncover and punish, often brutally, those persons alleged to be heretics.

Islam. Founded by the prophet Muhammad (570–632), Islam is the newest of the world's great religions. There are more than 1 billion Muslims (followers of Islam) worldwide, many of whom reside in northern Africa, Turkey, the Middle East, Pakistan, and Indonesia.

Lancaster. English royal family name (or "house") of Henry IV, Henry V, and Henry VI, who reigned between 1399 and 1461.

liege homage. A phrase referring to the relationship between a feudal lord in medieval times and his vassals.

Louis XIV (1638–1715). Long-time king of France (1643–1715), under whose rule the country fought numerous wars, persecuted Huguenots, and did little for the poorer classes. He increased royal authority and created at the Palace of Versailles the most extravagant royal court in Europe.

Medici. Powerful family from the Tuscany region of Italy, which amassed wealth and power in Florence through banking and business enter-prises between the fourteenth and sixteenth centuries. Although their rule was often brutal, the Medici were patrons of the arts and contrib-uted to the flowering of the Renaissance.

mudejar. The name given to Muslims in Spain who chose to live under Christian rule during the *reconquista.*

parlement. In France, this was a regional supreme court that handled both criminal and civil cases. Judges were royal appointees, and during the early modern period, the courts usually supported the monarch. Par-lements were abolished in 1789 during the French Revolution.

Plantagenet. Family name associated with the House of Anjou (or An-gevin). Plantagenet kings ruled England from 1154 to 1399, when the Lancasters came to power.

poll tax. A tax levied on each and every individual without any *quid pro quo.*

Ponce de Leon, Juan (1460?–1521). A Spanish explorer and administrator, Ponce de Leon was governor of Puerto Rico (1510–1513) and led an expedition north through the Bahamas to Florida, which he claimed for Spain and named. He died in 1521 during a second expedition to Florida.

Raleigh, Walter (1552?–1618). An English court favorite whom Elizabeth I sent to North America to place unsettled lands under English title. He explored the Atlantic coast from North Carolina to Florida, took settlers to form a colony on Roanoke Island, and later tried without success to establish settlements in Virginia. He fell out of favor and was executed during the reign of James I.

Salic Law. A law derived from the Salian Franks of the fourth century; used to exclude women from the monarchy.

Silk Road. A network of trade routes between Chang-an (now Xian), China, and Rome that facilitated trade between China and lands to its west. The route was opened to western Asia as early as the second century B.C.E., and trade with Persia and other Middle Eastern places flourished from the seventh century on. Direct trade with Europe fol-lowed the trek of Marco Polo in the thirteenth century, but was se-verely limited after the accession to power of the Ming dynasty in 1368.

Timur Lang [Tamerlane] (1336?–1405). Asian conqueror and descendant of Genghis Khan, Timur Lang first established his authority near Sam-arkand, but later conquered Persia and central Asia, and invaded Rus-sia as far west as Moscow. He also led military expeditions into India and Turkey. His nickname was, appropriately, the "Prince of Destruc-tion."

Tokugawa Shogunate. Set of powerful military governors who controlled Japan between 1603 and 1867.

Tudor. The Tudors were the ruling family of England from 1485 until 1603. Famous Tudors were Henry VIII and Elizabeth I.

Valois. Royal family of France, beginning with Philip VI (r. 1328–1350) and ending with Henry III (r. 1574–1589). Valois is a district in the Picardy region of France, northeast of Paris.

Appendix B

Timeline

1292	Marco Polo returns to Venice after 17 years working for Kublai Khan
1304	Giotto decorates a chapel in Padua, using a more realistic style than commonly used in the past
1307	Dante begins writing *The Divine Comedy*
1317	France adopts the Salic Law to exclude women from the monarchy
1337	Hundred Years' War begins
1343	The Black Death (bubonic plague) epidemic first seen in Europe, brought to Genoa by merchants returning from Asia
1353	Boccaccio publishes *The Decameron*
1393	Timur Lang conquers Baghdad
1400	Population of Europe's largest city, London, estimated to be 50,000
1415	English defeat French at Battle of Agincourt
1425	Portuguese take control of the Canary Islands, off the northwest coast of Africa
1431	Joan of Arc burned at the stake for high treason against God
1436	Leon Battista Alberti publishes *Della Pittura*, an explication of Renaissance aesthetic and scientific theories
1442	African slaves first sold in Lisbon markets

1453	Hundred Years' War ends; Ottoman Turks conquer Constantinople
1455	Wars of the Roses begin in England
1456	Johann Gutenberg publishes his Bible in Mainz, using moveable type and a screw press
1457	Scotland bans "futeball" and "golfe" lest sportsmen neglect their archery, deemed militarily important
1469	The marriage of Ferdinand of Aragon and Isabella of Castile unites the Spanish crown
1476	William Caxton sets up first printing press in England
1483	Tomas de Torquemada becomes grand inquisitor of Spanish Inquisition and carries out his duties with exceptional cruelty
1485	Henry VII becomes king of England, marking the end of the Wars of the Roses
1492	Spain completes *reconquista*; Christopher Columbus makes first voyage to America
1494	Treaty of Tordesillas establishes global line of demarcation between Spanish and Portuguese conquests
1497	John Cabot sails to eastern coast of North America; Leonardo da Vinci completes *The Last Supper*
1503	Canterbury Cathedral in England is completed, 436 years after construction had begun
1507	Leonardo da Vinci paints the *Mona Lisa*
1509	Henry VIII becomes king of England
1513	Machiavelli publishes *The Prince*; Ponce de Leon sees and names Florida; a Portuguese ship reaches China
1515	Thomas More publishes *Utopia*
1517	The Protestant Reformation begins with Martin Luther's public protests against the sale of indulgences
1519	Hernán Cortés begins conquest of Mexico; Ferdinand Magellan embarks on round-the-world expedition
1527	Henry VIII begins Protestant Reformation in England by seeking divorce from Catherine of Aragon; Spanish and German soldiers capture Rome, causing great damage
1533	Henry VIII marries Anne Boleyn; Francisco Pizarro completes conquest of Peru
1534	Henry VIII officially breaks with Roman Catholic Church

1540	Coronado launches his expedition into the American south-west
1541	John Calvin initiates a new government in Geneva, Switzerland, based on his religious tenets
1543	Nicholas Copernicus theorizes that the earth revolves around the sun
1545	Reform within the Catholic Church begins with the Council of Trent
1552	Signing of the Treaty of Passau, allowing rulers to determine official religion of their lands
1555	Peace of Augsburg brings end to religious wars in Germany
1558	Elizabeth I becomes queen of England
1565	Founding of St. Augustine, Florida, first permanent European settlement in North America
1567	Mercator projection map first published
1572	Massacre of 50,000 French Huguenots on St. Bartholomew's Day (August 23–24)
1580	Crowns of Spain and Portugal united after successful Spanish invasion
1587	Mary, Queen of Scots, is executed in England
1588	English naval forces defeat the Spanish Armada
1591	Running of the bulls tradition begins in Pamplona, Spain
1595	William Shakespeare writes *Romeo and Juliet*
1603	Elizabeth I dies and is succeeded by James I; Tokugawa shogunate is founded in Edo, Japan; London's population estimated at 200,000
1607	First permanent English colony in North America is founded at Jamestown, Virginia

Appendix C

Ruling Houses and Dynasties

ENGLAND

House of Lancaster

Henry IV	1399–1413
Henry V	1413–1422
Henry VI	1422–1461

House of York

Edward IV	1461–1483
Edward V	1483
Richard III	1483–1485

House of Tudor

Henry VII	1485–1509
Henry VIII	1509–1547
Edward VI	1547–1553
Mary	1553–1558
Elizabeth I	1558–1603

FRANCE

House of Valois

Charles VI	1380–1422
Charles VII	1422–1461

Louis XI	1461–1483
Charles VIII	1483–1498
Louis XII	1498–1515
Francis I	1515–1547
Henry II	1547–1559
Francis II	1559–1560
Charles IX	1560–1574
Henry III	1574–1589

House of Bourbon

| Henry IV | 1589–1610 |

HOLY ROMAN EMPIRE

Wenceslaus of Bohemia	1378–1400
Rupert of the Palatinate	1400–1410
Sigismund	1410–1437

House of Habsburg

Albert II	1438–1439
Frederick III	1440–1493
Maximilian I	1493–1519
Charles V	1519–1556
Ferdinand I	1556–1564
Maximilian II	1564–1576
Rudolph II	1576–1612

RUSSIA

House of Rurik

Ivan III (the Great)	1462–1505
Basil III	1505–1533
Ivan IV (the Terrible)	1533–1584
Fedor I	1584–1598
Boris Godunov	1598–1605
Fedor II	1605
Demetrius	1605–1606
Basil (IV) Shuiski	1606–1610

SPAIN

Ferdinand II of Aragon and Isabella of Castile	1479–1504
Philip I and Juana	1504–1506
Ferdinand V (II of Aragon)	1506–1516

House of Habsburg

Charles I	1516–1556
Philip II	1556–1598
Philip III	1598–1621

CHINA

Dynasties

Yuan	1280–1368
Ming	1368–1644
Qing (Manchu)	1644–1912

JAPAN

Ashikaya Shogunate	1338–1568
Tokugawa Shogunate	1568–1867

OTTOMAN EMPIRE

Bajazet I	1389–1403
Suleiman I	1403–1411
Prince Musa	1411–1413
Mohammed I	1413–1421
Murad II	1421–1451
Mohammed II	1451–1481
Bajazet II	1481–1512
Selim I	1512–1520
Suleiman II	1520–1566
Selim II	1566–1574
Murad III	1574–1595
Mohammed III	1595–1603

Index

About the Editors and Contributors

BLAKE BEATTIE received his Ph.D. from the University of Toronto and currently teaches courses in medieval and early modern European history at the University of Louisville. He has published numerous articles and book chapters on medieval church history and contributed an essay to *Events That Changed America Through the Seventeenth Century* (2000).

PAMELA BEATTIE received her Ph.D. from the University of Toronto and currently teaches courses in medieval history with an emphasis on Spain at the University of Louisville. Among her publications are "Eschatology and Llull's *Llibre Contra Anticrist*," in *Studia Lulliana* (1997), and "Pro Exaltatiuone Sanctae fidei catholicae: Mission and Crusade in the Writings of Ramon Llull," in Larry J. Simon, ed., *Iberia and the Mediterranean World of the Middle Ages*, Vol. 1 (1995).

JOHN K. COX earned his Ph.D. at Indiana University and is now associate professor of history at Wheeling Jesuit University in West Virginia. He is the author of *A History of Serbia*, a forthcoming volume in Greenwood's *Histories of the Modern Nations* series and has also contributed to *Statesmen Who Changed the World* (1993) and *Events That Changed the World in the Nineteenth Century* (1996).

CONNIE S. EVANS received her Ph.D. from Louisiana State University. She now teaches history at Baldwin-Wallace College in Berea, Ohio, and has contributed frequently to historical dictionaries. Her article on early modern Exeter will soon appear in the journal *Albion*.

JOHN E. FINDLING is professor of history at Indiana University Southeast. He earned his Ph.D. at the University of Texas and has pursued a research interest in world's fairs for nearly twenty years. He is the author of *Chicago's Great World's Fairs* (1995), and, with Robert W. Rydell and Kimberly Pelle, *Fair America* (2000). With Frank W. Thackeray, he has edited *Statesmen Who Changed the World* (1993) and the other volumes in the *Events That Changed the World* and *Events That Changed America* series.

ALISON GULLEY earned her Ph.D. in medieval English literature at the University of North Carolina at Chapel Hill and is now an assistant professor of English at Lees-McRae College in Banner Elk, North Carolina. She has published articles on medieval history and literary criticism in *Publications of the Medieval Association of the Midwest* and *Medievalia*, and has several pieces forthcoming in *The Chaucer Encyclopedia*.

DANIEL WEBSTER HOLLIS III is professor of history at Jacksonville State University in Jacksonville, Alabama. He earned his Ph.D. at Vanderbilt University and is the author of *The History of Ireland*, a forthcoming volume in Greenwood's *Histories of the Modern Nations* series. In addition, he has published articles on Machiavelli in *Statesmen Who Changed the World* (1993) and in the *Proceedings of the Year of the Renaissance Conference* (1993).

GERRITDINA (INEKE) JUSTITZ is an assistant professor of history at North Dakota State University in Fargo. She earned her Ph.D. at the University of California, San Diego, and is pursuing research on aspects of the German town of Naumberg in Saxony during the sixteenth century and of the German Reformation. She is also interested in animal imagery in sixteenth-century prophecy.

STEVEN E. SIRY is professor of history at Baldwin-Wallace College in Berea, Ohio. He earned his Ph.D. in history from the University of Cincinnati and has published articles in the *Journal of the Early Republic, Locus, Statesmen Who Changed the World* (1993), *Events That Changed America in the Nineteenth Century* (1997), and *Events That Changed America Through the Seventeenth Century* (2000)

CLIFFORD L. STATEN earned his Ph.D. in political science from the University of North Texas and is currently an associate professor of political science and dean of the School of Social Science at Indiana University Southeast. He has published articles in *Presidential Studies Quarterly,* the *Journal of Political Science,* and *Perspectives in Political Science,* and is currently working on a history of Cuba for Greenwood's *Histories of the Modern Nations* series.

LUNG-KEE SUN received his Ph.D. from Stanford University and is now professor of history at the University of Memphis. He has published widely in the areas of Chinese intellectual history, film studies, and historiography. Among his publications is *The Deep Structure of Chinese Culture,* first published in Chinese in 1983 and translated into German in 1994.

FRANK W. THACKERAY is professor of history at Indiana University Southeast. He received his Ph.D. from Temple University. He is the author of *Antecedents of Revolution: Alexander I and the Polish Congress Kingdom* (1980) as well as articles on Russian-Polish relations in the nineteenth century and Polish-American relations in the twentieth century. With John E. Findling, he edited *Statesmen Who Changed the World* (1993) and the other volumes in the *Events That Changed the World* and *Events That Changed America* series. He is a former Fulbright scholar in Poland.